WELCO~~ME TO~~ ...
MUSIC ...

- Branson, Missouri, has a population of under 4,000—yet entertains more than 4,000,000 visitors every year

- There are over 26 theaters in Branson— which, altogether, can seat 10,000 more people than all of the New York Broadway theaters combined

- Willie Nelson, Roy Clark, Cristy Lane, Mel Tillis and Ray Stevens are just a few of the superstars who own their own theaters— sharing the limelight and the applause with the likes of Waylon Jennings, Loretta Lynn, Tanya Tucker and Ricky Skaggs ... two shows a day, six days a week!

**NO GAMBLING, NO NIGHTCLUBS—
JUST GOOD, CLEAN FAMILY FUN!
PLUS THE BIGGEST STARS THIS SIDE OF
VEGAS ... AND THE BEST MUSIC
THIS SIDE OF HEAVEN!**

WELCOME TO BRANSON, MISSOURI:

**THE
TOWN
THAT
COUNTRY
BUILT**

WELCOME TO BRANSON, MISSOURI:

THE TOWN THAT COUNTRY BUILT

BRUCE COOK

AVON BOOKS ◆ NEW YORK

THE TOWN THAT COUNTRY BUILT: WELCOME TO BRANSON, MISSOURI is an original publication of Avon Books. This work has never before appeared in book form.

"Put Yourself in My Shoes" by Clint Black, Hayden Nicholas and Shake Russell © 1989 by Howlin' Hits Music, Inc. (ASCAP), Red Brazos Music, Inc. (BMI). All rights reserved. Used by permission. International copyright secured.
"I Hate Country" written by Michael Brewer © 1992. Quoted by permission of the author.
"Unwound" words and music written by Dean Dillon and Frank Dycus copyright © 1981 Songs of Polygram International, Inc. and Musicor Music, a division of Music Corporation of America, Inc., Fast Ball Music and Hall Clement Publications. All rights administered by MCA Music Publishing, a division of MCA Inc. Used by permission. All rights reserved.

AVON BOOKS
A division of
The Hearst Corporation
1350 Avenue of the Americas
New York, New York 10019

Copyright © 1993 by Bruce Cook
Front cover photos by Alan Mayor
Published by arrangement with the author
Library of Congress Catalog Card Number: 92-97425
ISBN: 0-380-77095-4

First Avon Books Printing: June 1993

AVON TRADEMARK REG. U.S. PAT. OFF. AND IN OTHER COUNTRIES, MARCA REGISTRADA, HECHO EN U.S.A.

Printed in the U.S.A.

RA 10 9 8 7 6 5 4 3 2 1

Contents

1

"Where Is the Town I Used to Know?"

We're talking serious sprawl, calamitous clutter. Just look at it! Through a five-and-a-half-mile stretch of Missouri State Highway 76, you have the opportunity to experience practically every sort of fast-food known to man—KFC (which in these hasty times is what they call Kentucky Fried Chicken), the ubiquitous McDonald's, the valiantly competing Burger King, and so on. If you're looking for something a little more distinctive, something regional in style, then you can duck in for chicken-fried steaks at Starvin' Marvin's Frontier Restaurant, or pig out at the lavish buffet spread at the Ozark Family Restaurant.

Feeling a bit stuffed? Well, you might want to take a leisurely stroll through the Wax Museum, or do some shopping at Silver Spur Western Wear or the local Wal-Mart, take a swift ride in a Go-Kart, or get an impressive overview of the 76 strip and surrounding countryside by jumping in a Jet Helicopter and rising above it all.

Shopping? You want to go shopping? There are a hundred or more places to shop along the way—plenty of room, just pull in and park—everything from the bottom-of-the-scale Dollar Store at the top of the strip to authentic Ozark craft shops that offer wood carvings by local artists, hand-sewn pattern quilts, and furniture made in the rude, old American coun-

1

try style. Or maybe you just want souvenirs, gewgaws, knickknacks; these are available in dizzying variety and overwhelming plenitude at scores of shops along the way.

It may be time to go back to your motel or hotel and rest up for the big evening ahead. Let's see, at which one of the many, many here on 76 Country Boulevard did you check in when you hit town this morning? Was it the local Holiday Inn? Or the Hillbilly Inn, which advertises "Fine Lodging and Vittles"? The upscale Dogwood Park Hotel, or the luxurious, brand-new Palace Inn? But there are others in such quantity and range of price that they can satisfy just about any taste or pocketbook—*if* you can get a reservation.

Now what? Why, it's what you came here for in the first place. You may have driven in from as far away as Wichita Falls, Shreveport, Indianapolis, even Chicago or beyond; you may commute regularly from nearby St. Louis, Tulsa, or Little Rock; but no matter from where, you probably came for one reason alone—to see the shows. That's why people flock to this little town in the Ozarks, just north of the Arkansas line— to see and hear the stars of country music perform nightly (and most of them at matinees, too, during the height of the season) at their very own theaters. These country show spots, some seating 2,000 and even more, are planted irregularly on and off Highway 76, offering visitors the greatest range of selection in this increasingly popular form of down-home entertainment that can be found anywhere in the country—or in the world, for that matter.

That's why some call Branson, Missouri (population, 3,706), "the Las Vegas of country music." But you don't hear that phrase bandied about in town. In spite of recent efforts to attract whole families to the city that Bugsy Siegel built, there remains about Las Vegas an aura of sin and sex that is altogether absent from Bible Belt Branson . . . and townsfolk want to keep it that way. No gambling, of course. And the theaters are theaters, just that—not nightclubs. There are only a few real bars in town. And anyone desiring an unencumbered view of those parts of the female anatomy above the knee or below the throat must journey forty miles up to Springfield (population, 140,000 and the third largest city in Missouri) to do so.

No, in Branson, they call it "Country Music's Broadway." That's what the sign says down near the bottom of 76 Country Boulevard, and at night the town's Great White Way is lighted nearly as bright as New York's. It boasts stars, too—more of them, and bigger stars, than you will find anywhere except . . . well, Las Vegas.

Up and down Branson's entertainment strip there are theaters at which country music stars and superstars perform twice a day, six days a week. Willie Nelson has a strong presence at his new theater, lives in a motel room next door, but lays off for a week or two at a time to give the stage to pals like Merle Haggard. Another one, just completed in 1992, is Andy Williams's $8 million Moon River Theatre, a new home base for the only noncountry personality presently performing in town.

Roy Clark, the "Hee-Haw" man, was the first name performer to come to Branson when he opened up shop in 1983 and played a seven-week season, bringing in other performers during the year; he now has a big, new theater of his own, where he holds forth through most of a long season. One performer who played Clark's original venue was Boxcar Willie, the Texas-born singer who created a persona for himself from his brief career as a hobo; he took a look at Branson, decided he liked it, and moved there, opening his Boxcar Willie Theatre and Museum in 1987.

Drive the strip and you see the show spots lined up, one by one, each of them identified by the performers who play there to packed houses—the Ray Stevens Theatre, the Cristy Lane Theatre, the Mickey Gilley Family Theater, Moe Bandy's Americana Theatre. Loretta Lynn has also done two seasons in and out of Lowes Theatre and likes it well enough to keep coming back as long as the audiences like her, which in her case probably means forever.

The biggest show in town, week in and week out, is the one offered at the Grand Palace. This huge showplace rises impressively behind a colonnaded antebellum mansion of a lobby. Out in front, at the entrance from 76 Country Boulevard, a sign flashes word to the passing traffic just who is currently playing the 4,000-seat theater and who will be there in weeks to come. During any given stretch you might see Waylon Jennings and Jessi Colter one week, Tanya Tucker another, followed by Ricky Skaggs. Yet even here the policy of resident performer holds sway. Glen Campbell and Louise Mandrell alternate as host and hostess to the visiting acts, opening for them and lending their own celebrity to make the big show even bigger.

There are over twenty venues along Highway 76. Just off the strip there are a few more. Among them is Buck Trent's, the only dinner theater in town, on Highway 165, just south of the action. North of it is the Shoji Tabuchi Show, home of the Japanese fiddler who may well become the first made-in-Branson superstar. And finally, beyond downtown Branson, boldly located in a fairly remote corner, Mel Tillis has built his new 2,100-seat theater and taken over the operation of the restaurant next door at the Branson Inn; one of the town's great boosters in country music today, Tillis has indicated that he is here to stay.

The Media Boom

Although Branson didn't happen overnight, the national media got the message out in a kind of rush of discovery in the fall of 1991. Beginning with a *Time* magazine story in late August, it kind of snowballed through the pages of *People*, the *Los Angeles Times*, and the *Wall Street Journal*. Yet, as so often happens, it took the power of television to make much of America truly aware of just what was going on in that little town in Missouri.

On December 8, 1991, "60 Minutes," the most watched show on American television, broadcast a well-produced segment on the country scene in Branson, titled "The Sound of Music." Reporter Morley Safer seemed quite amazed that a town the size of this one could attract over four million visitors during the season. Yet as they presented performance sequences, quick-cutting from Loretta Lynn to Waylon Jennings to Shoji Tabuchi and Boxcar Willie, it was more than clear what drew the crowds there.

Safer quoted statistics. The town does $1.5 billion in business annually, he said. (Perhaps a little high, though nobody quotes the figure at less than $750 million.) Speaking to Mel Tillis, he suggested that the stuttering troubadour must be pulling in about $1 million a month during the six months he plays there; Mel modestly allowed that wasn't too far wrong. Speaking of Branson's continued growth, Safer pointed out that while there were then twenty-two theaters in operation, there would be five more by next spring (1992), and that would give a total of 53,000 seats—10,000 more than New York's Broadway had available for live performance.

Impressive? Yes, impressive. Yet to anyone connected with the country music industry, an exchange between Boxcar Willie and Morley Safer must have made just as great an impact. "Box," as he is known universally in town, was explaining just why the economics of two-a-day, six days a week were so favorable to the performer.

"No promoters?" asked Safer.

"No promoters," said Box.

"No producers?"

"No producers."

"No agents?"

"No agents."

It's just him and the audience.

For most country musicians, the road is a way of life. Travel from town to town and date to date is usually undertaken on a band bus. Weeks of one-nighters can take quite a toll. This is another reason why performers welcome the opportunity to set up shop in Branson: relief from the road. Although he still does a bit of touring during the brief off-season, Boxcar Willie departs from and returns to his comfortable Ozark mountain home. The rest of the time he just does his shows and lets "the people come to me."

The others—including Mel Tillis, Moe Bandy, Ray Stevens, and Cristy Lane—take up seasonal residence and keep their suburban Nashville homes. Lane had an apartment for herself and her manager-husband built right above her theater. Pointe

Royale, the swanky condominium development out on 165, is home to a number of performers six months or more out of the year. Tillis, Bandy, and Stevens are dedicated golfers and like to put in a morning on Pointe Royale's championship course before doing their shows. Mel Tillis also likes to fish the three well-stocked artificial lakes in the area. His frequent angling companion, the Japanese-born Shoji Tabuchi, complains that Mel is always accusing him of eating the bait. With a laconic smile, Shoji tells his show audience, "I don't do that anymore."

Jim Stafford

Shoji Tabuchi is a year-rounder in Branson. Another is singer-songwriter-comedian Jim Stafford. He took up residence here after his first season in town, buying a home on Table Rock Lake and—a big plunge—buying a theater, too. No rental, no partners, just his name on the dotted line. As he said when the local music magazine, *Branson's Country Review*, made the announcement of the deal, "I've always wanted to be an entertainer . . . But never in my wildest dreams did I think I would end up owing this much money. When you sign a stack of papers two inches high and you know that every one of them is in the other guy's favor, it gives you something to think about."

So he, too, has found a home in the Ozarks. He has come to stay. When we talked about his move to Branson, he told me, "You know, I had a home in Florida and another one in Los Angeles. But we sold everything and bought a house here in 1991. I've lived in Nashville, Orlando, and Los Angeles. But each one just became a base for touring. This is a lot more like home. And the people come here. I don't know why exactly, but this is where they come to see me."

Perhaps they come because they remember him from what was in the late sixties considered a rather audacious show on CBS, "The Smothers Brothers Comedy Hour" (Stafford was chief writer and on camera, too). Or from his own summer replacement show on the same network. Maybe they have some recollection of his weird song with the trick ending, "My Girl Bill." Or maybe they remember his top 10 hit, "Spiders and Snakes." Or, finally, they just might have heard that the fast-paced Jim Stafford show is the funniest on the strip.

In any case, those who filled his 818-seat Jim Stafford Theatre (small by local standards) on opening night seemed to sense that they were in for a good time. There were many locals present. He is popular in Branson both personally and as an entertainer. But whether they had driven across town or two states, they were there for him, and he didn't disappoint.

Bill Mabe is producer of the Baldknobbers show, a couple of miles down the road, and one of the most experienced showmen in town. "We were here before the Nashville boys," he says, "and it's been to our advantage. We found out a long time ago that what people are looking for when they come here is a show, a whole show, with comedy and singing and maybe a little dancing. So what the Nashville boys are finding out is that they can't just come in off the road and do the same thing, two sets of songs over and over again. So now they're changing along our lines to suit the audience."

Whether Jim Stafford sat down on a cracker barrel and talked it all over with old Bill Mabe, or whether his own keen showman's instincts brought him to the same conclusion, the show he presented that night was just the sort that Mabe described—"a whole show."

As the curtains parted, an offstage announcer hollered out, "Rick McKuen and the Jim Stafford Band!" And there they were, jamming it out hard on "Move It On Over," going full tilt, electric bluegrass style. Maybe the influence here is Rodney Dillard, who, until Stafford hired him for the season, was one of The Dillards of bluegrass fame. Dillard plays second banana to the star of the show and was introduced with the "Andy of Mayberry" theme as a reminder of his running role on the TV show. The man can play guitar, sing a little, and has a lot of fun doing it. After a couple of numbers and a bit of joshing with the audience, he had established such rapport that he even got them to join in and sing, full-voiced, on

"Salty Dog Blues"—no easy job, as any performer will tell you.

There is more—a lot more—building up to Stafford's star turn. The backup-singing Brown Sisters—looking great in outlandish getup (cutaway coats over black tights and silver lamé dickeys), did a duet on "Little Liza Jane," and made way for feature singer Donna Falterman, who, dressed in a purple jumpsuit, did a cover rendition of Trisha Yearwood's then current hit, "That's What I Like about You," then proved she was from Louisiana with a medley of Cajun music, "Saturday Night at the Twist and Shout," and "Jambalaya." And *then* Jim Stafford. But the point is, everything up to the moment of his appearance was fast, high-energy, and pretty exciting. The audience had been taken on a roller coaster ride and was now ready to lean back and enjoy his sort of rather sneaky, low-key humor.

If you've never been exposed to Jim Stafford, then the loss is yours. The man is *funny*. Garbed in a brocaded tuxedo coat and black jeans, he paced the stage, shouting out in the style of a revival preacher, "I feel love in this room tonight. *Love* is happening here tonight!" And before you knew it, it was.

The jokes he told were in the nature of observations of the human scene: "Women are always complaining that they'll stop out on the road and ask directions. But their husbands—will they stop for directions? Nooo. If a man is lost but still making good time, then he's happy."

Or silly stuff that always gets a laugh. After making a half-hearted attempt to lead the audience in "Zippety-Doo-Dah," he said, "You know, one night I was doing this, and a man in the front row just kept singing, 'Zippety-doo-dah, zippety-doo-dah' over and over again. Then I looked down and saw that my doo-dah was open." (That's about as raunchy as he gets.)

A lot of his humor is self-deprecating. Enthusiastically: "Hey, I just signed a contract with CBS Records! Yeah, I get a record a month, and I can cancel it anytime I want to."

His jokes are interspersed among, and sometimes even used to introduce, his songs, some of which are at least as funny as his jokes—"That's What Little Kids Do," the naughty

"Wildwood Weed" (and he wanted it understood that he wasn't advocating the smoking of any controlled substance, just describing what happened), and the hilarious "Cow Pattie," which he wrote for Clint Eastwood's "Any Which Way You Can." There were others, more or less straight, like his hit, "Spiders and Snakes" and "Swamp Hattie," a story song in the grand old country tradition. And so on.

Somewhere along the way there was an intermission, another hell-for-leather warm-up by the various units of the ensemble, and an astonishing, gratuitous blimp launching which both impressed and mystified the audience. A whole show? music? singing? comedy? And yes, there was even a little dancing. Stafford took a go at clog dancing, demonstrating by his ineptitude both how difficult and how fundamentally silly this heavy-footed country ritual really is. He wound it up, as he usually does, with an instrumental rendition of Mason Williams's "Classical Gas," mostly funny but then, when he really got into it on the guitar, rather impressive.

Well, of course it's impossible to describe comedy. It's a case of you-have-to-be-there. And being there, laid low by his hesitant, rather puckish delivery, you find yourself at his mercy, eager for him to say anything—just anything!—so that you can laugh some more.

"We Work Hard Around Here."

A few days later, I talked with him in his office. The business area of the theater is located both behind and beneath the stage. I sat and waited for him a few minutes in a reception area as he finished up a rehearsal. Just at the end there was a great clattering and clumping from up above. I must have looked shocked and a little puzzled, for the young lady behind the desk then spoke up, explaining things. "That's Jim onstage," she said. "He's practicing his clog dancing."

(*Gosh*, I thought, *he better not get good at it. That'd spoil everything.*)

Jim Stafford entered, sweating, and led the way into his office—bare, spare, and unimpressive—but then, he'd just moved his business operations here from his home.

Settling into a chair across the desk from him, I began by burbling enthusiastically—but honestly—about the show I'd seen on opening night. Oil him up. Get him to talking.

"Well, we had a lot of rough edges," he complained with a sigh. "We work hard around here. This year we're doing a lot of shows—two a day. And I want to have a show where you just about feel you need a seat belt."

He wanted it understood, though, that his goal wasn't simply to get everything set, polished to a high-gloss shine and leave it that way. "Oh, we got a lot of plans, like that thing we did with the blimp. That was an experiment to get the audience involved, surprise them. I'm trying out a video screen and a transmitter. I'd like to do a radio show out of here, kind of an old-fashioned jamboree. See, these people come to see a show. I'd like them to feel they can come back and get something a little bit different every time."

It seems that having his own theater has released a lot of energy and given him the opportunity to realize plans he's had on the back burner for years. He grinned just thinking about it. "You know," he said, "ever since I was a child I wanted to have a theater where I could put on a show. Ever since I could walk I've had a passion for it—you know, dress up, come out from behind a curtain, sing a song. And all through my career I've preferred live performance to anything I've ever done. All my songs have been whittled out in front of an audience. My jokes came out of ad-libs. To have an area like this to live in and have a theater, too, well, it's just amazing."

I've got this theory that most people have a natural age. Jim Stafford's seems to be about thirty-three, although he admits to a chronological forty-eight. But whether thirty-three or forty-eight, he's clearly not ready for retirement. And that's not how he thinks of his new life in Branson. But he sure does like it here.

"I love the area," he declared. "I love everything about it. The people are friendly. I'm living on a nice lake. My friend Jud Strunk wrote a song where he asks, 'Where is the town I used to know?' Well, it's here! It really is. It's so nice to go to a downtown area that's thrivin'. Children can walk around here any time of the day or night. My little boy, Taylor, loves it here. He's just twelve years old, and that's a great age to appreciate what this place has to offer. He comes here summers. The rest of the year he lives with his mom in Savannah." (She's Stafford's former wife, Bobbie Gentry of "Ode to Billie Joe" fame.)

"Listen," he concluded, "I grew up in a little place in Polk County, in Florida, called Eloise, a town about the size of this one. It was adjacent to Cypress Gardens, but then they built Disneyworld just twenty minutes away, so it's all changed. I've played music since I was sixteen or seventeen, but I didn't really get out of Eloise until I was eighteen. But just figure it out—that's thirty years of touring. I've had enough of that. I'd just like to stay here and have my theater and my show and fish. You know, the Corps of Engineers stocks these lakes real good."

2

Who Comes to Branson?

Who are all these people you see in cars on 76 Country Boulevard? It's not as easy as you might suppose to generalize about those who come to Branson. Let me give you an example. I was standing in line to get my ticket to the Baldknobbers show. The man at the front was carefully counting out the price of the two $12.90 tickets in singles and fives. In his fifties, he was a hard-working farmer, sure enough, dressed in bib overalls and a workshirt. He looked like he'd just come off the back forty. When he completed his transaction, he turned away and started back to his car. As I edged up in line, I watched him go. He marched back purposefully, raising the tickets high above his head to show his wife he'd got what they came for. A rusty pickup truck? No. She waited in a shiny, brand-new, maroon Oldsmobile 98.

Detroit iron predominates, but there seem to be just about as many Cadillacs and Lincolns out there on 76 Country Boulevard as there are bottom-of-the-line Chevvies and Fords. Nevertheless, among the many domestic pickup trucks seen on the road, there were an impressive number of little rascals with names like Toyota, Nissan, and Isuzu imprinted on the tailgate. You saw the usual sprinkling of Honda sedans, but notably absent were Mercedes and BMWs. I spotted a silver Mitsubishi 3000 VR4 that looked like it was doing 140 mph parked right where it was. And oh yes, there was also the Rolls-Royce convertible I saw one evening tucked discreetly in a corner of the Holiday Inn parking lot.

It's not so easy to tell who the folks are who visit Branson by the cars they drive. Why, I remember a Mercury that looked kind of funny pulling up in front of the 76 Music Hall. The chrome had been stripped from it, the way they do street rods back in Los Angeles. But nothing else about the car said street rod. It was an oversized four-door from the mid-seventies. The original black paint job was faded and scuffed. Finally, the two couples who got out of the car were not at all what I expected to see emerge from any automobile. I took them to be Amish. The men, bearded but unmustached, were dressed in black from head to toe; the women wore gray, long-skirted dresses with white aprons in front and white coifs tied under the chin. But the Amish don't drive cars; their horse-drawn buggies and wagons are forever snarling traffic in eastern Pennsylvania. Lacking the nerve to intrude upon them and demand that they account for this discrepancy, I asked around town, describing them and their car. I was told that they were almost certainly Mennonites, who will drive internal combustion vehicles but believe chrome decoration to be showy, garish, and quite unnecessary. They are probably right about that too.

I wasn't usually in the least shy about approaching people in parking lots or theater lobbies and asking them where they were from and why they had come to Branson. I received all kinds of answers. What I learned was that there were as many from the North as from the South, and that there were many citybillies among them. They come to hear the music and see the stars from Des Moines, Chicago, from distant Detroit and Minneapolis—and even farther.

Then there was the time I was sitting at the Outback Steak & Oyster Bar and fell into conversation with the young fellow perched on the next barstool. He was dressed like a cowboy— jeans, high-heeled boots, beat-up Stetson—but then, many wear that disguise these days. I asked what he did for a living, fully expecting to hear that he sold insurance, or something.

But no, he let it be known that he was a cowboy, plain and simple, and proud of it.

"The real thing, huh? Where you from?"

"Florida."

I thought he was kidding me and told him so—in a respectful way, of course. "Cattle in *Florida*? Really?"

He proceeded to set me straight: "Well, you don't know as much as you ought to, mister. There's a lot of cattle ranching in Florida. Matter of fact, we run more cattle back home than they do in Texas. Look it up."

I did. They do.

He explained that he had decided to see a little of the world and lined up a job on a spread in western Kansas. He had loaded up his pickup truck and was now en route. "I went through Nashville, figuring to hear some music, but there's nothing there but Opryland, and that ain't open yet. Heard a little here, though. Think I'll come back."

They do come back. According to a survey taken by the Missouri Division of Tourism, nearly half of the 4.3 million who visit Branson during the season, between the months of April and December, are from within the state. They are on short vacations or getaway weekends of two to three days. And the residents of the surrounding states of Illinois, Kansas, and Iowa rank second, third, and fourth to Missouri among the visitors.

No statistics are available on how much of this is repeat business, but Dawn Erickson of the Chamber of Commerce assured me that quite a lot of it is. Why? "Well, it's a 'value' vacation destination," she said with professional conviction. What's that mean, exactly? "Well," she explained, "you can get by pretty easily and have a good time here for $75 per day per person, which is about half what you spend at most destinations." Most out-of-state people spend more than that, according to the Division of Tourism—though not much more.

But whether from in state or out of state, whether from near or far, visitors to Branson get here by car—or by tour bus. It is a "rubber tire destination." I first heard the term from Jan Eiserman of the Ozark Marketing Council, but I had grasped the meaning of it during my first full day in town. The stretch of Missouri State Highway 76 that wends from the Ray Stevens Theatre up at the top of the hill to downtown Branson near the shore of Lake Taneycomo is just three lanes wide—westbound, eastbound, with a left turn lane in the middle. At the height of the season, it is crowded with cars, buses, and recreational vehicles in the mornings, impossibly packed in the afternoons, and a creeping parking lot in the early evenings when people are trying to get themselves fed and move on to the shows.

It can take up to two and a half hours to inch along the five-mile stretch. This leads to frustration, stress, and short tempers. Physical altercations occur.

"Oh, sure, it's true," said Branson Chief of Police Steve Mefford. "As the season approaches peak it gets more hectic. . . . We anticipate major problems, maybe even gridlock. A city built on a strip, so to speak, has a real problem right from the start. This will be the year we're put to the test."

Stephen W. Mefford is young, completely professional, and nobody's idea of a small-town police chief. Although he was born and grew up in the area and attended Southwest Missouri State in Springfield, he moved to Davis, California, and began his career in police work there. He returned with his family to Branson eight years ago as chief and up to now has had things pretty well under control. We talked in his office in the city building in downtown Branson very early in the season.

"We currently have twenty-six full-time employees—fourteen in uniform and two detectives. I've got an assistant chief, and then there's myself. During the season, we put on a minimum of two part-time traffic officers, young fellas from the College of the Ozarks nearby, just for the traffic. We'll probably have more this year, though.

"Then there's the private security companies. We keep some control over them that we didn't have before. There were only two in town last year. Now there's eight or nine. We've got to know who's armed and who's not armed and just generally keep them under control."

How so? "Well, it took some training last year not to get them out onto 76 directing traffic in and out of the theaters. Through town, 76 is our responsibility. Up around the Ray Stevens Theatre, it's the Missouri State Police. With the Grand Palace, though, they're expecting fifty buses for some shows, so we're allowing their security people to direct after-show traffic onto back road exits. Not 76, though. That belongs to us.''

Yes, there are back roads, and the Branson/Lakes Area Chamber of Commerce is doing what it can to acquaint visitors with them. Stapled to a larger map of the entire Lakes Area is a smaller one, headlined, ''Branson is DOING SOMETHING About Its Traffic!'' The legend reads, in part: ''On August 6, 1991, Branson voters approved a plan to spend $10 million on new roads over the next few years. Work on the first project—a road that will run parallel to 76 Country Boulevard—has already begun. Six additional projects will follow, including construction of new roads and improvement of existing roads.''

According to the map, it is possible to detour around great stretches of the strip, though not all of it. This was what I found following the map, and it matched what local residents told me—yet there were always rumors of some fabled shortcut, like the Northwest Passage of yore, that would sweep wide around 76 and land you in downtown Branson in ten minutes flat. I never discovered it.

Traffic is Branson's biggest problem today. Its dependence upon auto transportation to deliver audiences for its theaters, guests to its motels, and diners to its restaurants is one of the two biggest obstacles to continued growth. (We'll get to the other in the next chapter.)

Even if you fly in you must rent a car to get to Branson— as of this writing. The local airport, three miles away at Point Lookout, handles lightplane traffic only. Springfield has direct flights in from Dallas and connecting flights from most other Midwest and mid-South cities. The airport there is expanding and is already set up to handle more than it does presently. But Branson has begun to think of itself as a national, even an international, tourist destination.

In a sense, it already is. Country music is big in America today, fast overtaking pop. Internationally, it has legions of fans all over the English-speaking world—in Canada, Australia, and Great Britain especially. A raise-your-hands survey at the 76 Music Hall's Brumley Show early in the season turned up a whole busload of snowbirds from Canada—and a few people from Germany. Why Germany? Never underestimate the power of the Armed Forces Radio Network overseas. And if Germany, why not Japan? Why not indeed? "Oh yes," said Jan Eiserman of the Ozark Marketing Council, "the Japanese are definitely interested. Executives from Nippon Travel are coming here to Branson in a couple of months to look it over as a tour destination." After all, they are represented locally on stage not only by Shoji Tabuchi, but also by another young fiddler, Mike Ito, who is in the Baldknobbers show.

Yet the traffic problem remains. It drives people crazy—and one it drove to song. Michael Brewer of the duo of Brewer and Shipley has put up permanently in the Ozarks not far from Branson. One unlucky day, when in a hurry, he found himself trapped in the creeping traffic along 76 Country Boulevard. With the radio tuned to Branson's country station, KRZK, he inched along past theater after theater, listening to record after record, and this was the result:

> *I hate country.*
> *I despise those barnyard sounds.*
> *Ricky and Earl and Randy and Merle*
> *Make me throw up on the ground.*
> *It might be heavenly to your ears,*
> *but it sounds like hell to me.*
> *All I know for sure is I hate country.*

And that's just the chorus. It gets pretty savage after that—especially when he declares:

> *Boxcar Willie makes me want to kill*
> *and maim with my bare hands*
> *and tap dance on his head in deep quicksand.*

Ah, well, poor Box! By this time I'm sure Michael Brewer must have recovered from his fit of pique. He might even like country again by now.

About the only person in town who seemed to have a good

word for 76 Country Boulevard is the Reverend Ralph La-
Forge, whose United Methodist Church is located right along
the way. He says it's just like any other resort town: "People
like to get out on the strip. It's exciting for them, even if they
are moving at a snail's pace. It's what they want to see."

There are dark mutterings that merchants along 76 like the
traffic just the way it is. Their reasoning, it is said, is that
when traffic is heavy and just creeping along, people get so
hot and frustrated that they need relief. So they pull off the
road to shop or maybe just to have some ice cream. Take away
the stress factor, and you'll cut into business.

Even if a few shortsighted businessmen see it that way, the
view of the town and the town council is much different. Not
only are roads being built, but proposals are also under con-
sideration for transit systems to move people up and down the
strip without adding to traffic. Plans for both trams and trolleys
have been submitted, some calling for tracks on both sides of
76, and others on one side only. The most radical, according
to a report in the *Branson Beacon*, proposed not only a tram-
way, but "ultimately making 76 a landscaped parkway closed
to automobiles." Well . . . maybe someday.

The Brumley Family

But who are all these people here in Branson, anyway?

"Basically," according to Dawn Erickson of the Chamber
of Commerce, "they are couples with children, whole families. They comprise the largest part, over 50 percent. Next are
couples over fifty years of age. A smaller group, but growing,
are the singles. Families and couples come here for the shows,
of course, but there are so many activities that don't cost anything—the fishing, the beautiful lakes, the scenery." By and
large, the singles come strictly for the shows.

The people who come to Branson are overwhelmingly
Christian.

There isn't a show in town that doesn't include a few gospel
numbers. Even hip, naughty, teasing Jim Stafford, who sati-
rizes most aspects of the country music ethos, has Donna Fal-

terman do a brief medley in the second half of his program. It consisted of the familiar "Amazing Grace" and a foot-stomping rendition of "Hallelujah, I'm Ready to Go," as hot as anything in the show. Don't think for a minute that even white gospel is all lugubrious wails.

The Blackwood Singers Show at Campbell's Ozark Country Jubilee is fundamentally a gospel show done up glitzy and sassy and presented at a pace just about as fast as its older audience can handle. The headlining quartet, two male and two female, is a lineal descendant of the Blackwood Brothers, who toured churches and the revival circuit throughout the rural South through the thirties and on into the fifties. What would the elder Blackwoods think of the streamlined, quick-change, nineties version? Well, they couldn't help but admire the showmanship that goes into it. And as the Blackwood Singers jump and dance through medley after medley with moves right out of Motown, they generate something of the old-time feeling for the new-time hits they recorded on Capitol. It's a brand of pop-gospel they pitch here, with such numbers as "One Day at a Time," "This Old House," and "Let Me Be There." But when they really want to generate some excitement they go to the old Pentecostal hymn known so well as a New Orleans good-time tune, "When the Saints Go Marching In."

The Brumley Show at the 76 Music Hall is the best little show in town. That's "little" in the sense of small theater and small group of performers. Although not as swift and sharp as some of the others, there is a nice relaxed feeling generated up there on the stage that seems to suit the paying customers just fine. It comes close to being a family ensemble that opens the program, with young Tod Brumley leading the singing, and his uncle, Tom Brumley, on steel guitar. When Al Brumley, Jr., Tod's dad, comes out to sing and strum his acoustic guitar, that makes the family complete. There's a lot of talent up there. Tom Brumley, one of the best steel guitar players in the business, backed up Buck Owens on most of his hits and has also recorded with the Desert Rose Band, one of the best new groups in country. The most impressive member of the band was lead guitarist Barry Bales, not a family member but the boss of the band. His solos blew the house down. He even sang creditably on a poor white piece called "Patches."

Jeannie Dee, "the Sweetheart of the Ozarks," did a few numbers—and did them well—most of them cover versions of current hits. And there was a bit of classic bumpkin humor by a comic with blackened teeth and ill-fitting clothes who went by the handle of "Chester Drawers."

What surprised me, coming into the show cold, was the emphasis on gospel. It seemed that just about every other piece in the Brumley Show was gospel—old-time, sing-along gospel and not the pale synthetic stuff you get out of Nashville these days. And here I must confess my ignorance, for the name Brumley didn't mean to me quite what it should have. Albert E. Brumley, Sr., father of Al, Jr., and Tom, was just about the most prolific and, well, the finest writer of white gospel music in the history of the music; his only questionable rival was A. P. "Doc" Carter of the Carter Family, who became better known through performance and recording.

Born in Oklahoma in 1905, before statehood, the elder Brumley toured with gospel choirs and quartets as a young man. But he settled down and raised his family about seventy miles west of Branson in Powell, Missouri. He brought his five boys up as musicians and singers—and at one time or another they have all played together in some sort of Brumley family band. But Albert E. Brumley was able to concentrate on his songwriting. He wrote nearly seven hundred of them, including a couple of hundred of what he called his "sentimental songs"—pop songs of the day. But, as Al, Jr., says, "His main bread and butter was his gospel songs." Over a hundred of them were recorded, and among them is the most recorded gospel number of all time, the joyous "I'll Fly Away." Nearly as well known is the quirky "Turn Your Radio On." Other Brumley favorites: "I'll Meet You in the Morning," "Camping in Canaan's Land," "Jesus, Hold My Hand," and "I'd Rather Be an Old-Time Christian."

Most of these and maybe a couple of others were sung during the Brumley Show. The audience loved it, applauding the songs they recognized, joining in when invited on the ones they remembered. At the end of the show, Chester Drawers appeared out of costume and without makeup, and revealed himself as Eddie Bowman, "a minister of the Gospel." He preached a little sermon and sent everybody out with a benediction.

It was easygoing, high-quality entertainment. When I cornered Al Brumley, Jr., at the end of the evening, he seemed pleased with the performance and the reception and said that what they try for is "that laid-back feel that Ozark people have."

When I commented that his father's songs were a big feature in the show, he was quick to say, "Yes, and they always will be!" Yet it's not just filial piety, it's also good show-business sense: "This is the Bible Belt area here. It's a family atmosphere. People want to hear country music but not in clubs. And they want gospel, too. That's part of it."

And a very important part. The new Celebration Theatre featured a half-season 1992 lineup of limited runs that was very heavy into gospel. It included Pat Boone, Marilyn McCoo (a black star who was the mainstay of The Fifth Dimension), and Bill Gaither. In addition to the Brumley Show, the 76 Music Hall also features an *all*-gospel program at 2 P.M. every Sunday afternoon. It's a kind of postchurch song service and is just about the only Sunday show in town.

Sunday is the Lord's Day in Branson, Missouri. The bars shut down. Bottled liquor, beer and wine, otherwise readily available, are not sold. People are encouraged to go to church—and they do. All the major Christian denominations are represented, and a few minor ones, too. Easily the most convenient to visitors is the United Methodist Church, a handsome new building with a large parking lot, located right on the entertainment strip.

The Reverend Ralph LaForge is the minister there, a nice man with a good sense of humor. The sign on the desk in his office signaled that he didn't allow himself to take his job too solemnly: "GOD, I love this business." He hasn't been in Branson too long—only since 1990—but long enough to have a feeling for the place. And he considers it a good, church-going community.

"We draw from Branson, and Hollister just across the bridge, and from people outside the city limits for about fifteen to eighteen miles. That's all through the year, including January and February when the entertainment business shuts down.''

And during the season? ''Oh, well, we notice it right away when the buses start coming. Sometimes they call in advance and sometimes they don't, but we try to make room for them in the parking lot. But buses or cars, our attendance certainly goes up during the season here. No question about it. We have to put out chairs in the narthex because the sanctuary just fills up completely.

''I have a feeling we get more visitors here than some of the other churches do because we're so visible on the strip. But you know, it says a lot about the character of the people who come here. I think it says a lot about you when you take time to worship during your vacation. It's an amazing thing to me. We welcome—encourage—casual dress just to make people feel easy about it. Seems proper in the summer, even for our own people.''

When I asked if there were many from the shows in his congregation, he thought a moment and shook his head. ''Not that many,'' he said, ''three or four who are members. There are two from the Foggy River Boys, and there's Brandy Chapman. She sings with Roy Clark. That's her professional name. She sings with the choir, did two solos last Sunday here.''

Has he noticed any change since he's been here? ''Well, it's a very exciting place to live. But the only thing that scares me is the possibility of getting gambling and stuff like that here. This is a family-oriented place. We'd like to keep it that way. That's one reason people come to church in such numbers here. Entertainers the stature of Willie Nelson and Johnny Cash will bring in a lot of people, all kinds of people. Don't get me wrong, though. Willie Nelson's my favorite.

''One thing you might be interested in, though, that's pertinent to change—or maybe to stability. We have this information on the area, projections for the year 2000, from the Ozark Ministerial Association in Springfield. What they're saying is that by that time, just through this decade, if you drew an eighty-mile arc south of Springfield, you'd have the greatest concentration of retired people in the country.''

Behind the Bar at Rocky's

Rocky's is located down by the railroad tracks, well off the strip in downtown Branson. Nevertheless it draws a steady year-round clientele that swells substantially in the season. The thing about Rocky's is, you have to know it's there and you have to be looking for something a little bit different. For one thing, pizzerias aside, it's the only Italian restaurant in town—and it's a good one. For another, its bar-lounge, open well into the night, is the only place in town to offer jazz—live jazz, good jazz, the real thing.

The owner, Chuck Barnes, though born in New York, grew up in Kansas City and has lived in Branson for sixteen years. He is one of the nicest guys in Taney County and certainly one of the most generous—generous with his time, with introductions, and advice. In the course of one of our many conversations, Chuck mentioned that his bartender, Beverly Spears, had been in the music business. "She sang country and quit," he said. "Maybe you ought to talk to her. She might give you an interesting perspective on the business."

I made a mental note, and one afternoon when things were quiet at the bar, I opened my notebook and began asking her questions. What is it about people who have been in show business? Once they've heard applause and been in demand, they carry with them a certain quality, a kind of charisma, wherever they go. Bev has it. Although never a real star, she still has that quality. Not that she's one of those who's always "on," straining to get attention. She kids with the customers readily enough but leaves them alone when that's what they seem to want. The perfect bartender. And yes, she was willing to talk.

"No, I'm out of it," she said. "I'm out of it to stay. Hot Springs was the last big job I had, but it wasn't enough to support my kids even then, so I just got out and got into bartending. I never had a drink until my thirtieth birthday.

"See, my Daddy was a Pentecostal preacher in Hot Springs. He was very strict but I always felt this pull to singing and performing. I was so shy in school, I'd take an F rather than give a report in front of the class. But somehow or other when

I got the chance to sing in front of people, that was all I needed. I could do that. I won every year in the talent shows until I was fifteen. That was when I ran away to get married. And then my husband became a Pentecostal preacher, too. So how did I wind up like this?''

"Yeah," I prompted, "how did that happen?"

"D-I-V-O-R-C-E. I had three kids to raise. I'd do anything to raise my kids. It's been very different coming from the religious background to the bar business, both sides of it, singing in 'em and working behind 'em. That's me. I've known the bar and the Bible worlds. It's a totally different life, but I'll tell you, I like both.

"The singing was easy for me, and it was fun. When I was Pentecostal I had a chance to be around a lot of the gospel singers and sang with them, too—the Henson Family and the Florida Boys. And to this day, I really prefer gospel to any other kind of music. But fronting the stars in Hot Springs was good, too. Just everybody came through, and I'd open for them. Got paid $30 a song."

It struck me then and seems to me now that it was a funny way to tally wages—sort of show biz piecework. But, depending on the number of shows and the length of her sets, she must have done pretty well there in Hot Springs.

A customer took a place at the other end of the bar and called for a beer. Beverly left me with a wink, drew a beer, and took a moment to exchange a bit of small talk with him. She's friendly but not flirtatious—with her looks she doesn't need to be. Indeterminately over forty, she's sort of a dark-haired, dark-complected Barbara Mandrell–type, if you can picture that.

She was back in a minute or two and picked up where she had left off. "We had a big home in Hot Springs that I bought, me and the kids," she said. "But after a few years of it there, I came down to Branson to look it over because I heard it was a slower pace here—and back then it was. I got a job right away with a show that's not here anymore called the Cotton-pickers. My kids hated it here at first, and my son, Tony, eventually moved back to Hot Springs. They're all grown now, but now the girls wouldn't live anywhere else but Branson.

"But it was here I really got behind the bar. I started managing Murphy's Pub down on Main Street, sang there but worked the bar, too. I found out I really liked that part of it. I love the bar business. You get real close to people, one-on-one, and that's good for me, good for my shyness. To make a living in a bar, you have to come out of that shell. To this day I find myself reverting to that old shell of mine."

There were rumors around town of a runaway love affair involving Beverly and producer-songwriter Bob Milsap, who until a few years ago ran Caravell Recording Studios, still the only 24 track setup in town. I didn't want to tiptoe around this, but as it turned out, I didn't have to. She brought it up.

"As far as music, I learned a lot about the business when I got engaged to Bob Milsap. He's written a lot of songs—'She's the Rock I Lean On,' 'You Needed Me,' and 'Jeannie Marie.' Most of his songs have been sung by Tommy Overstreet. We've got a song by him named after us—'Beverly.' The Oak Ridge Boys and Waylon have sung it."

And that's about as much as she wanted to say about that.

"A lot of people who know about me, how I was a preacher's daughter and how I was married to a preacher, they ask me, 'Don't you go to church?' And I have to say, 'No, I don't.' But I still have my belief. I still believe in God, and I've had some signs He still believes in me. When I was out on the road, touring—I did a little of that—there was a kid in Utah came by who had glasses on an inch thick. He couldn't see through them at all. I put my hand on him as I passed him by, and his eyes were suddenly okay. Oh, I've seen a few things like that, been around it with my grandmother and my dad. All of us have had cancer one way or another. All came out of it. I was treated for it, had surgery, and was up and around in six days. So much has happened in my family. You just can't dismiss it."

A couple came in then and sat down at a table. Beverly Spears called over to them and asked what they'd have to drink. She was back on the job.

3

"It's the Gold Rush."

During the first of a number of conversations I had with Chuck Barnes there at Rocky's, he cited two major problems that the town faced. The first was the traffic situation. Well, if I had not by then experienced it at its worst—that was yet to come—I had at least sensed the dire disaster that threatened. ("One of these days," said Barnes, "we're going to get total gridlock.") The other problem he mentioned was one I hadn't even considered.

"Where are we going to put the labor force as this town expands?" he asked. It wasn't a rhetorical question. He had no answer. "Listen," he said, "There are six big new restaurant operations opening in town—a Cracker Barrel, a Bob Evans, and oh, I don't know what all, but big. And these six are going to require 710 employees. We don't know where they're going to come from, or where housing for them will be."

Where will they come from? Well, the economics of recession may have taken care of that. When "60 Minutes" broadcast its report on Branson as "the live country music capital of the entire universe" and talked about $1.5 billion worth of business done there, a lot of those who were out of work in the Midwest and mid-South simply filled their cars with family and what possessions they could transport and headed for this new El Dorado.

The problem was, the word went out in early December, and all that was left of the season was the "Christmas in the Ozarks" celebration in which only a fraction of the theaters and shows took part. Most of those, literally hundreds, who answered the call of opportunity sent out on CBS arrived just in time to see Branson shut down for the winter. Many stayed. Some had no place to return to. There were families who suffered through the winter in their cars. It was a good thing that it was a mild one.

Branson, Missouri, is an honest-to-God, certified, A-number-one boomtown. They may not have struck oil here, but they have struck entertainment gold. The *Springfield News-Leader* reported that by late 1991 "building permits worth about $84 million were issued" in Branson and there were more on the way. "The magazine, *Missouri Business*, placed the number even higher: "In the past year, new developments totaling more than $100 million have been announced. These include nine theaters and a showboat which will add over 14,000 new seats for musical entertainment." (That showboat, by the way, will be moored well outside town and will ply the waters of Table Rock Lake.)

When I first arrived in town in March of 1992 there was so much building going on that it seemed that every tenth vehicle on 76 Country Boulevard was another cement truck emblazoned with an "Ozark Mountain Country" logo which quickly became very familiar. Among the more impressive construction sites along the strip were the $4 million Johnny Cash Theatre that was being put up by California mall developer, David Green; Andy Williams's $8 million Moon River Theatre; and most impressive of all, the $13 million Grand Palace. Off the strip, Shoji Tabuchi was remodeling the lobby of his theater extensively, and Mel Tillis, who has been a fixture in Branson since 1989, was building a $4 million auditorium of his own, leaving his old location to Willie Nelson, who had decreed some remodeling of his own. In addition, there were new hotels and motels (some of them very swank and expensive), and all those new restaurants Chuck Barnes was talking about.

How long will it last? Well, the business acumen of the Herschend family is greatly respected in these parts. It should be. They took a nearby hole in the ground (a cave attraction that was widely ignored by tourists) and built it into the multimillion-dollar Silver Dollar City, one of the most successful theme parks in the mid-South region. Among the Herschends' other enterprises is Dollywood, the Dolly Parton theme park just outside Gatlinburg, Tennessee. And their latest, of course, is the Grand Palace—not just the biggest theater on 76 Country Boulevard, but also the one offering the hottest entertainment lineup. Gloomy predictions are usually stilled with the question, "Would the Herschends be putting that kind of money into Branson if they didn't think it had a future?" Good point.

Challenge Jan Eiserman of the Ozark Marketing Council with talk of the boom going bust, and you get the feeling that she had considered the matter and thought out her answer beforehand: "Before the boom happened here the entire area showed a strong growth pattern. It's a strong tourism destination—on tourism routes since the turn of the century. The growth of the Branson/Lakes area coincides with the growth of this part of the country nationally. We're sitting on a solid foundation here."

Whatever Branson's future, the town's present seemed exciting. With all those big names coming into town—Willie Nelson, Johnny Cash, Andy Williams—and with even more visitors expected than last year, there was a certain understandable wish on the part of the smaller communities in the area to share the glory and some of the profits.

One nearby village paid Branson the ultimate compliment. It seems that Lakeview, Missouri, was due for a name change anyway. It lay across the line in Stone County, a bit west on Missouri State Highway 76. The trouble was, there was another larger Lakeview a good deal farther north in the state. Well, almost any hamlet would have been larger than Stone County's Lakeview, for it had only thirty-seven registered voters within its limits. In any case, postal confusion called for action. But when it was taken by Lakeview mayor Artie Ayres and the board of aldermen, it caused quite a stir.

Lakeview, Missouri, was renamed Branson West. A lot of those in town and around it argued against it. A petition was circulated. But the new name stuck. There was just too much power there to resist. As one of Lakeview's registered voters was heard to remark during the height of the controversy, "These days you could take a cow turd, say it came from Branson, and get a pretty good price for it."

Searching for Stardom

Right there in the middle of the entertainment strip is a shopping mall of modest size. It consists largely of a Wal-Mart on one side that sells the usual everything and a Consumers market that is just about as exhaustively complete in the grocery line. But connecting the two is a small arcade featuring boutique-size shops, such as the Fabulous Fakes jewelry store, an upscale sweet shop, and a fancy little coffee bean emporium.

In the middle of all this there is a small platform stage with benches placed around it. I'd been through the arcade a couple of times and wondered what went on there. Then I came by on a Saturday afternoon and found out. A young man of no more than twenty-five sat up there with his guitar on the little platform and sang into the microphone for the entertainment— no, call it the diversion—of the shoppers. They sat stolidly and listened as he went through a small repertoire of original songs, some of them notably all right, and a couple of hits off the country chart (I remember a good version of Alan Jackson's then current hit, "Dallas"). A free concert—and they were getting a lot more than their money's worth.

At one point, he accepted weak applause and said good-naturedly, "I don't take requests. But if you write it down and wrap it in a hundred dollar bill, I guarantee I'll sing it."

I guessed that he would. I never got his name, but I think of him as the anonymous representative of a gang of people, young and talented, who have come to Branson hoping to make it big. Maybe they tried Nashville first—and were rejected—or maybe they're working their way to Music City, U.S.A. But they have come to this little town in Missouri because they heard that this was where the action was.

Maybe some of them even got the word via "60 Minutes."

Most travel alone, manage to crash with friends among the working musicians, and avoid camping out in their cars. Some of them have day jobs as bartenders and waitresses, the kind of employment they can leave quickly, should the big break come their way. They are alert to any opportunity to show what they can do. They'll sing and play anywhere, even in a shopping mall.

The Copper Penny Restaurant has given them a venue in its lounge during the off-season. What they are calling the Branson After Hours Original Music Showcase runs every Wednesday night from nine to eleven right up until mid-April. Modeled after the songwriters nights at Nashville's Bluebird Cafe, the Branson showcase offers an open mike to the writers and singers in town to show what they can do. The music industry people who hang around Branson during the winter and early spring make it a point to come and listen. The showcase was such a success its first year—no bad shows, singers got hired, and songs were bought—that the coming year, the one leading into the 1993 season, plans are under way to videotape the Wednesday night sessions for later release on cable TV's Arts and Entertainment Network.

A real audition, one with a good band backing you up and an audience to play to, is something every unemployed singer in Branson prays for. I was present at one such occasion through the good offices of Bill and Janet Dailey.

Janet Dailey? The name rings a bell perhaps? It should. She is, of course, one of the reigning queens of the best-seller list. Her *Calder Saga* novels, as well as her more recent books, such as *The Great Alone* and *Aspen Gold*, have won her a readership that is worldwide. She and her husband were just about to begin their move into Belle Rive, the antebellum-style mansion they have built for themselves on the shore of Lake Taneycomo, three miles outside of Branson. Its grand, colonnaded entrance was visible from the window of the smaller house where we talked.

Before Bill made his entrance, Janet Dailey told just how they had come to settle in Branson. "My parents were here," she explained. "We started coming here in 1974 to visit them and bought this property in '78, and from 1979 on we've stayed. Dallas had been more or less our home base up until then. Ultimately I guess what drew me to this place was the small-town atmosphere and the people. And the country, of course. The Ozarks are just beautiful. We have all four seasons, but none of them are really severe.''

So the two of them were here to see the phenomenal growth of Branson take shape? ''Oh, yes,'' she said with a knowing smile—they hadn't exactly sat on the sidelines and just watched it happen. ''When we first came here, there was just the Presley Theatre out on 76, what was then way out in the country. Bill kind of sniffed the air and said, 'This is *not* going to be one time we *wished* we'd bought land.' So that's what we did. We bought land. We owned the three hundred acres that the Grand Palace now sits on, and we've got thirty acres across from it still.''

Bill Dailey entered the conference room where we were talking as his wife continued the list of acquisitions: ''Wildwood Flower, that club out on 165, was ours. We owned what is now Mickey Gilley's Theater—we called it Country Music World. And, let's see, we're investors in Lodge of the Ozarks. And what else, Bill?''

He shrugged and smiled. ''Oh, I don't know what all. Got it written down somewhere.'' You bet he has. Bill Dailey seems the complete businessman, an individual with vision enough to see opportunity in a situation that is only beginning to take shape—as he saw it in Branson—a tough opponent in negotiation, and one with a genius for detail.

He agreed that Branson was a boomtown. When I asked him if the boom would continue—or if it might possibly go bust, he thought about that for a moment, tugged at his lower lip judiciously, and said, ''I think the area will double. We'll have buses, a shuttle or trolley services to take care of that traffic problem, and in a short period we'll have an airport big enough to hold anything that flies in.''

''We got five busloads from England last season,'' said Janet. ''You can find international representatives in just about all the audiences.''

''We've got people like Andy Williams, his category, starting up here. Debbie Reynolds—she's going to bring in a good type of show. Julio's talking about it. Then there's the stand-bys—Mel Tillis, Johnny Cash, Willie Nelson, Roy Clark—Roy used to be in our facility.

"We would never have settled here if we hadn't seen the potential," he continued. "No matter where you go in the U.S., you're halfway home to here. It's a tourist area that's just a little bit out of the way—and people like that."

Knowing why I had come to town, the Daileys invited me out to Pointe Royale that night to meet Buck Trent. They said he was auditioning a girl singer for his dinner theater show. Buck would have some things to say, and they thought I'd find the audition interesting. I did.

Kathy Raye Auditions

Pointe Royale is about as upscale as it gets in and around Branson. This gated condominium development has one-, two-, and three-bedroom units available for days, weeks, months, or maybe even years. Completely furnished and equipped, they come complete with washer and dryer, and in general live up to the advertising claim of "affordable luxury." There are tennis courts, a swimming pool, and that championship golf course mentioned earlier. Located, as it is, just above Table Rock Dam, it offers trout fishing in Lake Taneycomo and bass fishing in Table Rock Lake. All this should account for the fact that many of the stars who play Branson for limited engagements put up there at Pointe Royale. Some stay the entire season. Buck Trent lives there all year long.

Driving out there that night, I took a left off 76 and headed down 165. Not far from the junction, I passed the Wildwood Flower, the club once owned by Bill and Janet Dailey, which features solid country music and two-step dancing; the parking lot was already starting to fill up. A little beyond that, I saw a big sign over a dark theater announcing the absence of Buck Trent and Jeannie Pruett; that was where Buck had played the previous season. It was a dark, narrow, winding road, and as I drove on with the oncoming headlights flashing in my eyes,

I became a bit uneasy that I might miss the Pointe Royale gate. No chance. Although not flashing neon, the sign placed there at the entrance was so well-lighted that there was no overlooking it. I turned left into the gate, told the guard where I was headed, and was waved through without further question.

Pzazz was my destination. That's the restaurant/nightclub located just inside the walls of the fortress which is operated for the pleasure of Pointe Royale residents too weary or too discriminating to journey into Branson for their fun. If they dress right and drive the right kind of car, visitors from the outside are welcome there, too.

It's one of those upstairs-downstairs layouts in a single-story building. The lobby of the ground floor restaurant was crowded with the kind of women who wear fur jackets over fitted jeans and the men who love them. Could I have made some mistake? But no, a passing cocktail waitress directed me downstairs to the basement club, spacious enough as I discovered but modestly appointed. The band was tuning up. The right table at ringside was, of course, the big one where the Daileys sat. Waving me over, they introduced me to Buck Trent. I grabbed one of the empty chairs at the table and pushed in beside Buck.

I knew him by reputation. For years he was known as about the best featured picker on banjo in the business. He toured twelve years with Porter Wagoner and Dolly Parton and did television with them, then he hooked up with Roy Clark and stayed on the road for another seven. Blessed with good looks and a fine Deep South singing voice (he's from Spartanburg, South Carolina), Buck decided it was high time he made his move, and what better place to do it than Branson? They liked him here, and he liked them right back.

"I'm going to be here forever." He said it like he meant it. "This is a boomtown, all right. It's the gold rush! My phone's ringing right off the wall.

"I still do a little touring, and to tell you the truth, sometimes I'd just as soon cut it out altogether. I'll tell you what it's like. I work as a single on the road, and not so long ago I had this date in Norfolk, Virginia, a club; I'd been told that all the 'arrangements' had been made in advance for me. That usually means Holiday Inn, at best. Anyway, this old woman met my plane, and it turns out she runs the club. She takes me to her house and upstairs and she shows me, 'This is where you sleep,' she says. It's the guest room. And then she says, 'Now, my grandkids will be ready to rehearse whenever you are. They're the band.' "

Buck Trent chuckled and shook his head, remembering. "I always wonder what Chet Atkins would do in a situation like that," he said. "The touring's done me some good, though. I admit that. All the people I've been playin' to for thirty years are the ones who are comin' to Branson.

"But really, it is such a pleasure to be here and live life at a regular speed. Branson's my kind of speed. I'm a golf nut, and I live right here at Pointe Royale on the fourth fairway. They got a tricky course here. Usually I get one good shot and then a bad one, but the worst I've ever played I never hit it in the water. To be home and just be able to walk over and do a show, man, it's like heaven."

Is the new dinner theater as close as all that? "You passed it, where it's going to be, coming down 165," he said. "The sign's not up yet. See, it's got to be on the neighboring property to be seen from the road. When I was at the theater today, the wife comes up to me and says, 'My husband wants to talk to you about the sign.' It's going to cost me. I guess you could say we're in negotiation. All these business things—now I know what it's like to be in business."

Just then a party of three descended upon our table, led by a blond woman carrying a guitar case and dressed in black— black jeans, broad black belt, black jersey top, black boots— black, black, black. People turned and looked from tables around. This was the kind you had to notice. Bill Dailey got up and introduced her around as Kathy Raye, the candidate for the female singer spot in Buck Trent's show. She, in turn, presented her friend, Melody, "who takes care of my little boy," and Melody's husband. Then she began coughing and ran off, apologizing, to the ladies' room.

Eyes followed her across the room. "I really don't know a

thing about her," said Buck. "Just that she's a singer, and I sure need one."

The band, which had been tuning and talking through all of this, suddenly kicked off in high gear. Buck leaned over to me and shouted, just to be heard, "This is really a good band!"

He was right about that. And who should I spot in the middle of that group up on stage but Barry Bales, the lead guitar whose work I had so admired a week or so before in the Brumley Show. He picked with the same high energy and good sense he had displayed then. He sang just as well, too, stepping forward to intone a rather solemn version of "Smell the Flowers." This was his off-night gig, his busman's holiday. I recognized the keyboard man from the Brumley Show, too.

We were yet to hear Kathy Raye sing but hadn't long to wait. Barry Bales stepped forward and announced her to the audience: "She's a fine singer. She's got a guitar and a voice."

The guitar was acoustic, flat backed, could have been a Sears Silvertone for all I knew. She tuned it in a hurry, then began fiddling with the microphones up front. "It's which one's got the most bass," she explained. "I'm really loud." Then, settling on one, she told the audience, "Ahmo sing three songs for y'all." Then she took a wide stance, stomped out the tempo, with the heel of her boot, and led the band into "Gone at Last!"

Her voice was loud, no doubt about that, and even without the cough would certainly be guttural—but it was what Kathy Raye did with it that was impressive. There are relatively few female singers in any musical genre who can muster a strong, confident attack. Janis Joplin had it, though there was always the nagging fear that she might do some damage to her throat with her all-out assaults. Dottie West could call it up but didn't always use it. Aretha Franklin had it, has it, and no doubt always will; it comes natural to her. It seems to come natural to Kathy Raye, too. There was nothing very subtle about the way she shouted it out on the little stage at Pzazz. But she had a way of throwing it in the face of the audience, letting them know what it was all about, that was just plain irresistible.

But what about Buck Trent? What was his reaction? He seemed oddly noncommittal as she returned to the table. He shook her hand and nodded in approval but really didn't have much to say.

I heard later that she didn't get the job. I guess she just wasn't what Buck had in mind. The last I heard of her she had gone back to Louisiana.

4

Las Vegas, Here We Come!

What was it Thoreau said when somebody asked him if he had seen much of the country? "I have traveled far in Concord." Or something like that.

Well, Shoji Tabuchi has traveled far in Branson. Although nobody came a greater distance to get here, nor by a more circuitous route, no other performer has achieved more spectacular success once settled in this, "the live country music capital of the entire universe." If not the biggest, his 2,000-seat theater is in some ways the most impressive (well, one way in particular) of them all. In it, he does two shows a day, seven days a week. Week in and week out, his is the hottest ticket in town. At every performance there are about a dozen tour buses parked in a special section of the lot reserved for them, and often there are more.

His fame has spread well beyond the Ozarks. It was only in February of 1992 that Shoji budged from Branson for the first time. He took his show out on the road briefly, playing in small and midsized cities in Arkansas, Louisiana, and Texas. Nevertheless, the Japanese immigrant star of country music is such an irresistible anomaly that he is sought out by every television crew that comes to town and given major attention in every magazine and newspaper article written about the Branson phenomenon. His well-publicized love of fishing has twice won him an invitation to one of then-President George Bush's angling parties. After returning from the first, he burbled enthusiastically to the local *Branson Beacon*: "This was an opportunity of a lifetime. How many people come to America with $500 and have the chance to get to know the president of the United States? This was a dream come true." How many indeed.

There are, sadly, scores like Kathy Raye who come to town looking for a break, and for whatever reason (not for lack of talent) leave without ever getting one. But there is really only one Shoji Tabuchi.

Born in 1946 in Daishoji, Japan, he grew up in Osaka. His father, a manufacturing executive, fully expected his son to follow him into business and toward that end sent him to college for an economics degree. But his mother had enrolled him as a Suzuki Method student at the age of seven. At first he resisted. He tells, during his show, how he used to climb a tree and hide when it was time to go for his violin lesson. "She is a great lady," he said, "and a great tree climber. She got me down every time."

Music won over economics when, during his sophomore year in college, Roy Acuff came to the campus and played a show. Shoji was quite overwhelmed: he'd been playing violin all these years; this was fiddle. Talking with Acuff after the concert, he was told by the "Grand Ole Opry" great to look him up if he ever came to Nashville. Years later he did just that.

Once graduated, he set off for the United States with $500 given him by his mother. Settling first in San Francisco, he worked as a waiter, polished cars, and formed a Japanese-country trio, the Osaka Okies. The novelty of the group won them work around the city, even at the renowned hungry i club. But it wasn't until he moved to Kansas City that he got his first steady job as a sideman and a membership card in the American Federation of Musicians. Roy Acuff passed through town, and when they met again he renewed his invitation and promised to put him on the Opry. Shoji didn't have to be told three times. He headed off to Nashville, and Acuff was as good as his word. Shoji played the Opry, got a standing ovation, and has returned many times since then.

That didn't quite change his life, as he hoped it might. He continued working as a sideman, moving on to Wichita (where he also held a day job as an X-ray technician) then touring out of Shreveport with David Houston. But return engagements on the "Grand Ole Opry" had given him greater recognition, and so finally in 1975 he began touring as a single, a tough life, playing with house bands wherever he was booked.

This went on for years, tough years of hard traveling, until at last in 1986 he received a bid to come to Branson as a featured performer at the Starlite Theatre—a whole season in one place! Season followed season: the audiences loved him there. He decided that this was where he would settle down. (The fact that he had married in Branson played some part in the decision, of course.) And so he took the plunge in a big way and began construction of what would be for a season or two the biggest theater in town—the Shoji Tabuchi Theatre, located just a quarter mile or so off the top of the strip on Shepherd of the Hills Expressway. It was there that the cameras of "60 Minutes" found him. And it is there that he holds forth to capacity crowds today.

People kept telling me that I just *had* to see the ladies' rooms at Shoji's theater. Well, of course the people who kept telling me that were all female. Just how did they suppose I would gain entrance? Go in drag?

Even so, I was curious. A construction crew had been working at the theater site all through the month of March, and the word was that Shoji was remodeling the theater lobby. That must have included the refurbishing of the fabulous ladies' rooms, because from opening day on they were the buzz around Branson.

Something remarkable happened on my way into the theater: they ran out of room in the parking lot. What happened? Had they oversold the matinee performance? No, as it turned out, there were just too darned many Greyhound-size tour buses taking up space that would normally be allotted to passenger cars. (Lucky Shoji! Every showman in Branson will tell you that the real money comes into town on twelve wheels.) The attendants were forced to direct cars across the road to the motel parking lot.

Was it my imagination, or was the crowd in the lobby a little giddier, a little louder than usual? They were certainly no younger. Then I decided these must be bus people. Group travel has that effect upon people, after all—gives them the chance to perform, vie for attention, leave their inhibitions back in Minnesota.

As I joined the file into the auditorium, I cast a sidelong glance at the door of the ladies' room nearby. Why were all the women who came out giggling? What could they possibly have found inside to whisper about so? The Shoji Tabuchi theater is terrific. Capacious and comfortable, its dimensions seem to suggest an even greater capacity than its advertised two thousand seats. As an example: there seemed to be greater space than usual between the first row of seats and the stage. But this was not, as it turned out, wasted space.

As the curtains part to the tune of "Everything's Coming Up Roses," a chorus of girls dances in, singing, whistles are blown, and suddenly, the front of the theater—that large space between first row and stage—is filled with chorus boys skating around in formal attire, passing out pink roses to lucky ladies in the audience. *Skating*! Wow! What an opener! The audience loves it. Women in the front two rows make unladylike grabs for the flowers. And finally, applause drowns out the last few notes of the song. Are they impressed? You bet they are—but they're not surprised. Previous visits and word of mouth have led them to expect this sort of spectacle in Shoji's shows.

A back curtain opens to reveal the band—all thirteen pieces, including a harp, probably the only one to be found in Taney County. A featured singer named Marvin Short comes on and begins a set of songs that he shares with girls of the chorus who step out to solo. Then the stage empties, and under a single spot (the lighting of the show is the most sophisticated in Branson), Short agonizes his way through Garth Brooks's big hit, "What She's Doing Now." And with barely a pause for breath, he launches into another Brooks hit, the hell-for-leather "Go Against the Grain." On comes the chorus, men and women, boys and girls. In just the time it took him to sing the first Brooks song, they have changed into cowboy duds. They carry short ropes. They twirl those short ropes. Nothing too fancy, mind you, no show tricks—but all eight members of the chorus keep those ropes in steady motion for a good three minutes or more, the entire length of the song. If you ever tried it as a kid, then you should be impressed. It's announced afterward that before the season, not one of them knew how to twirl a rope.

So. Two production numbers within a matter of minutes. But now . . . it might be time for—yes, it is! A white violin is projected onto a black scrim. A big construct of neon lights up: a large circle inside an even larger triangle. There is a deep drum roll and then a cymbal crash—and there he is!

It's Shoji!

He jumps through the neon circle, fiddle and bow in hand, acknowledges the tumultuous applause from the crowd with a wave of his bow and a nod of his head and swings immediately into the old hoedown tune, "Turkey in the Straw."

There is nothing particularly prepossessing about the man— and perhaps that is his secret. He appears to be a good deal taller than the average Japanese. His jet black hair is cut in a pageboy. He is dressed in a sort of modified tuxedo whose brocaded jacket is, in its own way, as bright and colorful as any creation Nudie ever put together. And the man plays the fiddle like a demon—fast-faster-fastest—really getting the crowd excited, getting them to clap time without any prompting. The people are there to have their temperature raised just a little, to be excited. They are disposed to like him—and like him they do. When he finishes and calls out, "Hiya, folks! Having a good time?" they answer with a wave of applause.

He asks how many are there from Texas? from Oklahoma? And then he announces they'll be playing a couple of western swing numbers—"music by Bob Wirrs" (Bob *Wills*—his accent sometimes gets in the way). And that's what they do— "San Antonio Rose" and "Time Changes Everything." He plays Bob Wills's fiddle part, and then sings them both,

Tommy Duncan–style, more or less—but again, his accent sometimes gets in the way.

It seems an asset to him, really, in the same way that Mel Tillis's stutter works so well for him. It sort of breaks down the barrier, makes Shoji seem sort of, well, cute. Although his English is hesitant, he doesn't hesitate to engage in chitchat with the audience. ''We try to do arr kinds of music,'' he tells them, as he begins the kitschy, vaguely classical ''Intermezzo'' from the 1939 Ingrid Bergman–Leslie Howard movie of the same name. And they certainly *do* try all kinds of music, from samba (''Brazil'') to big band (''Lady Be Good''), and so on, down the line.

After intermission, he talked about his parents' recent visit to Branson: ''My mother say, 'Oh, Shoji, your ladies' room is beautiful!' '' And he discusses the vicissitudes of learning English from stuttering Mel Tillis, his frequent fishing partner. And so on. Whatever he has to say or sing, the audience eats it up. They love him, and he loves them right back.

The second half of the program is mostly Shoji, although the blond singer and mistress of ceremonies, who turns out to be his wife, Dorothy, has a couple of solos. He winds up his portion with ''Listen to the Mockingbird'' (complete with birdcalls)—''This is the one that started me on everything.'' And finally, ''Orange Blossom Special,'' again rendered fast-faster-fastest. Are we through yet? No, we're not through yet. ''Now comes our patriotic portion,'' he says. ''The show's not complete without it.'' A huge American flag is hauled up behind the band as they play, and Shoji sings—an original, ''We're Comin' to America.'' The chorus joins in. The audience is on its feet, applauding. Then, while they are still up, Shoji and the chorus deliver a kind of adieu-encore, ''Put a Little Love in Your Heart.'' *Everyone* claps time at Shoji's invitation. Members of the chorus come down from the stage and begin shaking hands with people in the audience.

Sometime in there—who knows when?—the curtain closes and the show is over. Yet the crowd is left so high from it all it's as though they think it's still going on. Behind the curtain, the band keeps playing, and the audience keeps clapping time. At last the band winds down, and the people realize it's all over. They begin to move toward the aisles, still high from the experience. That's leaving them loving it.

What a showman Shoji Tabuchi is! He could take this production, just as it is, to Las Vegas, and when word got around, he would be king of the Strip.

He Smiles a Lot

And that was just the matinee. Shoji had an evening performance to do, just as he does every night during the season. What does he do between shows? Well, sometimes he and his wife, Dorothy, will go out for dinner; but usually he munches a sandwich. He's been known to sit in for a few hands of poker with members of the band. More often he stretches out in his dressing room and takes a nap. This time, however, he sat down and talked with me.

We were in his office, across from one another with no desk between us. Our matching chairs were upholstered in lavender, no less. There are pictures of family—Japanese and American—on the wall and on the big, executive desk that stands behind him. He doesn't seem entirely out of place in this setting. He may be an entertainer, but he is also very clearly a businessman.

I wondered if he had ever taken his show back to Japan. "No," he said, "that is my dream—to take entire company to Japan to perform in front of Japanese audience. Country music itself is not really big there, you know? But our show consists of everything—pop, Broadway, everything to classical, and of course country should also go there."

Shoji began in country, so why such variety in the show—particularly here in Branson? "Of course I love country music, you know? That's where I started making it. And I was classically trained, so I love to play some of that. Well, what happened was about ten years ago, since I came here, I started experimenting to mix with classical and country and actually, that was about 1982, 1983, somewhere along there, my wife said, 'Why don't you just try out different, like a Hungarian song and "Orange Blossom Special" together?' So we started doing it, and it went well, you know? The country audience loved the idea. And I love easy-listening song with semiclassical pop-type music.''

And how did he get to be the hottest ticket in town? ''Well, it's not only myself. It's the whole show. We have so much to offer. My daughter, eleven years old, she sings, and I think she does great—high A's. She can belt out and sing, you know, like hard songs from Disney—you know, 'Beauty and the Beast.' And the whole cast can do Broadway, you know, from Broadway musical. We have dancers. They can tap and even do a little, you know, ballet. And we have the special effects.''

He is smiling as he says all this. He smiles a lot; he always seems to be pushing hard, going that extra distance—during the show and afterward. He puts in time signing autographs and shaking hands with members of the audience after the show, as do just about all the headline entertainers in Branson. But once that is done, he runs out to the parking lot to bid good-bye to the tour bus visitors as they depart.

''The buses is important,'' he declares, ''the people. The contact with people is important to me. Without people, where are we? They're the ones help make me where I am. And also, I want them to have the best time while they're here. I love the feedback from the audience. I've done a lot of kinds of work, but the boss won't come to me every time I've done something good and say, 'Great! great!' But here, this job, they tell me how much they enjoy, and it makes you feel good. And also I don't mind to talk to people at all. I love it, and it's important to me.''

And where did he learn his English? ''In Japan I studied when I was in college. You have to take English course. They start teaching you in junior high, so I went to missionary church, and they have English-speaking class, and I went to that. But oh boy! What a surprise when I came here. I was lost. Had to start all over. People speak so fast, you know, and there's so many slang, too.''

Did he really come to America with just $500? He nods. It's true. Well, did he ever think he would own his own theater? ''You know, I did not know how far I can go, and I appreciate the opportunity this people and this country gave me." The smile is gone. He has leaned forward in his chair and speaks very seriously, very earnestly. "You know, the one thing I tell everybody is, I'm the best example of the United States. You can pursue the dream and make a living in this country. I brought $500, and sometimes I did two, three jobs. I'd go in the morning till nighttime, and then go back at seven o'clock again. But all of that taught me, you know, how to manage myself. I'm from a small country, very crowded, and it is very competitive. I appreciate the opportunity here. I used to play and pass the hat. Sometimes I didn't have a steady job, so I would pass the hat. And I want you to know, I made good money doing that. I always had dinner on the table, enough to eat and a place to sleep. And if you can do that, you can better yourself.

"My parents come here, you know, and they're very proud of me. This year, that was the first time they've seen this theater. They were really surprised at the size of it, and how pretty it was. My dad would like to move to the United States. He would do it. I went back six years ago. That's the only time in twenty-three years. And you know, when I was over there, I miss the U.S. Japan is a different country. I've been here so long, and I have a horrible time translating. I start thinking in English."

By this roundabout route he came to talk about how it was he had arrived in Branson. Given the opportunity to headline a show, he wasn't really so sure he wanted to come: "I'd never heard of Branson. This was 1980, maybe early 1981, and I was doing pretty good on the road. But then I came through here, and I saw what Branson look like, and I talk to my friend, Mike Ito, he was here already working at Baldknobbers. Look good, sound good, and so I decided to take an opportunity. I work at the Starlite Theatre four years—now it's changed into Cristy Lane Theatre. Then I moved to Country Music World, Bill and Janet Dailey owned, and I worked three years there. Then I had opportunity to go into business in my own theater, where Willie Nelson is now. That is my first theater. Then I sold that and built this one."

Mike Ito, whom Shoji mentioned, is the *other* Japanese fiddler in town, still featured in the Baldknobbers show. "I have to tell you a funny story about us," he said. "I hear from man at filling station, he told me this veteran from World War II went to see my show and got angry to see a Japanese playing. All this from the war, you know. He decided to see a real American show, so he went to Baldknobbers, and who plays there? It is Mike Ito! He can't win!"

Shoji laughed, but then he added, "We have so many World War II reunions, all kinds of veterans come here, and it's all good. One time gentleman wrote me letter, you know, nice letter, and I still keep it. He say, 'Your music and your show just made all the bad war memories go away.' He bought season ticket after that. But I never have any bad war memory. This was before me, you know."

About his wife, Dorothy: "She's the biggest support system, and she's the biggest wheel to this operation. She has foresight. She produces the show, and she put together the songs and song segments. She get together with the director, and they arrange it. She's very, very perfectionist. We have the hardest-working musicians and cast—they don't mind the practice—and she watches from every angle. She really helps me out, so all I have to worry about is go out there and play my part."

And their daughter, Christina: "She's doing pretty well, you know. She can play fiddle, too, but she don't want to practice. She loves to dance, though, and she can tap very well."

(Christina was missing from the show I saw—a weekday matinee—for a very good reason: she was in school.)

Challenged, he swears that he and Mel Tillis really do go fishing together. But does Shoji really eat the bait? It's an old joke by now, but he laughs anyway. "Oh, I try," he said. "You know, I kid him, too, that he's my English teacher. We have fun."

Finally, he admitted that he had just one unrealized ambition: "Well, you know, Branson is always my home, but I do like sometime to take my show to Vegas. That's one of my dreams."

How did I guess?

"I go there sometimes," he assured me. "I like Wayne Newton, his show."

Still unsettled, however, was the matter of the ladies' rooms. Somehow I couldn't work up the nerve to ask him to take me inside. I was quite willing to let the matter drop. But as it happened, the next night I found myself sitting next to a woman from Minnesota at the Willie Nelson show. It turned out we had been to the same matinee at the Shoji Tabuchi Theatre. She was one of the bus people.

"Oh, well," she said, "did you see the ladies' rooms?"

I don't remember exactly what I said to that, but when it turned out I was curious, though, she opened up her purse and produced a few Polaroids she had taken inside. As she showed them to me, she described it in some detail.

"Well, see this crystal chandelier? I don't know if you can tell, but it's lavender. Isn't it pretty? And, well, I guess it's all right to show you this, but this is how the stalls are inside. They're just like little rooms, see? Wooden doors with gold handles. And lookit here, they've got a maid who'll spray you with just any kind of perfume you want. The faucets have gold handles, and there's little angels all over the wallpaper.

"Now, isn't that something?"

Indeed it is. Not even Wayne Newton could top that.

5

Hats and Boomers

It happened toward the end of my first month in Branson. Of course it had to come eventually. But even so, a tremor of regret passed along 76 Country Boulevard, through Music Row in Nashville, touched Austin and Amarillo, and, well, it really hit Oklahoma City pretty hard.

Maybe you didn't notice it at the time, but Garth Brooks's *Ropin the Wind* album finally got knocked off the top spot on the *Billboard* pop chart (replaced by the original soundtrack album from "Wayne's World"!) Thus ended a reign that had begun the previous September. That was when the young, moon-faced country troubadour astounded the music world, and the recording industry in particular, by hitting the top of the pop chart his first week out. And he held on to the position, too, lording it over Michael Jackson and Madonna, for six months. Nobody at *Billboard* could remember that ever happening before with a country album.

There may have been a bit of envy among his country competitors, but nobody really begrudged him his success. Even in Nashville's lowliest precincts there was a sense of shared pride in what Garth Brooks had done. On Music Row they were calling his six months at the top of the pop chart "our finest season."

What had happened to bring this about? Two things,

really—a small mechanical matter and another of great complexity, one that may portend a great cultural shift and has pundits scrambling wildly to explain it.

First of all—and this is the easy part—*Billboard* is now keeping a more accurate count. Not long before the Garth Brooks coup, the bible of the music industry ended its practice of relying upon a telephone canvas of record shops (imprecise at best) to compile its all-important sales charts. It now pulls its numbers via SalesScan directly from the computer code imprinted on virtually every item sold in stores today. And this now includes sales information from Wal-Mart and K-Mart stores, where a horde of country music fans buy their albums. Given these new circumstances, it is not unlikely that Garth Brooks's considerable feat may soon be repeated—or duplicated by one of his hot new colleagues.

Second, there is a host of exciting new talent in country music today. Sure, the Nashville genre has enjoyed waves of popularity in the past. Individual performers—dating back to Hank Williams (Sr.) and Tennessee Ernie Ford in the forties and fifties, and Johnny Cash and Glen Campbell on into the seventies—have enjoyed so-called "crossover" success, moving from the country chart to rise on the pop chart (sometimes to the very top). In 1983, the movie *Urban Cowboy* brought a certain amount of attention to the country scene, but as it turned out, that had more to do with the apparel industry than it did with music—a fashion fad that soon faded. This time it's different. And one reason it's different is the array of young singers and songwriters who have come along in the last few years. It's the best crop of newcomers Nashville has ever had. Any one of them has crossover potential. Although Garth Brooks is very good, a performer with real staying power, he isn't necessarily the best—and he knows it. In accepting the Voice of Music award from the American Society of Composers, Authors and Publishers, he gave it to the industry audience in Nashville straight from the shoulder: "You and I both know there are people on the street here that can put me to shame, that can't get record deals." Right now he might be the foremost, but he's not the first—nor will he be the last.

No matter how young they may seem—and Dwight Yoakam, born in 1956, looks about half his age—the singers who comprise this new generation in country music actually represent a return to the roots of the music. The publicist who dubbed them, as a group, "the New Traditionalists," really got it right. It's a radical revolution, a return to the roots. And they had a lot to rebel against.

Country really hit its nadir in the seventies with what Nashville promoted as "pop-country." Glen Campbell's success on the pop charts inspired artists and producers to accommodate material and treatment to what they believed the big public wanted. They were actively pursuing crossover. Bill Anderson and Lynn Anderson (no relation) worked hardest at it—the former with an insufferably cute rendition of "The Unicorn" (he later even turned to "disco-country"), and the latter with the Grammy-winning "I Never Promised You a Rose Garden." But all over Music City singers were slowing tempos and producers were adding lush string tracks in the conviction that this was the way to sell a million copies of practically anything.

Through much of the decade it seemed that about all that kept the music honest was Merle Haggard and the "outlaws"—that loose confederation of bad boys that formed around Waylon Jennings and Willie Nelson and included, among others, Tompall Glaser and the very talented Larry Jon Wilson.

But one singer-songwriter came along then who proved to be a forerunner of the present-day New Traditionalists. James Talley came out of Tulsa to Nashville and was employed as a social worker in the poor neighborhoods of the city as he worked and waited for a break in the music business. When it came, he had a drawer full of songs which were about as different from the then dominant mode in country as they could be. His natural sympathies, as well as his experience as a social worker, informed every line of such songs as "Give My Love to Marie," about a Tennessee miner with black lung disease. They were not all so grim. "Forty Hours" was a hymn to the working man. "Red River Memory" harked back to his Meehan, Oklahoma, childhood. He sang them all in a nice country tenor against a backup that was pure, provincial honky-tonk. The content of his lyrics won him press attention outside the country field. Rosalynn Carter named him as her favorite. But Nashville wasn't listening. On pure quality James Talley got a couple of albums and his allotted fifteen minutes of fame. He came—and went—before his time.

If there was a first in this generation of New Traditionalists, it was George Strait. Texas-born, bred, and educated (he, like Talley, has a college background, as do most of the others who followed), Strait began singing with his Ace in the Hole Band through the Southwest during the late seventies. He had a sense of the country music tradition with emphasis on the old Western Swing style of Bob Wills—and he seemed to know just how he should fit into it. His own vocal style was influenced by George Jones (that name will recur). MCA scouted him and signed him, and he came into Nashville as an outsider. Nevertheless, his first single in 1981 hit the top 10 in country. Hit after hit followed. He was named Male Vocalist of the Year in 1985 by the Country Music Association and Entertainer of the Year two successive years, 1989 and 1990.

What made him different? Why did George Strait go over so well when James Talley faded so swiftly? Well, that first hit single of his provides a clue. It was titled "Unwound," and here's how it starts:

> Give me a bottle of your very best
> 'Cause I've got a problem
> I'm gonna drink off my chest
> Gonna spend the night gettin' down
> 'Cause that woman I had wrapped 'round my finger
> just came unwound.

It's not just a drinking song, and its not a George Jones–style hurtin' song. It's a *relationship* song, and its you'll-be-sorry-Charlie message appealed directly to women, who are the biggest buyers of country records—of records of any sort. This was the something new he offered in something old wrappings. He continued, issuing further warnings, "Since my woman left I'm down and out''; and promising reform, ''If you're thinkin' you want a stranger, there's one comin' home.'' And so on, through a whole list of hits.

Country's current male stars seem newly sensitive to women's wants and needs, at least in their songs. You sometimes suspect them of cribbing inspiration from pop-psych books. But then, Nashville is a big city; there are plenty of problems for them to study, just walking around on the street.

Born in 1962, Garth Brooks is just ten years younger than George Strait. He chose Strait as his musical model while still at Oklahoma State University at Stillwater. Until then, he had drawn his musical inspiration chiefly from quiet folk-rockers such as James Taylor and Dan Fogelberg. It's true that Garth's mother had been in country music herself long before he was born—as a featured singer on ''Ozark Jubilee,'' Red Foley's country television show, which was broadcast out of Springfield, Missouri, during the fifties. But Yukon, a good-sized suburb of Oklahoma City, was a place where high school kids back in the seventies thought country was corny. In fact, Garth got up at an assembly once and sang a country song for his schoolmates—and got hooted off the stage. That put his country career on hold for quite some time.

Then one day at college (where he majored, farsightedly, in advertising and marketing), he listened for the first time to George Strait's first album, *Strait Country*, and was won over completely by its featured track, ''Unwound.'' Garth Brooks made a major shift in his musical direction. He put together a country band and began singing Strait-style in and around Stillwater, where Oklahoma State is situated. He felt confident enough to take off for Nashville immediately after graduation. There he was quickly rebuffed. Humiliated, he went back to Yukon to lick his wounds; then he reorganized the band, gave it a name—Santa Fe—and took it out on the road.

After touring the Southwest a couple of years together, he thought they were ready to try Nashville again, this time as a group. They rented a house and swore to give it a full six months' effort—then one by one, they dropped out and left town. By the end of the period, Garth Brooks was all that was left of Santa Fe in Nashville. But by then, too, he had signed a management contract and another with a music publisher.

His campaign to break through in Nashville, though faster than most, was typical of the legion who go there every year and fight for recognition. He first attracted attention at a songwriters night at the Bluebird Cafe. Sandi, his wife, assured him she was ready to dig in there until something big happened for him, so they both took jobs at a specialty shop selling cowboy boots to locals and tourists. That's how they lived as he put together the necessary components for a country career—a songwriting contract, a management contract, a booking contract, and finally, the one that makes it all happen—a recording contract.

The first album for Capitol, titled simply *Garth Brooks*, was issued in 1989. Although it sold well, it took the release of the fourth single from the album, with an accompanying video, to really put the thing over. That single, "The Dance," by Tony Arata, is a look back at a relationship that is over. Quiet and moving in tone, philosophical in content, it ain't your average country song. But it certainly hit listeners right and gave a second life to sales of his first album; it went gold eight months after release.

Does the strange somberness of "The Dance" mean that Garth Brooks is no Traditionalist? No, it means he's a Traditionalist who is willing to take a chance on something different. On most of the tracks, as well as the next for Capitol, *No Fences*, that wonderful western sound predominates in the accompaniment—lots of steel guitar and fiddle. And most of the material, songs like "Cowboy Bill" and "Unanswered Prayers," is so old-fashioned that it must have pleasured old-timers like Roy Acuff and Hank Snow to hear it.

And *Ropin' the Wind*? Sure, it's got a Billy Joel song on it, "Shameless," a high-energy relationship song, a real declaration of love, as well as two others in that same new category—the big hit single, "What She's Doing Now," and "Burning Bridges." But there are also two trucker songs, "Papa Loved Mama" and "Cold Shoulder," a cowboy story song, "Lonesome Dove," and a sort of pseudogospel number, "The River."

In one way, certainly, Brooks has made a profound break

with country tradition—and that is onstage in live performance. Country singers, male and female, usually stay firmly
planted in front of the microphone. If not hampered by a guitar, they will roam around a bit with a hand-mike—but it's all
done with dignity. Garth Brooks, on the other hand, is posi-
tively rowdy. Impressed years back in Oklahoma by what went
on at a Kiss concert, he determined early that there was a lot
of room up there onstage to put on a show. And that is what
he gives them. He's been compared to Mick Jagger, the way
he jumps around, whipping the crowd into a frenzy on the up-
tempo numbers. In fact, he calls his brand of music ''cowboy
rock 'n' roll.'' He sometimes gets carried away, breaking his
guitar onstage a la Pete Townshend of The Who. One night
he got recklessly wild and fell down into the orchestra pit.

Then there's the matter of his hat. Garth Brooks is seldom
seen without it. It's said he uses it to hide a receding hairline.
And while that may be, the big beaver felt Stetsons he wears
in assorted colors declare his identification with the West and
acknowledge his debt to George Strait. Of course in the dear,
dead days beyond recall, when they called the music ''country
& western,'' virtually every male who could manage a guitar
and croon a ballad at the same time wore one of those things.
But that became embarrassing to those who cultivated the pop-
country image, and so one by one they shed them. Waylon
kept his—he was from Texas, and he was entitled. And David
Allan Coe went out and got the biggest, blackest ten-gallon
job he could find just to go along with his bad boy image.
Then along came George Strait, also a Texan, and he had
always worn one. Nobody thought of suggesting that he put
his Stetson aside, just as long as he kept selling records like
he did. But then a funny thing happened. He was followed by
a squad of the most talented young male singers country music
had seen, Garth Brooks among them, and they all had Stetsons
planted firmly on their heads, just like George. Nashville began referring to them collectively as ''the hats,'' and to each
one individually as ''a hat act.''

Who are they? Well, there's Clint Black, for one. The Hous-
ton-born singer-songwriter is Brooks's nearest rival among

them. He made an even splashier debut with his *Killin' Time*, which as fate would have it, was released the same day as *Garth Brooks*. Black set country music records for a first album; it sold well over a million copies. With a blazing start like that, it's remarkable that Brooks, who was quite openly in competition with him, eventually overtook him.

With Black's good looks and his purer country sound, he may well have greater staying power—without the crossover potential. Both in style and the content of his songs, he is about as traditional as he can get. Pure cowboy, he's got an outlaw number on his *Put Yourself in My Shoes* album that sings just like a Sam Peckinpah movie. The title, "The Goodnight Loving," may mislead: it's got nothing to do with amorous behavior on the doorstep. It was the name, rather, of a trail to the Raton Pass. A young outlaw is riding it with a posse on his trail. If he can make it before the snow sets in, he'll be free. Yet Black shows himself hip to the new male-female realities in the album's title song:

> *We've had our differences*
> *We're still the same*
> *Hear what we want to hear*
> *Now I'm head over heels in the lost and found*
> *It's a cryin' shame*
> *I thought we made a perfect pair.*

Clint Black will be around for years to come.

Dwight Yoakam? Well, there's no denying the country credentials of this Pike County, Kentucky, native. He put in a long apprenticeship on the honky-tonk circuit before even looking over Nashville. Then he headed for Los Angeles, where he hooked up with Reprise. His first album with the label, *Guitars, Cadillacs, Etc. Etc.* was such a smash hit, both on the country and pop charts, that it even got a country music club in Kansas City named after it. He continues to sell well and has undeniable crossover appeal. But just how seriously can you take someone who denounces Nashville as phony— then lights out for Los Angeles?

Although he's a sure-enough "hat" (a white one), Alan Jackson acknowledges a greater debt to George Jones than the one to George Strait. That makes him traditional, all right, for who could be more country than "No-Show George," who went through alcoholism, pill addiction, and Tammy Wynette to come out a hero at the other end? Jackson, from Georgia, exploded with the single and the album it headlined, *Here in the Real World*, a grown-up country song if there ever was one. What sold it was that sliding, wailing sound so reminiscent of Jones. He seems to fairly idolize the man. He pays him homage in the title tune of his album, *Don't Rock the Jukebox*, and again, on another cut, "Just Playin' Possum." And what do you know? At the end of the song, who should show up to join in the chorus but old No-Show George himself?

Mark Chesnutt, the youngest of the bunch (born 1964), hails from George Jones's hometown—Beaumont, Texas. Now, Beaumont is in east Texas near the Louisiana line, more Southern than Western. And that says something about Chesnutt's singing style too. It lacks the hard edge of Clint Black and George Strait; his style, as well as the settings of his numbers, are sort of generically Nashville. He's had his hits, though—"Brother Jukebox," "Old Flames Have New Names," and "Too Cold at Home." And to his credit, he turns the last-named into a real, old-fashioned hurtin' song, and he slips and slides and slides Jones-style just like a human steel guitar, through its barroom refrain.

According to *Time* magazine, Vince Gill turned down an offer to join the soft rock band, Dire Straits, to sing country. Well, good for him; he's doing great in country. But he's no "hat." Meaning more, in this case, than that he mounts the stage bareheaded, outfitted in the kind of cazh-dress featured in the pages of *Details* and *GQ*. What's missing is that hard-edge cowboy sound. What he offers lacks a certain masculinity that you would associate with a male country singer. He has a way of pushing his voice into a key a bit too high for him on most numbers, so that what you get from him is close to a falsetto. That works just fine on the sweet stuff—and nobody sings sweeter than Gill on relationship songs such as "Look at Us'' and ''If I Didn't Have You in My World''—but is altogether unconvincing when he tries to pass himself off as a working man, or a drinking man.

What we're talking about here is authenticity. That's always been the standard in country music. From the days of Jimmie Rodgers and Woody Guthrie, on to Hank Williams and Merle Haggard, the tone of voice and the choices made in phrasing have constituted a kind of code that is immediately understood by the hard-core country audience. This, perhaps even more than what is sung, identifies the singer as pure country. Willie Nelson, for example, never sounded more truly Texan than he does on those pop standards from the thirties and forties that he recorded a decade or so ago. A certain sort of hard-won experience goes into the making of that sound—whether it be manual labor, jail time, or years of singing in the kind of honky-tonks where the band is protected from the crowd by chicken wire. The pure country sound can't be faked: John Conlee, fat, forty, and a former undertaker, has it; Whispering Bill Anderson, a one-time journalist and disc jockey, never did, never will.

Randy Travis has it. You could say he came by it naturally—and you'd be right, for there's no hint of anything studied or practiced in his style. His is an easy baritone, slightly nasal, and reminiscent of Charley Pride's. And oh, how that young man phrases! He finds more subtleties in a song, adds more fillips and sudden, drop-down swoops, than you could ever imagine were there in the notes on the page. You have to look to jazz and blues to find singers who phrase as boldly as he does.

You could also say he earned that authentic country sound of his—and you'd be right there, too, because in spite of the fact that he was in his mid-twenties when he burst upon the scene, Randy Travis had by then done a lot of hard traveling. He grew up on a farm in Marshville, North Carolina, out in the rural reaches beyond Charlotte. The father that life gave him was both a blessing and a curse. While he loved country music, played and sang it, and sent Randy off for guitar lessons at the age of eight, he was also a drinker, a hell-raiser, and the town's angry man. And so it was not surprising that Randy himself soon earned a reputation as a pretty wild kid. He dropped out of high school at fifteen. And when he was not putting in a full day's labor, and then some, on the family farm, he was out drinking, getting high, driving drunk, breaking into stores for petty theft, and often getting caught at it. As a result he did many an overnight in the county jail and spent some time in the Juvenile Detention Center. Just about the only positive thing in his life at that time was country music. He and his older brother Ricky were playing at dances and picnics when they were just kids. They graduated to honky-tonks before they were old enough to drink—but of course they drank anyway.

At last, at the age of eighteen, Randy found himself at one of those dramatic crossroads in life that prove fate sometimes writes the best fiction. He had won a talent contest, at Charlotte's biggest country music club, that included in the prize an engagement there. At the same time, he was coming up for a court date, facing a five-year sentence for stealing a pickup truck. (He swore he had just hot-wired it to drive it home and meant to return it in the morning.) Well, the owner of the club, a woman named Lib Hatcher, went to court and stood up for him. Randy was put on probation in her custody by the court, removing him from his father's influence and example. The judge warned the young defendant that if he ever came up before him again he had better bring his toothbrush because he was going directly to jail.

From that moment on, Lib Hatcher managed his life and his career. She recognized Randy's talent, showcased it, and won him a local reputation that none in the area could match. They began making reconnaissance trips to Nashville, sounding out the situation there. When she thought he was ready, she sold her club, and they moved there. Then came years spent trying to establish him, struggling to get a record industry still fundamentally hung up on pop country and crossover possibilities to accept a singer whose style and basic instincts were opposed to what they were doing there at that time.

But what Nashville was doing wasn't working. Sales and

interest in country music fell to a low in 1985. That was the year that Warner Brothers Records, rethinking the pervasive strategy, countered it by signing Randy Travis. They tried him on four singles, were encouraged by the results, and the following year released an album, *Storms of Life*. It went right through the roof, setting a sales record for debut albums (later broken by Clint Black) and winning him the Academy of Country Music's award as best New Male Vocalist. Other awards have followed in the years since then. It looked like he had started something.

He's not, strictly speaking, a "hat act" (he doesn't wear one onstage), but he is certainly a New Traditionalist. He grew up on Lefty Frizzell and Hank Williams and is obviously in sync with the styles and goals of the best of today's younger get-back-to-it country talent. In 1985, before he was firmly established, he approached George Strait at an awards function determined to meet him. But Strait recognized him immediately, stuck out his hand, and said, "Hi, Randy! I like your music!" Travis subsequently opened for Strait on dates during 1986.

He records songs by Alan Jackson and frequently collaborates with him. In fact the best tune and biggest hit of his recent album, *High Lonesome*, is credited to the two of them. "Better Class of Losers" suits them both, a lyric that thumbs its nose at yuppies and snobs of every sort.

But back up! Hold on! Randy Travis is now a seven-digit star, so firmly established that not even Garth Brooks could hope to blast him loose. True enough. But what happened to the woman who put him up there? who saved him from jail and managed his career? What happened to Lib Hatcher?

Reader, she married him.

She still runs the business end of the operation, has taken on other clients, and is now just as firmly established as one of that growing number of women who operate behind the scenes in country music and day-by-day help to make it all happen. No, not loyal secretaries and cute receptionists, girls Friday and dependable assistants—give Nashville a little credit. After all, the vice-president of A and R (artists and repertoire) at Warner Brothers Records who showed the good sense to buck the trend and sign Randy Travis was also a woman named Martha Sharp. Pam Lewis is the star publicist who made the world beyond country aware of Garth Brooks, bagging covers on *Forbes* and *Time*. And for every woman like them in top spots, there are scores in middle management positions. Women are establishing themselves in this corner of the music business, in spite of its macho traditions, just as they are in pop, rock, jazz, you name it.

But that's behind the scenes. You must have noticed that the roster of the bright new stars of country I've called off are all men. It's not a plot against women that has established overwhelming male dominance among performers in the country field. In fact, women themselves are to blame—that is, women as consumers. By and large, they determine how entertainment dollars are spent. They are certainly, as noted earlier, the major buyers of records and tapes—and the country field is driven by success in record sales. And the simple biological fact is this: women choose men. Ladies love outlaws. They love those great big hunks in cowboy hats who now seem to know better how women feel. And sometimes they get downright demonstrative. A number of times, as Garth Brooks whirls and jumps around at concerts, he's been joined by a female fan who just wants to boogie with her boy. Sandi (Mrs. Garth) Brooks has been known to run on from the wings on such occasions and toss the volunteer dance partner bodily off the stage.

What all this adds up to is lots of problems for women who try to make it as country singers. It wasn't until after World War II that Nashville got its first female star. Kitty Wells was homegrown, and got her first big break singing on a Nashville radio station at age eighteen. Yet it was many years after that she got her first record contract, and she didn't really hit it big until she recorded "It Wasn't God Who Made Honky-Tonk Angels," her "answer" to Hank Thompson's "Wild Side of Life," when she was thirty-four. She had many hits after that during the course of a long career. But then, she never had much competition from members of her own sex.

There haven't been many female country stars—and here I

suppose we mean superstars, headliners who could pull in big audiences on the strength of their names alone. Patsy Cline? She's remembered for the quality of her work, rather than her successful career (she died at age thirty-one in a plane crash). Loretta Lynn? Tammy Wynette? Dolly Parton? Absolutely! No argument there, yet when we continue and name, say, Tanya Tucker and Barbara Mandrell, there is an immediate sense that we are discussing stars of a lesser magnitude, no matter how many hits they may claim.

Women looking for onstage careers in country music need all the help they can get. Have you noticed how many who come along are relatives of well-established performers? Let's see, there's Crystal Gayle, who is of course Loretta Lynn's sister, Stella Parton, sister of you-know-who, LaCosta, Tanya Tucker's sister, Louise and Irlene, sisters of Barbara Mandrell. And then the daughters—Shelly West, the late Dottie's kid, Pam Tillis, Roseanne Cash—and even a niece, Carlene Carter, June Carter's kin and, I guess, niece-in-law to Johnny Cash.

In an odd sort of way, Wynonna Judd is in a position similar to all of these relatives of the more famous. Not that her mother, Naomi, was the star of their very successful duo, The Judds. But Wynonna is now going out on her own, following Naomi's retirement because of chronic hepatitis. She must draw what glory she can from the nine-year run she enjoyed with her mother, yet at the same time demonstrate that at twenty-eight she is her own woman and quite capable of making it on her own as The Judd. She put her problem neatly to *Los Angeles Times* writer Robert Hilburn when she said that "people forget I hadn't been the star. *We* had been the star."

Nevertheless, the years of recording and live performance she had as half of the duo have given her an immeasurable advantage over any other female vocalist beginning a career in country. After all, she sang lead, and Naomi Judd harmonized. And anyone who remembers her contribution to the crossover hit, "Mama, He's Crazy," will be certain she will make it by herself.

Yet making it is one thing and standing up to the competition that "the hats" offer is quite another. Curb/MCA Records certainly showed faith in her, pressing and shipping 600,000 copies of her first solo album, *Wynonna*. And her fans from the duo days responded, too, putting it up on the pop chart's top 10 within a week or so of its release—a respectable debut, certainly, virtually assuring that the album will go gold soon. Still, it's certainly not likely to equal, or even come close, to the showing Garth Brooks made with *Ropin' the Wind*.

The quality of the album is good—of course it is, *she's* good—but it indicates that Wynonna Judd hasn't quite chosen her way yet. When she's not growling out the lyrics to bluesy, rocky numbers against a driving beat, she's showing off her range on gospel-tinged love songs and a few of those secular anthems to faith, hope, and verity. One of these last, "It's Never Easy to Say Goodbye," is especially touching, considering this is Wynonna's first album without her mother aboard. (Strictly speaking, Naomi Judd participated in her daughter's debut; she cowrote one of the songs, "My Strongest Weakness," and sang harmony on another.) The best thing on Wynonna's first album is one pure gospel piece, "Live With Jesus," which Wynonna sings just about as dirty as the First Baptist Church allows. It is done very simply, in contrast to some of the rather heavily arranged material leading up to this, the album's last cut.

Part of Wynonna Judd's difficulty is that she is not a songwriter, and so she must always depend on others to provide her with sentiments she must make her own. Well, of course singers do that all the time, but because the singer-songwriter has done the work at one time or another, he or she has at least considered what is to be said choosing material by others. The singer-songwriter *has* something to say. You can't be sure, from the material compiled on the debut *Wynonna*, that The Judd really does.

A female country singer is in a curious position, for she must appeal to the same female audience as the males—though she lacks their sexual advantage. She must sing woman-to-woman, expressing their fantasies, giving voice to their complaints, disappointments, and joys. She can't be too far ahead of her audience, nor can she fall behind them. In writing and choosing her material, she must, by some sixth sense, know what women, her women, have on their minds. At the same time—and this is the tricky part—she can't be completely cynical about it, choosing only what she expects to have commercial appeal. No, when she sings, she's got to mean what she says, has to make their truth her truth, and vice versa. For if she doesn't, her fans will drop her as fast as you can say Barbi Benton. Now perhaps you understand why there are so few female stars in country.

The great ones—Loretta Lynn, Tammy Wynette, Dolly Parton—understand all of this instinctively. Loretta Lynn knew, for instance, in 1971, that it was just exactly time to record "One's on the Way," in spite of the fact that it had come from that madman, cartoonist Shel Silverstein, hardly a recognized country music writer. She sang it like she believed its message of (mild) protest because she did believe it—and she got her first real crossover hit. Ditto for Tammy and "D-I-V-O-R-C-E." And Dolly? She has been so prolific as a writer and remains in such close contact with her country fans that she seldom, if ever, seems to go wrong.

One female vocalist with Dolly's instincts is Reba McEntire. Their voices are even somewhat alike—which is to say, pure country and a bit plaintive. A fine, college-educated musician, Reba writes songs, too, though not nearly as many nor as apparently easily as Dolly. But whether she writes or chooses what she records, a fair number of songs on each album seem to go right to the hearts of her female listeners. Going back to 1976, her first hit single, "I Don't Want to Be a One Night Stand," expressed what a lot of women felt all too keenly—and it was considered a rather daring song by conservative country standards. There was a whole string of hit singles and albums during the early eighties, including a cheater's anthem, "You're the First Time I've Thought About Leaving" and the rousing "Why Do We Want What We Know We Can't Have?" Today, she sings more pointedly of independence in songs like "Is There Life Out There?" in which she offers a belated college degree as a way out of marital miseries. She understands her audience, all right.

The moment Reba McEntire steps on stage she distances herself from most of her competition, male and female. She is a very sophisticated performer who understands the importance of dazzling costumes and imaginative lighting. The way she moves around the stage you'd swear she owned it; and as long as she's up there, she does. She's come a long way from Chockie, Oklahoma—and she still has a long way to go. Although there are talented younger performers around today, such as Trisha Yearwood and Kathie Mattea, not to mention Wynonna Judd, Miss Reba seems likely to outlast them all. Except for Garth Brooks, she is the best and most consistent seller on the MCA label. Down the line, she may even give him a run for his money.

If country music is winning acceptance today from a wider audience, it would be reasonable to assume that it has changed in some important way. And has the music, in fact, changed? Yes, but the newest, youngest, and most popular of the male performers represent a return to a more traditional mode. It's back to the future as Garth Brooks, Clint Black, Alan Jackson, and Randy Travis return to those thrilling days of yesteryear when Lefty Frizzell was always late, and Hank Williams swore he'd never get out of this world alive. And the strongest of the female singers are just as conservative in their own way. So yes, country music has changed—by becoming more old-fashioned, less accommodating, *less* pop-driven than it has been in decades.

Then it must be the audience that has changed. And it is this possibility that has cultural pundits hopping, demographers crunching numbers, and pollsters charting popular taste. Are you ready for some statistics?

Time's famous cover article (March 30, 1992) on the country music explosion was titled "Country Rocks the Boomers." It sought to prove with some overwhelming figures that the impressive chart standings racked up by country artists could be attributed to the embrace of the music by the baby boom generation, who number some seventy-six million. Who are they? According to D. Quinn Mills in his book, *Not Like Our Parents*, they are Americans born between 1946 and 1966. In spite of the fact that the recording industry has for years paid most attention to the 15- to 19-year age group, they no longer buy the most records (just 18 percent), the biggest buyers are those 35 to 45, the baby boomers (29 percent). And it does stand to reason that this largest segment of the record-buying public is tipping the balance toward country. Just how are they demonstrating their new preference? Quite impressively. In 1991 (the most recent figures available at this writing), no fewer than thirty-three country albums went gold (500,000 units sold) and another thirty-five went platinum (1 million sold). Garth Brooks—the champ—has sold a total of 16 million copies of his three albums.

Although the point has been made that the average country listener and buyer today is a solid dues-paying member of the middle class, the pundits attribute the rise in country to the recession. Well, maybe. This recession has hit the middle class harder than any in the past. Why shouldn't segments of it come to identify more closely with what in the past has been considered blue-collar music? And why shouldn't country openly appeal to them? This may account for the cultural confusion on a Mark Chesnutt album in which he tells us, "It's too hot for golf," and also includes a cover version of a Garth Brooks hit, "Friends in Low Places." Clearly he is attempting to communicate with two separate constituencies in the same album.

But these are just songs. Are we trying to draw too much meaning, too many hints, from their lyrics? No, because in country, the lyrics have always been the point. They are more mature, more real, more adult in their concerns—and have just about always been. Way back in the Depression thirties, when Fred Astaire was inviting everyone to fly down to Rio (fat chance!), Jimmie Rodgers was passing on the last words of a dying hobo. Even during the dreary days of pop-country, there were honest souls who sang of jail time, of alcoholism, of cheating and divorce, of all of life's miseries experienced by real, grown-up people. And that is still the content of much of country music today. It's misery music, hurtin' songs, white man's blues—and white woman's, too. Oh, there is still a certain amount of macho chest beating, but it is balanced by a new awareness of the complexities inherent in male-female relations.

If anything has drawn the baby boomers to country, it is not some sudden sense of solidarity with the hard luck working class brought on by economic stress, but rather the simple process of growing older—and all that it entails. You take a forty-five-year-old in a modest suburb, fighting a mortgage, trying to come up with college tuition payments for the kids— what possible sense of identification could such a man—or woman—have with Axl Rose? What interest in anything he might have to sing? No, they, men and women, are far more likely to take seriously the words of George Strait or Reba McEntire.

And so it's really not that country music has changed; it is more solidly centered than it has been in years. No, it's that its audience has expanded into a new class, a new age group, a whole new segment of the population. Professionals who deal in such matters will tell you that the demographics are great. Country can only get bigger.

The View from Branson

In a way, what has happened in Branson, Missouri, is a reflection of all this. As for the performers, while a great many of the old stalwarts of country have opened up theaters and taken up residence, the newcomers are also in evidence there on 76 Country Boulevard. Most of the young leaders in country will play this year at the Grand Palace. But not Garth Brooks. Rick Todd, the man in charge there at the Grand Palace, is frank to say, "We couldn't afford him. If he wants to come, he will. We're not counting on him until on down the line sometime, maybe." (It was later announced that Brooks had chosen stadia as venues for his new concert tour.)

The demographics of country are also Branson's demographics. Remember that the largest segment of those visiting the area are couples with children. They are middle-class, and they spend money on shows, on lodging, on food and incidental shopping and entertainment. And the fastest-growing group is made up of young singles who are drawn by the big names in country music.

The latter group is especially interesting to Ed Anderson, editor and publisher of *Branson's Country Review.* "There's no question but that country is appealing to younger people," he says. "I'm talking about a wide variety of acts, from the Kentucky Headhunters to Garth Brooks who have that cross-over audience today. They're not just appealing to hard-core country fans but to an adult contemporary, or even a yuppie audience."

We were talking at his office located out on Fall Creek Road, a turnoff from 76 at the Holiday Inn. Anderson came here nine years ago from suburban Chicago to manage a group of local newspapers. After he had been here awhile and watched the entertainment scene grow, he decided that Branson needed a publication that would report specifically on country music and deal in general with vacation activities in the area. *Branson's Country Review* was born. Once the strip began to boom, advertising and circulation begin to increase. And so, after a few rough years in the beginning, the publication enters its sixth season in a very healthy state.

"What other city of three thousand could support a city magazine?" he asked. "Without the music shows helping me then, I couldn't help them now."

As for his own musical taste, he said "I like *good* country music, not so much the twangy kind. But you get everything here. Although Branson is specifically identified with country, a lot of Branson shows are pure entertainment. The American public doesn't have blinders on. People have a lot of varied interests and varied tastes. Mostly, they come here to be entertained—and that's what they get, entertainment.

"The big country names, all the young singers, may not have much to do with the national popularity of Branson, but in a way they go hand in hand. Most of them play The Grand Palace—Vince Gill, Ricky Van Shelton, Pam Tillis, Mark Chesnutt—but I think it would be foolish for the hot country acts to locate here and open up a theater."

Does that mean that Branson is sort of the end of the road for country performers?

"Oh, I don't think you can say that," he said. "When you can get as many in the theater as they do here, day after day, you can cut costs and stay off the road. That's attractive to a lot of performers. Willie Nelson is not a dying act. The Gatlin Brothers are coming here, and they're not a dying act. The acts I've heard who are considering coming her are *not* at the twilight of their careers. Once the Kenny Rogers and so on come, this place is *really* going to shine."

6

"Hometown Radio"

Most urban baby boomers get their first serious exposure to country music driving across the country. Maybe it's happened to you. Out there on the interstate where there are more *Gas Food Lodging* exits than real towns, you find that all across the radio dial, FM as well as AM, the sound that dominates the airwaves is the skating whine of the pedal steel guitar. When you hear that, then you know you're in country country.

What is it that persuades such strangers to the music to surrender and really listen to it? Well, for one thing the lyrics are understandable, as they seldom are with heavy metal rock. And the lyrics mean something, too, addressing situations they know and emotions they feel. There is something appealing, too, about those comfortable regional accents. The guys sound like guys, and the women—full-throated and strong—sound like real women. There's more to this stuff than might have been imagined.

I've driven across the country a lot of times—twelve, as of this writing. More often than not I take Interstate 40, which, in its western reaches, follows the path of old Route 66. And whenever I do, I always search out one of my favorite stations as I get near the Arizona-New Mexico line—KTNN, on the AM side, over toward the left, 660 on your radio dial. Try it sometime, and you'll have one of those only-in-America experiences.

There won't be any trouble picking it out from the rest. When you hear a concatenation of syllables as strange as any that ever touched your ears, you'll know you've got it locked in. KTNN, broadcasting from Window Rock Reservation, is the Voice of the Navaho Nation. Yes, it's a Navaho language station—most of the time. Commercials for Ford Escort and Jeep Eagle, announcements for meetings of the Navaho Rodeo Cowboys Association, interviews, are all delivered in that solemn-sounding, unstressed, vaguely Asian tongue. You may not love listening to languages you can't understand quite as much as I do, but just hang in there for a while, and you'll find out that it's the NBC affiliate for eastern Arizona, and you get the news in English piped right in from New York. And then the nicest surprise of all: KTNN has a country music format. They play the old cowboy stuff—a lot of Willie and Waylon—and some of the new guys, too—Clint Black and Alan Jackson—long sets that seem to match perfectly the wide open terrain that surrounds you out there. You get the feeling that God made country music just so it could be listened to in places like this.

As I said, only in America.

Today, you can hear country anyplace in the land. Drive Interstate 95 from Washington to Boston, the main stem for the Northeastern corridor, and you can have Nashville sounds every mile of the way. And even beyond, out across the great Canadian prairie on Route 1, you'll hear as much Garth Brooks and Wynonna Judd as you will below the border on Interstate 90. If you've got a radio, you can listen to country just about anywhere in the United States or Canada.

Whether cause or effect, radio has played a big part in the rise of country music. *Forbes* magazine noted in its 1992 report on country: "Ten years ago there were 1,800 country radio stations. Now there are more than 2,500. . . . According to a study by Simmons Research, more people with household incomes of $40,000 or above listen to country music radio than any other format." The message is clear: country demographics are *great*!

Cause or effect? That's a good question. For while each of these stations wins new converts to country every day, no medium is more sensitive to audience preference than radio, nor more willing to change in order to accommodate it. The legion of stations that have switched formats to country have done so, by and large, because surveys told them that this was what their listeners—and potential listeners—wanted to hear.

That's what happened, anyway, in Branson, Missouri. When Rod and Carol Orr bought KRZK-FM and KOMC-AM in Branson, neither station was on the air. The former owner had essentially gone out of business. All he had to sell were the station's physical facilities and the Federal Communications Commission's license to broadcast. That was in 1986. The Orrs went on the air with a modest signal of 3,000 watts. After boosting KRZK's power a bit to 4,200 watts, they went to 25,000 watts on June 1, 1992, and now hit a hundred-mile radius around the little town that lies just twelve miles above the Arkansas line. "But we don't want to lose the hometown flavor we've established," says co-owner and station manager Carol Orr.

They all say that, don't they? Well, in Branson they mean it. When you're out on 76 Country Boulevard, and George Strait is coming in loud and clear, deejay Jessica James will tell you that you're listening to "KRZK, hometown radio in Branson." It's a signature that's put out over the air a hundred times a day or more. Not quite so often, a mellifluous male voice comes through with a slightly cryptic reminder: "You asked. We listened." That means something, too.

When they came on the air in 1986, the lead station, KRZK-FM, carried an adult contemporary format, and the AM station, KOMC, was doing country—more of a golden oldies country playlist. Rod and Carol Orr felt at the time that the combination suited Branson pretty well. But they kept their ears to the ground and began regular surveys of their listeners.

"But what we wanted, right from the start," said Carol, "was to show a real commitment to this area, this town. We did a lot of local news from the lakes area, heavy local weather. But after a while, people began asking, 'Why don't you play country music on the FM station?'

"Since we have so many visitors to this town, we try to be there for them, too. During the show season, you've got to broadcast with two audiences in mind, the local people and the summer visitors. Now, how do we serve the visitors? Well, we've worked out an emergency message procedure with the local police. We work real close with the police department on that. It might be an emergency message from home. What we do is give the name and description of the people we're trying to reach, the kind of car they're driving, and we say, 'Please contact the Branson Police Department.' Sometimes we have as many as ten different parties we're trying to get through to on a single day. But people drive around town with their radios on, and a lot of them, maybe most of them, have us tuned in. Chief Steve Mefford says we've got an 80 percent success rate on this."

And what about the local people? How are they served?

"Well," she said, "we do publicity on scams." She smiled a little smile as she remembered. "You know, this is an ordinary town about three months out of the year, and people around here are as gullible as they are in any small town. A couple of years ago, a lot of people came through Branson, working some deal where they were going to pave driveways here. It was a scam—get the money and run—and we publicized it. People around here listen to the radio. They put a lot of trust in us.

"Then, too, we've helped raise money for some projects I'm proud of. There was the money we raised for a safe house overnight shelter for women. I'm on the board of the Women's Crisis Center—also on the board of the Taney County foster kids project. Then there was another interesting thing—the addition to the hospital. Peter Herschend—I guess you've heard about the Herschends and Silver Dollar City—well, Peter came and asked us to help raise money for Skaggs Hospital here. In a lot of rural towns, the hospitals are going broke. But we're in a special position here because of all the visitors we have. We need a good one. So naturally we pitched in with appeals and a lot of public service announcements. Seven million dollars was raised. We're proud of that."

All this was in her office. We had talked there after a short tour of the KRZK-KOMC studios. But now it was time for lunch. On our way out of the building she pointed to a plaque mounted prominently on the wall. It said, "Never expect more from a community than you're willing to give it in return." Her comment: "If you do that, it comes back to you."

On the drive over to the Koi Garden, a good Oriental restaurant in town, she said, "I suppose you really ought to talk to my husband, Rod, but he's out of town at our other stations. He's real involved in this community." Then, she added with a smile, "I am more than he is."

We drove through town, then turned up 76 Country Boulevard as she gave me a little of their background in broadcasting. The way Carol told it, they sounded a little like radio gypsies: "He got me into radio in Des Moines, where we met. He was on KSO at the time, and he'd done everything—been on the air, into sales, everything. He's just got a great background. We lived in Salina, Kansas, and worked on a station there together, and then we owned a station in Lake of the Ozarks with Al Sykes, who's now the head commissioner of the FCC."

But Branson gave the Orrs their first venture completely on their own, and provided them with an opportunity to put to the test their theories on community service. Their efforts have brought them recognition: in 1991, the Orrs, KRZK and KOMC, were presented with a Crystal Award, the highest honor in broadcasting for community service. "They only give ten of them each year," she said proudly, "and ours is only the third ever to be awarded in Missouri."

We were in a Chinese restaurant, and talked during that kind of lunchtime hush, over green tea and Chinese chicken salad. And I look back on the scene as slightly ironic, for even the fact that there should be good Oriental restaurants in this out-of-the-way corner of the Ozarks seems somewhat anomalous. The fact that we should be discussing hometown radio's switch to country over bamboo shoots and bean sprouts strikes me as a bit odd. Does Merle eat Chinese? Do Waylon and Willie? Maybe this is another one of those only-in-America situations.

"Obviously we watched the market," said Carol Orr. "We

saw the heavy trend of country music stars coming to Branson and all the crowds they were drawing. And some of the local people were continuing to ask, 'Why aren't you carrying country on KRZK?' Probably we should have made the change earlier, but we like to do our homework. We figured, if we make a change we'll do it right. So we did a lot of surveys. Five years ago country wasn't what they wanted. But now the surveys indicated that's what they did want. Finally the research indicated that the preference was very clear. That's when we came up with that tag line, 'You asked. We listened.' "

The switch was made on August 30, 1991. Essentially, the formats of the FM and AM stations were traded—though not quite even-stephen. KOMC inherited the adult contemporary format, but KRZK came up with what was not simply generic country, but a rather distinctive format, one designed to fit the special needs and tastes of a very special place like Branson.

"The basic playlist is the Country Hot 100," Carol explained. "But we try not to say that because even though we play so many current hits each hour by people like Garth Brooks and Alan Jackson, we mix in a lot of the old stuff to get variety, things by Johnny Horton and Tennessee Ernie, singers like that. But one time each hour we play something by one of our locals—not just those who're playing that week at the Grand Palace, but those who're really associated with Branson, like the people in the Baldknobbers Show and Shoji Tabuchi. Our reasoning here is that if people are coming to town to see them, they'll want to hear them on the radio, too. It gives them a kind of sample of what's available.

"Then there's the interview show that Jessica does—Jessica James, she was an entertainer herself, on the Opry and everything. She does interviews several times a week—'Branson Backstage.' The idea is to catch all the excitement and mystique of what goes on behind the scenes. Then the performers come to the studio, too, and do a 'celebrity set.' Mel Tillis might read the weather report; someone from the Baldknobbers might play some records. The listeners like that."

Is listenership up? "Well, the service we use is Auditair, and I can tell you our listenership has increased substantially after the format change. But with all the visitors in town, well, a tourist market is hard to survey. There's a new way to rate that—Audiscan—and we're going to do that this summer. But basically, there's no way to answer how many listeners we have here during the season. I tell advertisers that if only half the people in town for the shows are listening to us on a typical day—and that's not unrealistic—then we've got 75,000 to 80,000 tuned in locally. We know we've got a large basic Branson listenership. We judge that by when we do call-ins and giveaways.''

Now, with KRZK's power expanded to 25,000 watts, it is sending out country sounds twenty-four hours a day. Carol Orr feels that they're riding the crest of the wave: "I know that they say country is now programmed on one of every four radio stations in the United States. The number of country stations is up 92 percent since 1978. You know, years ago, in the seventies and eighties, a lot of people listened to country but didn't want to admit it. They were sort of closet country fans. But now, suddenly it's all right to admit it.''

Rod and Carol Orr feel the next wave is coming their way, too. They've acquired FM and AM stations in Sevierville, Tennessee. "That's the Gatlinburg area in the Smokies,'' said Carol, "and that's going to be the next Branson. It's a very big tourist area, especially now that the Herschends have opened Dollywood. Better believe it's Dolly Parton country. Our FM station, WDLY, is the first radio station she ever sang on—and we have the mike she used right in the studio. As a matter of fact, we use her butterfly signature in the station logo.''

And of course it's country format. "Just think about it— one station in every four broadcasting in the U.S. That makes country the dominant radio format today. That's a pretty big audience.''

7

Nashville: The Industry Town

I bought a T-shirt at a gift shop in downtown Branson. It had on it a cartoon picture of a light bulb. The legend it bore was that line Waylon Jennings attributed to Mel Tillis: "Will the last one leaving Nashville for Branson please turn out the lights?"

A funny little joke, but let's get real. Nashville is a city of about half a million. It is the capital of the state of Tennessee. It is the financial and insurance center of the mid-South area. One of the South's major universities, Vanderbilt, is situated there. And on November 28, 1925, when Uncle Jimmy Thompson sawed away on his fiddle for an hour in front of a WSM microphone and began *"The Grand Ole Opry,"* Nashville became a center of country music.

On radio, Nashville was preceded by a more sophisticated show on WBAP in Fort Worth and a much more sophisticated show on WLS in Chicago. Actually, *"The National Barn Dance"* on WLS was the first big-time country show on radio, and it continued to be through the thirties and forties (in a depleted state, all the way into the sixties). It established some of the early stars of country music—Red Foley, Patsy Montana, Lulu Belle and Scotty—while *"The Grand Ole Opry"* was just struggling to get established. The big move for the *"Opry"* was its relocation from the WSM studios to the Ryman Auditorium in 1941. The old tabernacle in the heart of Nashville, site of hundreds, perhaps thousands of revival meetings, gave country music a home, a focus, and claimed it for the South.

Listeners to "*The Grand Ole Opry*" began to make pilgrimages to Nashville from all over the surrounding territory. They would sit in the uncomfortable church pews all Saturday night to see the stars of country music—Ernest Tubb, Roy Acuff, Cousin Minnie Pearl, the whole grand galaxy—that they listened to religiously on the national broadcast each week. Those in the know might slip around the corner to Tootsie's Orchid Lounge, the bar on Broadway that backed onto the stage door of the Ryman, where stars and sidemen slipped in for a quick one before going onstage, or maybe stuck around to unwind after their part of the show. The Ryman Auditorium and its raffish annex continued to be the center of country music activity until 1974, when "*The Grand Ole Opry*" show moved out to the suburbs of Nashville to its new home at the theme park, Opryland USA.

Both the Ryman and Tootsie's are still there. The neighborhood around them began deteriorating in the sixties, bottomed in the seventies, but is gradually making a comeback. What had become Nashville's skid row seems to have taken on a sort of bohemian aspect. There are a couple of art galleries, a commercial art studio or two, and a lot of young people on the street who don't look like they are there to visit the Ryman.

But many still come; older visitors mostly, they arrive on tour buses, some all the way in from Opryland, which owns the Ryman Auditorium and maintains it as a kind of shrine to country music's past. The grand old place stands empty; people wander in, listen to the lecture given them by the guide, heave a collective sigh, then wander out again.

At least Tootsie's Orchid Lounge still functions as it once did, though the proprietress who gave it her nickname is long gone, dead of cancer sometime in the seventies. Yet it certainly isn't what it used to be. Inside, it is dark in the daytime. A few patrons are scattered along the long bar. They look like practiced afternoon drinkers. I had come to Nashville to get the industry's response to Branson, and Tootsie's was one of the first places I hit. Finding an empty barstool, I ordered a beer and listened, along with them, to a man with a guitar and a microphone who was sitting on a little stage near the door. He groaned and wailed his way through a couple of numbers. The last of them, I remember, was Conway Twitty's "Hello Darlin'." The amplified guitar and voice were almost too much for the restricted space; sound seemed to reverberate against the walls. Then he told a joke—a pretty bad joke: "Seems the new preacher in town was makin' the rounds, and he looked just a lot like Conway Twitty. He knocks on the door of the first house on the block, and the lady of the house opened the door, and she says, 'Why it's Conway Twitty!' And he says, 'No, ma'am. I'm the new preacher, and I sure would like to see you in church this Sunday.' This went on right down the block. All the ladies thought he was Conway Twitty, but he set 'em right and invited 'em to church. Finally he comes to the last house on the block, and the lady of the house there had been taking a shower, so she just threw a towel around her. She opens it up and says, 'Why, it's Conway Twitty!' And the preacher takes one look at her there in her towel, and he says . . . 'Hello . . . darlin'.' "

There were a few generous cackles along the bar. Then, as he swung into Hank Snow's "Movin' On," it occurred to me that his joke, mild as it was, could never have been told to an audience in Branson—too racy, too disrespectful of the clergy.

That was about as much fun as I could stand all at one time, and so I left Tootsie's and returned to wander on Nashville's lower Broadway. This was, at one time, where Nashville's country music industry was centered. About all that is left to remind you of that former glory is the Ernest Tubb Record Shop, which offers just about the greatest store of recorded country music you are likely to find anywhere. The word is that the Tubb enterprise is scoping Branson for the right location to put a branch shop.

Today, the vast complex of buildings, offices, and studios that make up Nashville's very large piece of the country music industry are to be found farther west on upper Broadway, leading into West End Avenue and the important loop known as

Music Square. Along the way you will see a variety of tourist shops—the Elvis Presley Museum and Gift Shop, the Barbara Mandrell Gift Shop, the Hank Williams, Jr., Museum, and so on. They are there for the fans, of course. Yet it's in those big buildings that remain closed to visitors that the real business gets done. Take a stroll around Music Square, and what do you see? The United Artists Tower, one of the tallest buildings on that side of town, dominates the view. Just as impressive is the newly opened ASCAP (American Society of Composers, Authors and Publishers) Building; BMI (Broadcast Music Incorporated) is close by, as is the older, solid presence of RCA, always one of the leaders in the country music field. Country has now gone international: what used to be known as Tree Publishing (along with Acuff-Rose, one of the biggest music publishing houses in Nashville) is now Sony Tree.

It's in places such as these that the deals get made, the songs get written and recorded. But the flocks of tourists who come to Nashville must take all this on faith. And after all, just how interested would they be if they could see papers being passed from hand to hand to be signed, composers tearing their hair, or even, with proper exposure, the long, boring, repetitious recording process? No, tourists want specifics. They want to be entertained, surprised, fascinated. That's why virtually all of them who come to Nashville visit the Country Music Hall of Fame and Museum.

There they can view such stunning objects as Elvis Presley's "solid gold Cadillac," Hank Thompson's Nudie jacket and boots, Willie Nelson's *Red-Headed Stranger* outfit, Merle Travis's Gibson Super 400 guitar, just to mention a few of the exhibits of every sort in the museum hall. There are demonstration exhibits, too—of the recording process, a how-to-play-it lecture on the pedal steel guitar—and all sorts of artifacts to stir the imagination and satisfy the fantasies of visitors from every state and from nations far beyond our borders. The half million who visit the museum annually seem to leave it satisfied, too.

Yet behind the scenes the Country Music Hall of Fame and Museum serves a function that is arguably far more valuable. It has a vast archive and library that is available to scholars, journalists, writers, filmmakers, anyone, in short, with a qualified professional interest in the field. It contains thousands upon thousands of recordings, and nearly as many books, magazines, photos, and pieces of sheet music—documents of every kind. There is really nothing like it available for research in any other form of American popular music. Tulane University's jazz archive would probably fit in a small corner of the Country Music Hall of Fame Library.

With all this to see, why are visitors to Nashville so often disappointed? Because, unless they trek out to Opryland USA and are lucky enough to get tickets to the "*Opry*" or to the concerts held there, they may indeed go the entire length of their visit without hearing any live country music. And for some, it may have been chiefly for this reason that they came to the city. Nobody told them that while Nashville is indisputably the seat of the country music *industry*, it is not, nor has it ever been, a place to catch the music in live performance.

Like most of those who have theaters in Branson, Ray Stevens has a home in Nashville (or just outside it). Yet he will spend half the year in a little town in the Ozarks, playing two shows a day and competing with attractions at twenty-six other theaters to bring in paying customers. Visitors not only have a chance to hear live music in Branson, they are offered a wide selection of shows.

Stevens declared to *Atlanta Journal* reporter Cynthia Mitchell, "Nashville's just not a performance town. You could book Elvis and the Beatles and you'd never fill the place up every night like you do here [in Branson]."

Those who go to Nashville, having studied the problem in advance, will of course be able to hear music while they are there. They will have ordered their tickets at Opryland in advance. They will have heard about the Bluebird Cafe and its songwriters nights, and they will know that the rest of the week it offers a showcase for up-and-coming acts. There are a few other small clubs in town that serve the same function. Randy Travis, for instance, played regularly for a couple of years at the Nashville Palace, just down the road from Opryland, before he got his big break.

A singer may fight, as Randy Travis certainly did, for any sort of exposure he can get there in Music City, U.S.A. How will the industry know what he can do if they can't hear him? Yet, as soon as he gets close to a recording contract, his voice and style become a "property," and he is jerked back from live performance until he can be established via singles on national radio. As he stood on the brink of his first national exposure, Garth Brooks was instructed by his managers to make no more appearances at songwriters' nights or at any clubs around Nashville. They didn't want his voice, or his material, to become too familiar.

Why Are They so Touchy?

Having acknowledged that Nashville is mighty and Branson's only importance is in the specific area of live performance, I must say that it is remarkable just how touchy people are in Music City about the existence of this modest little place in the Ozarks. They just don't want to hear another word about Branson.

When I talked with Jerry Bailey, who is director of Media Relations for The Nashville Network, he fairly exploded with scorn when he heard I was writing a book on Branson. "Let me tell you," he said, "the lowest thing on my list of priorities is to be included in a book about Branson, Missouri."

I don't know exactly what I said then, but I was trying to be persuasive. TNN is an important part of the story. A large segment of those who visit Branson are regular viewers of this country music network. But Bailey wasn't to be persuaded.

"When is the press going to get off this? Why, there was an article in the paper here just today about a couple of clubs opening up. It said, 'The competition is heating up!' Meaning the competition between Branson and Nashville. Why, that's silly!"

(I had seen the piece in the business section of the Nashville *Tennessean.* Staff writer Adam Tanner reported that a local developer, John Hobbs, "has launched a salvo in the live music battle with Branson, Mo." Both the 800-seat Celebrity

Theater and the Night Life Theater, seating 600, are to be located in the Opryland vicinity. Tanner commented in the article: "During the last few years a chorus of tourist voices have complained that Nashville lacks venues for regular, big-name country shows outside of the Grand Ole Opry and Opryland." Then he went on to say: "At the same time, the once-obscure back roads of Branson are attracting an increasing number of top country music acts to its ever expanding array of music arenas.")

Jerry Bailey wasn't through saying no: "Listen, Austin has had terrific live entertainment for years—Texas in general, Austin in particular. Why, you can see more live entertainment *there* than in Nashville!"

Sort of proving the point, wasn't he?

He admitted that he had never been to Branson but added that "a number of people I work with have been there. We did a video on Branson—but we also did a video on Little Rock. These are our travel shows."

Then, reluctantly: "I suppose that in a sense Branson has helped country music in general. It's an excellent venue. But most of the artists there are not in the developing stage. Well, as a matter of fact, a lot of them are past their peak. And frankly, I think that most of the boom in country music is happening with younger listeners—younger performers. Branson's audience seems to be a little older."

Of course, he's never been there.

I asked how TNN's demographics compared with that. "Well . . ." he said, "your TNN viewer is a little older, but the viewer for Country Music Television is a little younger. They're both under the same umbrella, both owned by Gaylord Communications and distributed by Group W."

Then, backpedaling a bit, Jerry Bailey said, "I really have to admit that everything I've heard about Branson has been quite positive. It is important, I guess, but so is the appearance of country music shows in Atlantic City and Las Vegas. They all contribute to the rise of country music in popularity."

That was as far as we got. There was no invitation to tour the TNN studios. There would be no introduction to Ralph Emery, the talk show host—the most famous man in country

music who doesn't play a guitar. No Cruise and Chase, no—
Well, I was disappointed.

Bailey did relent and agree to have sent to me a packet of
information on TNN's 54.9 million subscribers, a demographic
profile. When I got hold of it, the profile confirmed my pre-
conceptions, except for one. I knew the audiences I had seen
in Branson were made up, for the most part of prosperous,
middle-class people, but they also seemed to be a little
younger than the TNN average. Still, both groups fit into the
baby boom category. This is how TNN sees its audience:

The typical TNN viewer is

- 44.4 years old
- With a median household income of $30,828
- Living in a household with an average of 3.2 people
- Living in a household with an average of 2.1 children
- 70% own their own home, with a median home value of
  $60,167

Although there is no breakdown on TNN's penetration of major metropolitan areas such as New York, Los Angeles, and
Chicago (except the note that 30 percent live in an undefined
"metro central city"), it is reasonable to assume that more
than 70 percent live in towns and cities where the dollar figures cited on income and home ownership would be worth
considerably more. So yes, The Nashville Network is in direct
communication with middle-class America.

As for Country Music Television, although there were no
figures provided, you can bet the viewers are younger, for this
is country's equivalent of MTV. Videos by country's top
young artists are run nearly nonstop twenty-four hours a day,
with just the usual breaks for commercials, a pitch by the host
or hostess, and time out for the occasional drop-in guest. CMT
was a competitor until Gaylord Entertainment Company
bought them out in 1991 for $24 million. Because its audience
is quite distinct from TNN's, Country Music Television continues to operate separately.

Essentially, Gaylord Entertainment is Edward L. Gaylord,

seventy-three. He came out of Oklahoma but now operates from Connecticut. According to *Forbes*, he is a media billionaire, and his move into the country music field was swift and impressive. In 1983 he acquired TNN by buying Opryland USA and all its holdings for $270 million. Besides the cable network, these also included the "*Grand Ole Opry*," the old Ryman Auditorium, a tour bus operation, radio stations WSM FM and AM—and who knows what more? He also owns a healthy 20 percent of *Country America* magazine, and 14 percent of the new San Antonio theme park, Fiesta Texas. In 1991, he took all this, together with his four independent television stations and twenty-six cable franchises and went public with a 24 percent share of Gaylord Entertainment Co. The offering brought $200 million. And today it is considered a very hot stock.

Craig Lamb, a public relations representative for Opryland USA, proved quite hospitable and invited me out to see him. He gave me directions out on Interstate 40 to Briley Parkway, even specified the gate I was to enter. But sure enough, the place is so big that I turned in the wrong gate, got redirected and, with time to spare, took a comfortable car tour of the place. The park workers were busy preparing for opening day, which was coming up that weekend, but there was still room to maneuver through the streets as there would not be in a few days' time.

I had been there a couple of times before but only to catch the "Grand Ole Opry" show. It is telecast now, of course, carried in part nationally on TNN; the whole show is heard on WSM, both FM and AM. But coming in at night, whisked in and out of the park quickly, I had never really gotten a good look at the Opryland Hotel. It is immense—a 1,891-room convention hotel with 320,000 square feet of meeting and exhibition space. It operates year-round at an annual average of 86 percent occupancy. There were guests moving in and out of the entrance and cars pulling away. I spotted tennis courts around one corner, and I understand there are also swimming pools—that's plural—and an 18-hole golf course. Everything on the grand scale, as you might expect from Gaylord Entertainment.

Craig Lamb's office was in a sort of nondescript, temporary-looking building not far from the Opryland Hotel. There was a second gate to go through there. The guard called up to him, and Lamb came down and led me to a conference room where we had our conversation. There seemed nothing temporary about the interior of the building. Walls were plastered and painted and on them were hung a succession of beautifully printed, colored promotional photos taken around the park. The conference room was very handsomely appointed with the same sort of photos in evidence. Hollywood studio buildings are like this: much classier on the inside than on the outside. This wasn't the only thing about Opryland USA that reminded me of Hollywood. A few days later, when I returned as a paying customer, the place seemed to me like nothing quite so much as one huge movie set.

If not exactly a pitchman, Craig Lamb proved so voluble and well-informed that it seemed there was no stopping him once he had begun; all the figures and all the facts were right on the tip of his tongue.

For instance, when I mentioned to him that I had been quite impressed by the Opryland Hotel, he was ready with all those numbers already quoted. But he wanted me to understand that it is "primarily a convention hotel."

Meaning? "Well, the exhibition space, which is all below ground. You'd never guess there was that much there. We get big 2,000- to 3,000-delegate conventions, like the AMA and the GM dealer show because of the exhibition space and the hotel's convention services. And our staff, too—we've got two lobbies, and our staff has handled 3,000 delegates and their luggage in a matter of three hours."

But, of course, tourists come too: "Oh yes, during the season, that's what we're here for. You can't see all we have here in one day. It really takes several days to do it all. We offer a three-day package and longer stays, try to assemble a complete vacation for them, all the way up to a week—go to Nashville, play golf, fish."

And they come in tour groups all the way from Japan, where country music is in growing favor. Like the rest, who arrive from all parts of America and Canada, they are attracted to

Opryland because it is the home of the "*Grand Ole Opry*." It's *the* attraction that has put Nashville on the world map.

"We have up to 250 performances of the "*Grand Ole Opry*" here each year—every Friday and Saturday night, with shows added during the season just to make sure everyone who comes here gets to see the show. It's been, well, modernized quite a bit—a lot of young people are brought on. The caliber runs from Roy Acuff to Garth Brooks."

Lamb emphasized that Opryland is a theme park—"though it's sometimes mislabeled an amusement park"—and the theme is country music. "On any day," he said, "you can see seventy-two live shows here, performed by 175 performers—actually, it's a total of 400, since they don't work seven days a week."

Where in the world do they find four hundred country music performers? They must have cleaned out all of Nashville. But no: "We have a forty-three-city audition tour, from New York City to Los Angeles and all the points between," he said. "This year we auditioned 15,000, and we boiled that down to four hundred for here and three hundred for Fiesta, Texas, our other major theme park. Why, there are forty ex-Opryland performers now in first-run Broadway musicals. This is sort of the last springboard to the top."

That said, Craig Lamb couldn't really name any who had used that springboard to reach the top—except "the one who played opposite Kevin Costner in *Robin Hood*—Mary Elizabeth Mastroantonio." Didn't know the lady could sing.

"In addition," he continued, "we've got an amphitheater here that will seat 3,500 people, and we'll have 284 concerts in that, separate from the Opry and separate from the shows we offer all around the park. Now, if you'll look at the schedule, you'll see that it features a lot of the hot young performers in country, like Vince Gill, Trisha Yearwood, Ricky Skaggs, and Pam Tillis, as well as others more established, like the Gatlin Brothers, Tanya Tucker, Ronnie Milsap, and Crystal Gayle. It's really pretty well balanced. It took us two years to set this schedule up.

"Then, do you know what happened when we announced it? The Associated Press called it 'Opryland's answer to Branson.' Now that's just plain silly. We're not doing this to compete with Branson. We have nothing to lose or gain in competition with Branson. If you ask me, Branson is using us—Nashville—as part of their marketing strategy.

"I mean, it's said that there is a problem in finding live country music performance here. But 284 concerts and approximately 250 performances of the *"Grand Ole Opry"* tells me that's just not true!"

It's remarkable, isn't it, how people in Nashville react to Branson? Craig Lamb brought it up; I didn't. They seem really supersensitive to the attention that little town has received. But why should they be, really? If Branson has proved anything, it's that there are more than enough country acts— and country fans—to go around.

And if Craig Lamb convinced me of anything, it's that yes, there certainly is country music in live performance available in the Nashville area—but that Opryland USA and Gaylord Entertainment Company have a lock on about 90 percent of it.

Recording in Branson

What makes Nashville Nashville? Well, to country music fans it's the *"Grand Ole Opry,"* but to the music business it is the considerable chunk of the recording industry that is located there. All of the major labels have full-scale operations in Nashville. Recording is the lifeblood of country music. This is why artists—even most of those who perform in Branson during the season—live the rest of the year in the Nashville area. It is so much a part of the history of country music that the Country Music Foundation has taken over RCA's famous Studio B and made it part of the Museum's tour, using it to explain to visitors patient enough to listen the intricate nature of the recording process.

You might suppose that the country recording began right there—but if so, you would suppose incorrectly. The first sessions featuring white Southern artists singing and playing their kind of music were made on "field" trips to the South by a man named Ralph Peer beginning early in the 1920s. He came down from New York for Okeh Records and visited a number of cities and towns, such as Bristol, Tennessee, Asheville, North Carolina, and Atlanta, where he recorded both white and black artists. Among the "hillbillies" Peer recorded in those early sessions were The Carter Family, Jimmie Rodgers, and Fiddlin' John Carson—some of the first "stars" of country music.

This so-called "field recording" continued through the thirties and into the forties. Studios were set up in some cities, usually at radio stations big enough to have the proper equipment on hand. In fact, the first recordings made in Nashville were done at WSM. In the spring of 1945, Red Foley, who some years before had left the WLS "National Barn Dance" for the "Grand Ole Opry," cut two sides for Decca. The next year a couple of WSM engineers opened up an independent studio operation of their own. And when, a few years after that, Owen Bradley opened up his studio, Nashville was well on its way to becoming the recording capital it is today.

Nothing underlines Nashville's preeminence as the center of the country music industry quite so indelibly as this fact: in Nashville there are 124 recording studios with full 24-track capability. Branson, by a contrast that fairly shouts the disparity between the two situations, has just one.

That's not to say, however, that Branson's single recording facility surrenders anything to Nashville's top independent studios in its capabilities, nor that the man who runs it is anything but a top professional in his field. Although born and raised in Los Angeles, Keith O'Neil, who owns and operates Caravell Studios out on Fall Creek Road, is about as low-key and easygoing as any Branson native. He's had some drama in his life, though—one of the toughest breaks that life has to offer. Keith O'Neil is blind.

Long before he had any difficulty with his sight, he played drums with various bands around Los Angeles, even gigged with Freddy Fender out on the road in Texas. But then he settled down and went to radio and television school in Los Angeles. He first worked in radio and then graduated to television during eight years in Nebraska. Television was his love and video was his craft. Although he had begun experiencing problems with his left eye from glaucoma, he accepted an offer to work on the production of the long-running "*Ozark Jubilee*," which was really the first network country music television show. In the course of directing forty-one segments of the show, he lost the sight of his left eye. Then, in 1982, he lost the sight of his right eye because of a detached retina. His career in television was over.

So what did he do? He set out to master audio recording. He knew a good deal about it from radio and having worked as a musician, "on the other side of the glass." But he became as skilled on the board as any sighted individual. And when, in 1987, the opportunity came, he begged and borrowed what he could, put it together with his savings, and bought Caravell Studios.

It is located in a good-sized, single-story building that went up in 1984. It is about a mile and a half from 76 Country Boulevard, out where the edge of town merges into the countryside. From this same location Ed Anderson published *Branson's Country Review*.

Keith O'Neil came out of his office and took me on a brief tour of the studio. This is his territory. He knows it by heart. There was never a misstep as he led me quickly through the place. He didn't even fumble for the doorknob as he took me into the control room and switched on the lights. Nothing was going on just then, and to a layman—that's me—all control boards look equally impressive. I did notice, though, that the performing space beyond the glass was more spacious than usual and had at least one of every kind of microphone I'd ever seen before. All O'Neil had to say about the facilities was, "It's 24-track, of course. As far as mixing and putting any sort of finishing touch on what's down on tape, we're capable of doing what needs to be done."

Then to his office at the same brisk pace. He settled behind his big desk and started to talk: "Well, you see what's happening in this town. Branson is getting its fifteen minutes of fame. Oh, it's more than that, of course. Country is huge right now, and Branson is in the right place at the right time with the right product.

"It's just confusion to ask if Branson is going to be another Nashville. Except for the Opry, Nashville is business, strictly business, and Branson is live performance. There are some support industries forming up here—songwriting and us, recording. When I need to consult an entertainment lawyer I go to Los Angeles."

Keith O'Neil didn't need prodding. He just continued, giving voice to some things he thought needed to be said: "It's very competitive for entertainers here. Some of them who come here from Nashville don't realize how strongly so it is. Yes, it's very competitive, and it's going to be more so. They've got to think more about putting on a real show, better lighting, better sound. Ticket prices have gone up, and so has the quality. The next couple of years are going to be important here—pivotal. If the built-in problems we've got do get solved—the roads and so forth—and if the cable network gets started, people are really going to see this town take off."

But then I did put a question to him. I asked how Caravell would be changing to meet the new situation.

"I'll be making improvements," he said. "I want this to be the kind of place where people come from outside to record. As it is right now, we do a lot of demo tapes, but we've also done a lot of albums. Boxcar Willie and Jim Stafford have done album sessions here, and we have had two albums we recorded come up as final nominees for Grammys in the bluegrass category—*Heartbreak Hotel* by the Doug Dillard Band on Flying Fish in 1989, and *Let It Fly*, by the Dillards on Vanguard in 1990. So right there the studio has achieved a level of acceptance. I like the recognition we've received. We'll probably have another nominee this year. Right now I have people who want to record here because we've become known, not because they're in the area.

"You know, for a long time Muscle Shoals, Alabama, has been one of the alternative sites for Nashville. People like to go there because it's out of the spotlight, and it's comfortable for them to relax and create. They developed a unique sound there, too. Now, those same ingredients are here potentially. What we've got to have for total acceptance is a number one record on the charts done right here in this studio. And some of the acts right here in Branson are capable of that.''

Keith O'Neil paused, then took a moment to ruminate over what he had said. His final word then was more than a summary. It had the resonance of a kind of credo.

"What is success?" he asked. "How do you measure it? I can't sit here and say I'm going big-time, that I'm going to take over RCA. No, but I can make successful recordings here at Caravell. What I want to be successful is to be doing the best I can in a town like this where the entertainment business is alive and growing. I don't think that down the line this will be the only recording studio in town. I just want it to be the best.''

8

Who's Hot and Who's Not?

All right, let's get this out in the open. Ed Anderson of *Branson's Country Review* alluded to the matter tactfully. TNN's Jerry Bailey used it to dismiss Branson's relevance to what is happening in country music today. How was it he put it? A lot of the artists there, he said, "are past their peak."

Well, in a way it's true. Nobody would ever mistake Mel Tillis for a "developing" talent. He's just about as good as he'll ever get—and, of course, that's very good indeed. The same could be said of any number of other performers who have established themselves on 76 Country Boulevard—Ray Stevens, Mickey Gilley, Cristy Lane, Moe Bandy—but they keep packing them in, season after season.

What's the matter with those 4.3 million visitors to Branson? Don't they know who's in and who's out? who's hot and who's not? More like, they don't care. Let me tell you something about country music fans. They are the most loyal, the most devoted to their favorites, of any who follow any style of American popular music. It's been estimated—though I don't know exactly how—that whereas a rock performer, once established with a recording contract, has an average career expectancy of three years, a country music singer can look forward to a run of fifteen years or more.

In the case of Mel Tillis, the career in country is now well past the thirty-year mark. He had his first hit in 1958, "The Violet and the Rose," and before the decade was out, he had two more, "Finally" and "Sawmill." And that was just the beginning. Through the next three decades he racked up hit after hit on label after label. In 1976 he was named the Country Music Association's Entertainer of the Year. Along about that time he began playing in and around Branson. "I first started here in the seventies," he says, "singing at the Baldknobbers. Then, later on, I worked for Bob Mabe who started Bob-O-Links, and I worked there. I worked over in Lampe, Missouri. I worked in Lake of the Ozarks. And I thought of it at that time as just another gig. And then, about six or seven years ago, I started to working the Roy Clark Theatre. I worked at his place for about three or four years, and I noticed I drew pretty good, had good crowds, about every performance."

That was when he started thinking about opening up a theater of his own in Branson. Mel went back to Nashville and announced to his friends, "Boys and girls, there's gold in them there Ozark hills!" He leased a theater for two years—it's the one that Willie Nelson now shares with Merle Haggard—and his fans came flocking in. By Branson standards, it was medium-sized, seating just a little over a thousand. With more visitors coming in each year and the town's getting national publicity, the future looked good to Mel Tillis, and so he plunged even deeper and began construction of a completely new $8 million theater.

There is a lot about the new Mel Tillis Theatre that bespeaks the keen business sense of the man who built it. First of all, there is the matter of location. He chose, rather daringly, to place it well away from the Highway 76 entertainment strip. While he may have lost a little something by refusing to be one of the crowd, he gained a good deal more in accessibility. His theater may be on the other side of town from the rest, but driving down on US 65 from the Springfield airport, or from I-44 (the nearest east–west interstate), it is the first thing in Branson you will see. There it is—Mel Tillis's name in lights and his portrait illuminated, night and day. No need to join the creeping traffic to get there; just turn off at the first

Branson exit and buy your tickets to the next show.

And another thing. Mel located his new theater next to the Branson Inn, one of the biggest and certainly one of the best motels in town. Yet he is more than a neighbor. He has entered into a kind of partnership with this Best Western operation, taking over its restaurant and bar operations, giving his name to them, and personally supervising the hiring of the staff and the choice of menu. Mel Tillis has his name all over the place, and it has benefited both him and the Branson Inn.

Finally, there is the theater itself. It is brand spanking new and looks it, both inside and out. It may not be as large as the Grand Palace, as it only seats a little over 2,000, but it is almost twice the size of the one Mel left on the strip. Both his theater and the Grand Palace provide especially comfortable seats and extra space between the rows of seats. (You can get from the aisle to a seat in the middle of the row without mashing a single foot along the way!) The lobby boasts three refreshment stands and the biggest souvenir shop this side of Boxcar Willie's Railroad Museum.

Inside, settled in your seat, you find Mel looking out at you from either side of the stage. Two large screens provide the audience with a video warm-up of about forty-five minutes' duration. Mel sings a lot of his hits—mostly in close-up, it seems. Then, as it nears showtime, the video ends, the screens retract, and two concession stands light up. Up on the stage a pitchman appears and pushes a big line of Mel T-shirts, his recently recorded cassette, which features Tillis and the Statesiders and their new "Texas sound in the glorious tradition of Bob Wills," etc., etc. It seems that the video which has been on view up until a few moments ago is also available for a mere $20. Personal checks are acceptable. Such huckstering is part and parcel of any country music show today—probably any music show at all, short of grand opera and symphony. Mel's man doesn't push too hard, nor does he take up show time.

When the curtains part at last, they reveal not the star of the show, but a set depicting an old-time Ozark cabin with granny on the porch and full-grown kids lounging around. Then, the youngest of them (he looks about twelve) rushes in and announces, "Company's comin'." It's a production number, featuring the boy singing (he's third-billed Levi Hare), and the six others onstage dancing up a storm, country-style—even granny struts her stuff on her cane (they're the Melody Greenwood Dancers). All of a sudden you realize you're in for a real show—not just a couple of sets of Mel in front of the band. Why, he could take this to Las Vegas—and maybe he has, for he still plays there during the six months or so he's away from Branson. The man's a real showman.

With a big ta-DAH! the curtains close on the Ozarks and those energetic mountaineers, and then the pitchman's voice comes from offstage: "And now, our star—the stutterin' boy himself—Mel Tillis!" And there he is before the greatly augmented Statesiders. The nucleus group of seven has been expanded to twelve, now a big band that includes trumpet, saxophone, and four fiddles. But the pitchman had it right: all this *is* in the glorious tradition of Bob Wills and the Texas Playboys, the man who shaped the "Western Swing" style of the late thirties and forties. If Mel, a Floridian, has no territorial claim on this musical mode, at least he knows that the time is ripe for revival. (Strictly speaking, Texan George Strait led the way with his two-fiddle band.)

And Mel Tillis fits right in. He hasn't altered his style of singing to suit the music; there was no need to. No, Mel, as Mel, is just right for Western Swing—and he proves it from the git-go with a long set before he so much as says a word to the audience—a set that includes the Bob Wills classic, "San Antonio Rose" (white roses are projected onto the blue backdrop behind the band—nice touch).

When at last he does speak, he calls out to the crowd, "How do you like my new theater?" And he is answered by thunderous applause. "You just keep comin'," he says, "and it'll be paid for in ten years." Tillis is the kind of performer who has an immediate, close rapport with his audience. His famous stutter helps. It makes him one of them. Everybody here knows about it and has heard or read that it's the rhythm of the music that makes it possible for him to sing without being troubled by the impediment. The stutter is by now part of the act. It is in evidence as he tells the folks how he's working on it. "B-b-but I ain't k-kicked 'em yet," he adds. He calls his two female backup singers "the Stutterettes," and at one point he threatens to keep the crowd there all night while he attempts a recitation. They love it.

Without piling detail upon detail (describing the return of the Melody Greenwood Dancers, young Levi Hare's short solo set, and wonderful Barbara Fairchild's long one), let me assure you that what is presented in that classy new theater is a class show, and the gentleman who put it all together is himself a real class act. Look at him up there. He's dressed conservatively in a western-cut tan suit and wearing a neckerchief tied four-in-hand-style. He doesn't use the guitar much. Mostly he's just leading the band, keeping tempo with an energetic crooked arm, or singing into the mike. But there's no question who's in charge. The man has presence and thirty-five years of experience behind him. He knows just what he wants; he's gotten it; and the audience loves it.

Melvin Tillis was born in Tampa, on August 8, 1932, and grew up in the much smaller town of Pahokee, Florida. He put in some time at the University of Florida but enlisted in the Air Force during the Korean War. It was while he was in the service that he began his singing career, found Air Force audiences appreciative, and decided to try for a career in country music. Soon after his release—in 1957—he headed for Nashville, made it first as a songwriter, then began recording on his own. And the rest, as they say, is history. His has been one of the longest, steadiest, and strongest careers in country. But in the early eighties things began to change for him.

But why not let him tell it?

"About 1981 or '82, the record companies started to change the image of their labels. They wanted to attract the younger audience, and they dropped a lot of artists who had been on the labels." Mel Tillis would find himself one of them.

"I had had fifty-eight albums. I suppose," he laughed, "it was time for me to go, but I still had fans out there, and I wasn't ready to retire. I continued to work as much as I wanted to because I'd had a lot of exposure on national television— 'The Johnny Carson Show,' 'The Dinah Shore Show,' 'Dean Martin Show,' Tony Orlando show. I was on all of them, and I continued to work, but then, oh, about four or five years ago, it began to tell. I wasn't getting as many fair dates as I usually had and, because my records weren't being played as much as they were before, and I was finding less and less places to work, I was being forced out of the business by the new image of the record labels. The Country Music Association was not behind it, but they cooperated with the record labels. Nashville is record-driven, and unless you're recording, you're not wanted very much.''

Along about that time, Mel Tillis decided to set up shop in Branson. It has obviously worked very well for him. Now over sixty, he looks great—clear-eyed, with a full head of hair, and only enough wrinkles to make him look distinguished. "I've always taken care of myself," he says. "I don't abuse my body." By the way, that speech therapy has worked far better on his stutter than he let on to his audience. Every few sentences he may hesitate over a word, but if you weren't aware of his problem, you probably wouldn't notice. A couple of times his lips quivered as he searched for a word. But none of this slows him down much. He's an interviewer's dream: the man likes to talk.

For instance, about how he's come to fit into the community here in Branson: "Oh, yeah, I go to the First Baptist Church. I've got some time to do things here—I may even join the Rotary, I don't know. I get to go fishing, and some of my children are here with me, some help run the theater. When my daughter Pam gets to the point when she no longer wants to tour, I'm going to have me a family show–type thing. She's going to work one time this year in town over at the Grand Palace. But I couldn't get her for the dates that I wanted her—she was unavailable, opening for George Strait. She'll be at our theater next year."

With all the competition in town, won't some of the smaller theaters suffer? "Well, some of the bigger ones may, too," he said. "It depends on if they got their act together. You gotta give a show, and you have to respect the people, and you have to sign autographs—and I mean, that's a must. I feel like I owe the people something. I mean, mercy, where would I be if these people hadn't accepted me. And I feel like I owe them something. I feel like that when I'm onstage with my band. Listen, I've got over $100,000 in uniforms for that band of mine. They got thirteen suits apiece, and they're $800 suits. They wear $400 boots like I wear, and I think I owe that to the public.''

About that remark he made in the show about paying off the theater debt in ten years. What if—well, just suppose— the people stop coming? What if boomtown Branson goes bust? ''I don't see that happening,'' he said seriously, confidently. ''And I intend to stay here until they stop coming to see me. Every year I'm going to put on a different show. I've already laid out my plans for next year, but I think if we keep up with it, keep entertaining and keep our senses, if I don't go senile or get Alzheimer's, I'll be here.''

Then the boom will continue? ''Sure. They announced a billion-dollar development that'll take twenty years to finish, that South Branson thing. I understand Kenny Rogers is coming in. It won't be long before Barbara Mandrell'll be coming, and you'll see some of the other acts, like Randy Travis. As they get older, and the new recording acts sign to the labels, they'll be coming along. You know, that's just normal attrition.''

What about that figure he dropped oh so casually to Morley Safer—something about making a million a month? Mel laughed. ''Well, you figure it up,'' he said. ''If you can put them in the seats, you can do it. And that was at the old theater. I've got more seats now. It really is just amazing.'' He grinned and shook his head, like he just couldn't believe his good luck—but then he added, ''Of course I don't get to keep all that. You've got your expenses. You've got your band, your other acts, and your help to pay. In my organization I've got over one hundred employees. I've got a farm in Tennessee that has six employees. I got my office in Nashville where I have my recording studio and all, eleven employees. I got four employees at my house in Florida who look after that stuff down there, and then I got about sixty over here at the theater. You even have to have a caretaker for the grounds.''

Mel kept on talking about how much he liked it in the

area—just as someplace to spend time. He mentioned "the mystique of the Ozarks, the lakes, the rivers, and everything." And then he returned to the question of finding a place in the community, getting attached to it by way of fund-raising and participating in community events.

"Well," he said, "you have to give some of it back. We have a fountain over there at the theater that was dedicated by the head Shriners. They had a little ceremony there, and it was real nice. Then I got petitioned to be a Mason. Stuff like that is so important. You need to get involved with the community, because then you have a small voice in there. And I think I need to be heard from time to time, just as well as the guy who owns the filling station right down the road here. I'm not just making him up for an example, you know. There really is a guy who owns the filling station down the road. He's a buddy of mine I was in the Air Force with. He needs to be heard, and I need to be heard. I think in order to be part of the community, you have to be involved in it. I want to be."

"Shower of Stars"

As we all know, summer belongs to kids. School's out. Mom and Dad have planned the vacation. If they live within driving distance, there's a good chance they may wind up in Branson. They'll find a lot to do there—rides for the kids, a couple of theme parks, fishing on the lakes. It's a great town for kids. That's why families with children comprise slightly more than half of those who visit Branson. Yet the overwhelming number of them come, of course, during the summer months of June, July, and August. The rest of the season belongs, for the most part, to couples without children, some of them older, some of them retired.

That's the picture of Branson that Nashville seems to promote. Whether they've been to the town or not, industry people seem certain that it is nothing more nor less than the playground of the Social Security set. And while, in the spring and fall months the audiences at the shows tend to be a bit older, they are clearly the kind of people who get out and do things, who are willing to drive six or seven hundred miles to see some good shows, and who are willing to spend money once they get there. If they are in general older than the summer crowd, they are certainly not "old folks." They have their favorites. They have their memories. Their notion of who is and isn't a star of country music is not derived directly from Billboard's Hot Hundred.

As I sat there in the Cristy Lane Theatre waiting for the show to start, I looked around and tried to get a fix on the audience. If I were asked to determine an average age for this group of a few hundred, I would have placed it at about forty-six or forty-seven—old enough for their kids to have moved out of the house and young enough to pick up and go off to hear some music whenever they had a mind to.

It was a little before ten in the morning. I hadn't come to see Cristy Lane, whose "One Day at a Time" superhit put her briefly in the superstar class, or Ray Price, whose hit-studded career in country stretches even longer than Mel Tillis's. They would play their regular eight o'clock show that night. No, I was there for the so-called breakfast show, "Shower of Stars." Ferlin Husky was the headliner. I had heard the Ozark-born singer-comedian interviewed on KRZK, and when he named the lineup of talent appearing with him, I knew I had to catch that early show the next morning.

It included Melba Montgomery, a personal favorite. Born in Tennessee, reared in Alabama, she first gained recognition as George Jones's duet-partner—before the days of Tammy Wynette—and as a single she notched a number of hits with her hardscrabble sound before Nashville decided she was "too country." Bobby Helms was also on the bill, a singer whose "Jingle Bell Rock" is heard again and again every Christmas season. And finally, Dick Curless, whose deep, resonant voice had popularized a dozen or so trucker songs, including the well-remembered, "Tombstone Every Mile."

Good show. Ferlin was funny, both as himself and in the person of his comic creation, Simon Crum. And he showed he could still sing, too—particularly well on his old gospel hit, "Wings of a Dove." Sharing the spotlight with his son,

Terry Preston Husky, who has something of the voice and style of Vince Gill, there was a nice moment when the crowd called young Terry back for an encore and Ferlin leaned into the microphone and said to them, "I was hopin' you'd do that."

Dick Curless

There were probably only about three hundred there for that early show, but they were about as enthusiastic as a full house at the "Grand Ole Opry" when the applause sign lights up. They went wild for Bobby Helms's "Fraulein." And when Melba Montgomery recited and sang her paean to motherhood, "No Charge," there were a few tears, and afterward, cheers and an ovation. But for me, the emotional high point of the show came very early on, during Dick Curless's set.

He emceed the entire show at just the right pace. A tall man made taller by boots and Stetson, gray-haired and with a black patch over his right eye, he has a rather commanding presence, helped considerably by a wonderfully resonant voice. Curless is sixty, but he still sings well, maybe better than he ever did. He remarked that it was "nice not to be on the road," then he sort of contradicted himself by swinging into a lusty truck-drivin' song, "The Big-Rig Cannonball," to the tune of "The Wabash Cannonball." But then he followed that up with his memorable "Tombstone Every Mile," about a deadly stretch of Maine highway, which could in no way be interpreted as a hymn of praise to the open road.

I don't know when it was exactly, maybe it was after he did a couple of gospel songs—"When the Roll Is Called Up Yonder" and the old Pentecostal hymn, "When the Saints Go Marching In." Anyway, it was well into his set when he stood up to the microphone and told the audience that the only reason why he was here was because he met the Lord Jesus on August 12, 1976, that he had had a problem with alcohol and drugs, was drinking two fifths of vodka a day—when God made it possible for him to turn away.

They call it testifying, I guess—"amazing grace that saved

a wretch like me''—and a lot of us don't know quite how to handle such abject professions of faith. But I'll tell you, I was moved. There was something profoundly affecting to hear this big, dignified, one-eyed man standing up there in front of people he'd never met and telling them about his failure and a triumph that wasn't his to claim. And more, for it was nearly sixteen years after the date he had cited, and here he was, carrying on, giving the best he had to give. There was courage in that, a strength of character that you had to admire.

But just to take the edge off things, Dick Curless went into ''I Love My Rooster.'' It's an old play-party song, fundamentally a children's piece in which the audience joins in with barnyard animal sounds. It worked just fine. He got everyone to join in, and by the end of it, he had them all set up for Melba Montgomery.

At intermission, as he was selling his tapes at the table beside Melba, I asked him if he'd be willing to talk about things at greater length. He said he would, and we agreed to meet at Starvin' Marvin's the next day way out on 76 beyond Silver Dollar City.

Although there is a Starvin' Marvin's on the strip, the one Curless suggested was out in Branson West. Remember the name change? What was once Lakeview is now officially Branson West. Citizens, the Board of Aldermen—everyone, it seems, except the State of Missouri's Department of Highways—has recognized the new name; the green highway signs haven't yet caught up with the march of progress.

Although I was there early, Dick Curless was there first. I came in surveying the tables and the waitress asked me if maybe I was looking for that gentleman over there—''gentleman'' was the word she used, and it fits Curless perfectly. I got the idea he was a regular at Starvin' Marvin's.

He rose to meet me, and we shook hands. He'd been drinking coffee, and with the waitress shuttling back and forth, we must have put away a couple of gallons between us before we ever got to lunch.

Dick Curless is from Bangor, Maine. Country is, of course, a brand of music closely identified with the South. There always have been and always will be, however, a certain number of performers who come from north of the old Mason-Dixon Line—Johnny Paycheck and David Allan Coe from Ohio, Janie Fricke from Indiana, and so on. If anything, as the popularity of country music spreads nationally, that number is growing. Yet of them all, past or present, only Hank Snow, from Nova Scotia, hails from farther north than Curless. There is nothing of the clipped, slightly querulous accent of northern New England in his talk, though. Years of rambling around the country and a stretch in Bakersfield, California, have softened his articulation and settled him in one of those generic middle-American styles of speech. He could be from almost anywhere—and by now he may feel as though he is.

I commented first on the enthusiasm of the audience at the previous day's show, saying they made more noise than a lot of full house crowds I'd heard at other theaters. He told me then that there were twice as many at the show he'd just played—good word of mouth around town. "After Memorial Day it really starts," he said. "This is the best situation I've had in all my forty-three years in the business. I go home to the same bed every night. My wife Pauline and I are living up the road in Ozark. Bought a house there."

Forty-three years in the business! He started out at the age of seventeen, having grown up in a home in which records by Jimmie Rodgers, Ernest Tubb, and Roy Acuff were always on the turntable. His mother, French-Canadian, provided what he calls "the Cajun influence" and taught him how to keep time with spoons, the old, country way. Guitar he picked up on his own. The family had moved down from Maine to Massachusetts, where his father worked as a heavy equipment operator. By the time Dick was a senior in high school, he had a little program of his own as the Tumbleweed Kid, singing and playing the guitar, on the local radio station WARE in Ware, Massachusetts.

That was how he happened to attract the attention of a New England country performer, Yodeling Slim Clark, who invited him to join the band and go out on a tour of the Maritime Provinces with them. "The only thing was," said Curless, "this was right before the end of my senior year. If I went, I wouldn't graduate from high school. It was okay with my mom and dad, but they wanted me to talk it over with the principal. So I did, and it turned out he was a country music fan, too. He wished me good luck and asked me to remember to play 'The Wabash Cannonball' for him. Well, I went, and I liked it just fine. Then on the way back home we all took a week off and fished. And man, I thought, this is it, this is how to live.''

He stuck with Slim Clark until he married Pauline at the age of twenty in 1952—"same woman, forty years"—and then he went to work for the *Bangor Daily News* "for the benefits." But the move he made toward the straight life didn't take him far. Two months after his marriage, he was drafted into the Army and sent to Korea.

It was wartime. He was glad to be in the motor pool and not up there permanently on the MLR. But he was even happier when his radio and performing experience won him a spot as a disc jockey on the Armed Forces Network. As the Rice Paddy Ranger, his tagline, "Welcome to the Oriental Cow Pasture Jamboree" went out to twenty-two stations in Korea, Japan, Okinawa, and Hawaii. Korean War veterans still remember him and the surprising hit he made of the Japanese pop tune, "China Nights."

Out of the Army, he returned to Bangor in 1954, went back to his old job on the newspaper, which had been held for him. "But," as he said, "I just couldn't fit in. I went to clubs and started playing. All that rowdiness was where I wanted to be. I started drinking pretty heavy back then." He did all right working on his own and also with a little band he headed. People in the area recognized his talent. In 1957, local fans pushed him into auditioning for the Arthur Godfrey network talent show.

He took Lenny Breau with him to New York to audition. Breau, a Bangor native, was a brilliant guitarist even as the teenager he was then. They had formed a close association as the two top talents in town. Breau eventually moved toward jazz and relocated to Los Angeles where he recorded, did studio work, and generally established himself as the fastest guitar in town, with the possible exception of Joe Pass. He died there in 1984, murdered, a case that police said was drug-related. But in 1957, he was a straight, happy, terrifically talented kid, and he helped Dick Curless win first place on the Arthur Godfrey TV talent show with a rendition of "Nine Pound Hammer."

Curless went right back to Maine and recorded it along with four others—his first records—and yes, he got some airplay outside his home territory. That, together with his national television exposure, got him a manager, Saul Tepper, who at that time was handling Dean Martin and Jerry Lewis. Tepper got him booked into Las Vegas and Hollywood. Things were looking rosy—and then Tepper died, and Dick was back more or less where he started.

There he stayed—although his trips out of Maine did take him farther and farther afield—until a young man named Dan Folkerson came to him with a song he had written called "Tombstone Every Mile." "Dan lived in Blaine, Maine, and was courting a girl in Bangor," Curless explained, "and he used to hitchhike there every weekend. It seemed like the truckers were the only ones who would pick him up. He'd ride with these fellows along a particularly deadly stretch outside Bangor, and they'd tell Dan, 'This is where so-and-so bought it,' and another mile or so, they'd point out another place where there was a big wreck and another trucker died. Well, it was a great song because it was real, you see, so I recorded it on my own label, Allagash. Capitol Records pressed it. We took it all over as a single and got it played. WBEZ in Boston really jumped on it. It started to take off, and so Capitol took it over and signed me up. The next thing I knew I was number one on the country charts, and that record stayed right up there in the top five for a long time."

In the middle of all this, he got a call from Buck Owens inviting him to join his show: "So we moved to California Pauline and I—to Buckersfield, as he called it. I continued what proved to be a fairly long and satisfactory association with Capitol while I toured with Buck. We played everyplace—from the Hollywood Bowl to Carnegie Hall and everything in between. It was really quite a lineup—Merle and the Strangers, Wynn Stewart, Tommy Collins, Kay Adams, did some songs with her—the Buck Owens All-American Music Show."

This led to other package tours—"all those West Coast people, all the biggest places you could get into." He remembers one night when he was booked into Detroit's big Cobo Hall with Dotty West and Charley Pride. "It was Charley's first night," he said. "He had his first hit record but hadn't been on the road. They announced him, and the applause started, and then he appeared, and it was suddenly just silent. They weren't prepared for his color, you see. But then he started singing, and then everything was fine—just that initial shock."

He eventually left Buck Owens and Bakersfield and went to Nashville where he did shows with Porter Wagoner and Dolly Parton and concentrated on recording. He feels that it was then and there that he finally found his sound, with the help of George Ritchie his producer, Harold Bradley, who led all his sessions, and "that amazing musician, Charlie McCoy, who plays harmonica, vibes, and everything else."

But all this time the drinking continued—and of course increased. There were pills, too, uppers and downers, to get him through the day. And it finally caught up with him. He collapsed in pain in a motel in Wheeling, West Virginia. He checked into a hospital—"my insides were messed up from all that drinking." Surgery followed with a long period of recuperation. At the end of it he went right back to the bottle.

What was it that brought him to that day in August in 1976? "I had a blackout," he said, "and when I came out of it, I had my hand around my wife's throat, throttling her, squeezing. My God! How could I?" He shuddered, not for effect but because telling it seemed to make that moment real again. "Well," he said, "she left, stayed away three days—and that's what it took. I quit!

"But I actually thought I could do it alone. I didn't touch the stuff, but those first days without it were just, well, indescribable. I finally begged God to let me die. And you know what He did? He let me feel it, what it would be like. I suddenly felt heavy as a rock. I was surrounded by complete silence. I was in the blackest of black of eternity. And I thought, 'If this is it, I don't want any of this.' And so I prayed again, and I said, 'If you'll just spare my life, I'll make amends to all I've hurt—especially to those who love me.'

"Well, from then on I started to get better. I got cleaned out, and then I found out about Jesus. Where do you find Jesus? In my case I was sitting in a rocking chair on my front porch, getting well. Just this voice: 'Sit down and learn and know My word.' I started studying the Bible then. A neighbor of ours, a truck driver's wife, took Pauline and me through it, a chapter a day. That's when my life really started to improve."

But not materially. The crisis and recovery had taken years from his life, years in which he all but dropped out of sight on the country scene. He managed to get a few dates back in New England. Capitol had dropped him, but he recorded an album for Belmont, a small label out of Boston, *The Great Race*, that kept his name out there and got him a little airplay. But it wasn't until 1984, when he happened to be in Nashville, trying to drum up business that he heard an announcement on WSM about a group called the Reunion of Professional Entertainers, that was organizing a kind of nostalgia tour. "I went right over there and bared my soul to them, told them I'd quit drinking and that I was in a condition now where I could be counted on. Old Smoky Rogers was kind of in charge of it all, and he listened to my story, talked it over with the others, and said to me, 'Well, you've got a job in October in New Orleans if you want it.' Man, I wanted it, and I've held on to that job ever since. 'Shower of Stars' is basically the same show. The promoter of the ROPE show is the promoter here. Smoky emceed the ROPE show, then he had some strokes, and I more or less took his place as master of ceremonies."

That's it. End of story. It's a good one too—one about bravery (Dick's), and loyalty (Pauline's), and divine intercession. Meet Dick Curless today, and you'd know, too, that it's a story with a happy ending, for he truly does seem to be a happy man.

We parted in the parking lot, shaking hands, wishing each other well. I jumped into my rental car, and he climbed up into his old GMC van, the one he said had 336,000 miles on it. I watched it in the rearview mirror better than halfway back to Branson. Then he turned off and headed for Highway 65 and headed for his home in Ozark.

9

Outside Branson

I don't know about you, but to me, the word, "resort" conjures up the picture of big, beautiful beaches, palm trees, and rolling surf, perhaps a high-rise hotel looking down onto the beach where, in the evenings, music from a small orchestra wafts over couples turning dreamily on an outdoor dance floor.

In Branson, it means something different. What they call a "resort" is really a collection of vacation cabins. You know the kind of family accommodations I'm talking about. They sleep a good many for their size, offer rudimentary kitchen facilities, and in this case are not much more expensive than the many motels located along the entertainment strip—if at all. And around Branson, located as it is in the "Tri-Lakes Area," you are usually guaranteed direct access to water.

I stayed in one such resort cabin during my temporary residence in Branson. It is located right at the junction of man-made Lake Taneycomo, a narrow, river-shaped body of water that snakes down from Powersite Dam, and Roark Creek (pronounced locally Ro-ark), nearly as wide as the lake at that point. My cabin was a little A frame with a separate bedroom. The front porch was located so close to the water that if I'd had a fishing rod and a mind to, I could have stepped out in the morning and cast into the shallows of Roark Creek. And chances are, that with a little patience, I would have pulled in a trout or two, for they are that plentiful there.

But it wasn't life below the surface that fascinated me so. Right at the junction of the creek and the lake, only about fifty yards from my front porch, was a bird refuge—a narrow island on which, at any time of the day, you could count scores of water birds. There were ducks, plenty of them, and it seemed like the last thing I heard at night and the first thing in the morning was their quacking chorus from the island. But mixed in with their sound was the deeper, sort of nasal, honk of the big wild geese. Although not so numerous as the ducks, they seemed more assertive, more in command of the turf. They strutted around, mostly in pairs, just below my porch, demanding respect from anyone who might happen by and generally getting it. I used to watch them goose-stepping in the space between the cabins and the creek bank for minutes on end. I remember a boy of about seven or eight from the next cabin decided he would chase a pair of geese, as he had been doing with all the ducks in the area. He took off after them, but they refused to be spooked. They turned, stood their ground, and honked at him sternly. The boy skidded to a stop and sized up the situation. True, they weren't as big as he was, but there were two of them and only one of him. And so, with what looked like a shrug, he left them alone and went back into the cabin.

I thought the geese were boss out on the refuge and along the creek bank until one morning four or five big birds showed up and took charge completely. It's funny how deferential behavior seems so plain when observed in other species. Perhaps, from the proper perspective, it would be just as evident in our own. I'd never seen birds quite like these before. They looked a lot like pelicans but without the big lower bill. Although larger than the ducks and geese, they weren't huge. But to see them take off, skimming along the surface of the water, big wings flapping, was impressive—stirring, you might say. There was something about them—the long beak, the narrow skull, the gaunt configuration of the neck, body, and legs—

that reminded me of the pterodactyl, the old dinosaur bird of yore.

I found out later they were herons, not native to any part of the country I've lived in before. You can tell I'm no naturalist. And I'm only likely to do my bird-watching early in the morning when I have a front porch with such a commanding view as I had there.

The Ozarks

Drive the winding hill roads surrounding Branson, look around you at the thick, deep woods that cover every rise and hollow, and you know those woods are thick with wildlife. And they are—yet nothing that a camper should have to fear. The number of rabbits and squirrels hereabouts would probably equal the human population of New York City. There are foxes and deer and a few wildcats. Once there were bears and wolves as well—but no longer, all of them, they say, were chased south from Missouri and down into Arkansas.

The country looks wilder than it is. It is hilly enough to have great, long vistas at the high points. When a road sign says, "Scenic View," you'd better believe it. Take the turnoff, get out of your car, and give it a long stare; you'll find it worth the trouble.

You're looking at the Ozarks, folks. It is one of the most distinctive regions in America. Sparsely settled for long decades of the nineteenth century, it was considered a semiwilderness area well into the twentieth. It stretches from a line bulging northward from just above St. Louis and Jefferson City south through the Ozark Plateau area; then below Springfield it abruptly rises up into these high hills. Southward into Arkansas, the hills rise even higher into the Boston Mountains, skip a wide valley, then rise up again into the Ouachita Mountains. There the Ozarks end, dropping off a little to the west into Oklahoma.

The hills and mountains are formed mostly of limestone and dolomite. You see outcroppings along every road, wherever the highway cuts through a rise. The tops of some hills show through as bare limestone. These are the "bald knobs" that gave their name to a violent group of vigilantes called the Baldknobbers, who met upon them after the Civil War. Like most of America, from the Appalachians to the Rockies, all this was under water eons ago; sea fossils can be found easily in the limestone throughout the Ozarks.

How did the Ozark region get its curious name? It may sound Indian, but it's actually French, or partly French. The early explorers of the region established an outpost in the south on the Arkansas River. The way they saw it, this whole dense, wooded area—plateau, hill, and mountain—was simply a rough transit to that outpost on the Arkansas, and so the French put it down on their maps as *"Aux-Arcs,"* abbreviating the name of the river, which they had accepted from the Indians there. "Ozark" is a rough approximation in English of the French.

Marquette and Joliet were the first explorers of the region, and the French were the first Europeans to settle it. It belonged, if they could have claimed ownership, to the Osage and Missouri Indians. Very late in the eighteenth century and early in the nineteenth, two new groups began to move into the Ozarks. The first was made up of the Scotch-Irish-English who had entered through Virginia and moved westward through Kentucky and Tennessee; their descendants populate the area to this day. The second were Cherokees, one of the "civilized" tribes, who began losing their tribal home in the Carolinas and northern Georgia, bit by bit, to white settlers. The final forced resettlement, the "Trail of Tears," came later. The whites stayed, but the Native Americans—Osage, Missouri, Cherokee, and whichever else—were eventually pushed off into Oklahoma, the "Indian Nation," where they were at least permitted to own land and keep it, even after the opening land rush of 1890.

The Ozark area was more deeply and tragically involved in the Civil War than any other region west of the Mississippi. Arkansas was one of the Confederate states. Missouri was nominally neutral, in spite of the fact that nasty, bloody raids were carried out all through the state by Quantrill's Raiders, who were called "irregulars," "guerrillas," but more often downright "outlaws" (Jesse James was one of them). Other guerrilla groups were led by Bloody Bill Anderson and George Todd.

The two bloodiest battles fought west of the Mississippi took place in the Ozarks. The first, the Battle of Wilson's Creek, came early in the war on August 10, 1861, at a point just south of Springfield off U.S. 65. It resulted in more than a thousand casualties on both sides. It led, after much maneuvering on both sides, to the Battle of Pea Ridge, fought March 6–8, 1862, in the northwest corner of the state of Arkansas. There were terrific losses, including many Missourians, on both sides. In the end, as was so often the case, the Union artillery proved the difference, and the Confederate forces fled southward to the shelter of the Boston Mountains. After that, military activity in the Ozark region was limited to raids and guerrilla activity.

The fact that the James brothers, the Youngers, and others learned lawlessness when it was sanctioned in wartime had a long-term effect during the years afterward. Their gangs and others not so well remembered continued to rob and pillage through the Ozarks, and from it, in every compass direction. There were plenty of places to hide out in the deep Ozark forest and limestone caves of such a size that horses could be stabled in them. Whole counties had been sympathetic to the Rebel cause and were willing to shield the boys who had ridden with Quantrill.

For this and other reasons, says Ed Marshall, a local historian and a member of the *Shepherd of the Hills* outdoor drama troupe, "settlers moving westward were advised to give the Ozarks a wide berth. And mostly, they did."

In 1885, right in Branson's Taney County, a group formed to counter the lawlessness. Calling themselves the Baldknobbers after their secret nighttime hilltop meetings, they were vigilantes, pure and simple. Riding masked through the country, they dispensed rough justice, burning, delivering beatings, and ultimately murdering. When they killed two men in nearby Christian County, men whose only sin was stirring opposition against them, they brought upon themselves retribution by the state and the federal government. There were mass arrests, trials, and three of the Baldknobbers were hanged for the murders. This ended their reign of terror in Taney and its surrounding area, although a few survived to form their own outlaw gang.

I remember asking Jim Mabe, one of the original cast members of the Baldknobbers show, why they had adopted the name of such a lawless bunch. His answer, while not exactly satisfactory, deserves repetition, for it offers a sample of the way that people in Branson look upon the town's history.

"Well, the Mabes used to play Baldknobbers in the *Shepherd of the Hills* show," he said, "so that's where we got the name. But in a way, the Baldknobbers weren't so bad. They started out as real good people for law and order and stuff, then they were vigilantes, and finally they robbed banks and so on, became kind of an outlaw group. But I guess we think about them the way they were when they first started out. We're the *good* Baldknobbers."

Taney County

Not long after I arrived in town, Kathy Oechsle, who is the Branson bureau for the *Springfield News-Leader*, took me out on a Sunday drive through a big piece of Taney County. We covered a lot of territory and took a lot of time. It was then, I guess, that I began getting a sense of Branson as a part of the Ozark region.

She pointed out to me that thick as the trees are over these wooded hills, everything we saw was second growth. During the post–Civil War era and into the first years of the twentieth century, there was a great need for timber as America expanded in every direction. Through most of the West timber was not at all plentiful. It was needed not just for building construction but also for the railroads—those crossties which support mile after mile of steel rails. The Ozarks, with its sparse population, had trees to spare, and so the timber companies took all the Ozarks had to spare—and then some. It wasn't long until the hills had been shaved clean. Today, with its ever-increasing value as a retirement and recreation area, it won't happen again.

We had lunch in Rockaway Beach. Kathy described it as "the Branson that never was." Most of Lake Taneycomo (TA-NEY COunty, MO) laps against banks; there are few real beaches there, but Rockaway Beach has a nice, small one. It became a very popular recreation area from the time Powersite Dam was constructed and the lake was created. In a way it became *too* popular—with the wrong people. As Branson police chief Steve Mefford had told me, "In the fifties it became a major hangout for bikers." He said he remembered driving through the little town as a boy with his parents and seeing the streets lined with motorcycles, practically no cars at all. Some of the biker gangs were pretty rough. There were some major disturbances that culminated in a riot-sized battle between two gangs. The state police were called in and many arrests made. That ruined the family trade in the town for decades, but it is now on its way back up.

We drove down the road to Powersite Dam, certainly a modest construction as dams go, built in 1913 by the Army Corps of Engineers. This created Lake Taneycomo, a cold water lake filled with rainbow trout and brown trout. Further work by the Corps of Engineers after World War II gave the area two more considerable bodies of water that are just right for fishing. The warmer waters of Table Rock Lake and Bull Shoals Lake make them great for bass fishing, and there are also plenty of crappie and catfish. When Mel Tillis and Shoji Tabuchi talk about this area as a fisherman's paradise, this is what they mean.

Kathy Oechsle took me up a high hill overlooking the dam to visit a friend of hers named Scarlett. (You're probably way ahead of me, but the lady is from the South, and she was named by her mother after the redoubtable heroine of *Gone With the Wind*, Katy Scarlett O'Hara.) Scarlett has a few nicely appointed cabins and a lovely, eccentrically furnished home that overlooks lake, dam, and countryside. A steady stream of guests come to her, mostly from cities within easy driving distance—St. Louis, Kansas City, Tulsa.

"Is it for the fishing they come?" I asked her. "Do they drive into Branson for the shows?"

"Oh, some do," she said, "and some just fish. But mostly they come here just to chill out. I had one businessman come down from St. Louis, and he just sat out there on the porch with a book open on his lap for two days. I don't even think he read much."

A little later, I sat where he had and took in the view. It is deep, steep, and long. I believe I understood then how you could sit there two days enjoying it and the quiet of the hills and the warmth of the sun.

There were a couple of places I particularly wanted to see on this tour, and Kathy dutifully drove me to them. The first was the College of the Ozarks, located just south of Branson off Highway 65. It's a fully accredited four-year college that operates along the work-study lines for which Antioch College in Ohio is so well-known. The 1,200 students at the College of the Ozarks earn their tuition and keep maintaining the campus (in beautiful shape), operating a restaurant and museum there open to the public. Students even run Branson's small local airport.

Then, nine miles above Branson, north off 65 on the way toward Springfield, is Bonniebrook. It was the home of Rose O'Neill, an artist—for the most part a commercial artist and illustrator—who was born in Wilkes-Barre, Pennsylvania, in 1874, but lived off and on just outside Branson in a magnificent old mansion of a house from 1893 until her death in 1944. Why is she famous? Why is her home a landmark? She was the creator of the Kewpies, those fat, little, round-eyed babies with the pointed cowlick hair that for decades after their first appearance in the *Ladies Home Journal* in 1909 were everywhere in evidence—not just in America, but all over the world. The famous dolls made from her drawings became an industry in themselves. Kewpie dolls were the sensation of their age. Every middle-class home in America had not just one, but a collection of them.

The original Bonniebrook was destroyed by fire, three years after Rose O'Neill's death, in 1947. Yet it is now in the process of being restored by Kewpie fans and collectors who have banded together as the Bonniebrook Historical Society. Eventually it will house, as it does on a small scale now, a Rose O'Neill–Kewpie museum. It is the site of the International Rose O'Neill Club's Kewpiesta, held annually in April. Hundreds come to Branson for it and make the pilgrimage to Bonniebrook.

Driving back to Branson, Kathy Oechsle took us through Hollister, which I knew simply as the smaller town across the bridge. Yet going through the center of it, I was interested to see that it seemed to have been laid out according to a plan. Nearly all the buildings were of substantial construction and done in the old English Tudor style—timbers and stucco. I asked Kathy about them and she hadn't a clue. I later found out—from Janet Dailey, no less—that Hollister originated as a real estate development promoted by a W. H. Johnson in 1906, who planned a whole town in the style of an English village. It is sufficiently unique to have found a place on the National Register of Historic Places.

Bluegrass in the Ozarks

All of this then—wildlife, lakes full of fish, long pages of history—are represented in Branson's Ozark region. And if it is truly distinctive, the point should be made that it also has a native style of music. Country music? Certainly—but not the comparatively sophisticated brand that is served up there along 76 Country Boulevard. Not to take anything away from Mickey Gilley, Moe Bandy, and the young stars who parade in and out of the Grand Palace, but theirs is a kind of music that the majority of Americans can and do adjust to with little difficulty. It has been somewhat homogenized with influences from other forms and styles of American music—blues, pop, swing, rock, you name it. Mel Tillis, for instance, often sounds more like a forties-style crooner than he does a lineal descendant of Jimmie Rodgers and Hank Williams.

But Ozark music is something different. It is not one of a kind, for it merges with Appalachian music so seamlessly that it is virtually indistinguishable from it. The reason, of course, is that it was brought to the Ozarks by the Anglo-Saxon and Celtic settlers who came from Virginia, eastern Tennessee, and Kentucky. Generally classified as bluegrass, this purer form appeals to a comparatively small audience, most of whom think of themselves as folk music fans.

If you know pornography when you see it, then you know bluegrass when you hear it. It's a sort of down-home jazz, completely improvised, even through the long, intricate ensemble passages that prevail in virtually every number. It's string music—trio, quartet, sextet, whatever—in which guitar, banjo, sometimes mandolin, fiddle, and acoustic bass are the instruments that carry the burden and back the singers. What songs? Oh, there's a whole repertoire of traditional bluegrass material—"Salty Dog," "Liza Jane," "The Wabash Cannonball," and so on, lots of white gospel, and all the old hoedown tunes, like "Fire on the Mountain" and "Sally Goodin."

But there's a new repertoire, too. Or perhaps better put, the old repertoire has been extended by new groups, such as the Seldom Scene, out of Washington, D.C., and the Dillards out of Taney County, Missouri. That's right, the Dillards, the grand old men of the new grass revival make their home right down the road from Branson in Kimberling City. As noted, Rodney Dillard has taken (temporary) leave of them for a featured role in the Jim Stafford Show. He brings a breath of authentic Ozark to 76 Country Boulevard.

Then, too, just to remind all those folks who journey to Branson to hear those slick country sounds that the hills were alive to the sound of music long before Roy Clark arrived, they held a bluegrass festival over Memorial Day last year at Coffelt Country Crossroads—right on the strip. The three-day affair (during which "no electrical instruments" were heard) featured performers and bands from all over the South and Southwest—Jim and Jesse, from Tennessee; Prairie Wind, out of Kansas; and Brushy Mountain Bluegrass, from Oklahoma. Just to mention, as they say, a few. It went over well enough that a second annual Coffelt Country Bluegrass Festival is now being planned.

The two oldest shows in Branson—and year in and year out, among the most successful—began as Ozark music shows of the more authentic kind. Today, although the Presley Show and the Baldknobbers mount productions just as slickly professional as the rest on the strip, something of the old style remains. And for his part, Gary Presley, boss of his show, swears it will always be there. "I feel like my mission is to keep people in this area mindful of our Ozark flavor here," he says. "If we lose our Ozark roots, then there's no difference between us and anybody else up and down the road."

And although Gary Presley is certainly his own man, that attitude was no doubt instilled in him by his father, Lloyd Presley. With fifty-eight years' playing experience behind him (he started at age ten), Lloyd still slaps the bass in the Presley show. "I bluff a lot," he says modestly.

He himself grew up in the Ozarks and raised his family right here in the area. Some of the best times he can remember go back "before TV." As he tells it, "We'd get together in the living room, and just anybody who had an instrument would join in. We'd have a big old jam session. If you couldn't play, then you sang. Just got the whole evening long like that. Oh, I'll tell you, it was an enjoyment.

"My kids still remember one time, and they still tell the story, when they all got so sleepy while we was makin' music, they just couldn't stay awake. So we made a little pallet for them under the kitchen table, my two sons and two daughters, and they just slept away, while we kept right on havin' our jam session in the living room." He laughed. "Oh, those were good old times."

I'll bet they were. It seems a shame, doesn't it, that they can't be revived right here on 76 Country Boulevard? This, after all, is the musical tradition that shaped Branson. But with Shoji Tabuchi going Vegas, Andy Williams presenting a show (and a good one) that would be applauded anywhere in the country, and with rumors floating through town that Debbie Reynolds and Wayne Newton are on their way—with all this, it would seem that the trend is away from tradition.

10

A Novel Beginning

It may seem strange, but it was a book that first brought visitors from the outside to Branson in great numbers. It was no travel guide, no history of the Ozarks, but rather a novel that created such widespread curiosity about the place and the region. Readers of the book came to view the setting for themselves. They braved the backcountry roads, some of them no more than wagon tracks, in their Model T Fords. Ed Marshall, who knows more about the history of the Ozarks in general and Branson in particular than anyone I met in town, says they started coming down every summer after the book was published, and it continued for years. "I've heard tell," he says, "that they had to back their cars up these steep hills because those old Model T's had gravity feed gas tanks, and if they tried to take the hills head-on, they'd just dry up about halfway to the top. But even so, they kept right on coming."

The book that proved such a magnet to readers was *The Shepherd of the Hills*, by Harold Bell Wright. It is a novel still remembered in the book trade as the first runaway best-seller. Published in 1907, it sold over a million copies back when the population of the United States was less than half what it is now—under a hundred million. No book before had electrified its readers quite so completely as this one. It is hard for a reader today to understand why. Yet its mixture of violence, piety, and romantic love, its advocacy of virtue and the simple life, hit readers in the first decade of the century as both absorbing and elevating. The book's best-seller reputation and the fact that it was constantly in print (and is today) led to a couple of movie versions. The latest of them, a kind of Ozark western, made in 1941, starred John Wayne.

Harold Bell Wright was a minister in the Christian Church who had held pastorates in a number of small towns in the Ozark region and then in the much larger town of Pittsburg, Kansas, right on the Missouri line. Sickly since his college days, Wright's health declined sharply under the demands placed upon him by the bigger parish in Kansas. And so, in 1903, a friend took him off to what was considered one of the most remote corners of the Missouri Ozarks to spend a summer recuperating. He stayed with the Ross family in a section known as Mutton Hollow. There he found not only the peace that helped him regain his health, but also a group of people and a way of life that fascinated him. He felt well enough upon his return to accept an even larger ministry in Kansas City. But he returned to Mutton Hollow for the summers of 1904 and 1905, nominally for the sake of his health but also to observe and take notes; he had decided to make use of what he had found there in a novel. *The Shepherd of the Hills* was finished late in 1905 and published two years later. It made him a rich man. Ultimately, he left the ministry altogether and moved to Arizona for his health. There he worked full-time as a writer and had one later significant success with the novel, *The Winning of Barbara Worth*. He died at his home near Tucson in 1944 at the age of sixty-eight.

Wright made no secret of the fact that he had set his novel in an actual place and that his characters were based on the people he had found there. People wanted to see that place and meet those people—and so they came in their flivvers, jalopies, and runabouts, their carriages and buggies. They came searching for Mutton Hollow . . . and found Branson.

The two were then separated by only about six or seven

miles, most of which go to make up what is the entertainment strip today. But they were distant worlds apart in their separate ways of life. Branson, named for its first postmaster in 1882, was certainly a very small town, but it had made a firm entry into the twentieth century when the railroad came there in 1905. Prior to that it had depended on the White River and a fairly primitive road system for travel in and out of town. The logging industry made use of whole sections of the river too. The only significant agriculture in Taney and nearby Stone counties was tomato growing; canneries operated right on the spot, in and out of town. But Branson had a good-sized hotel—a big frame house of a place still in operation today that is located north of the railroad depot; it had a college nearby (then known as the School of the Ozarks), and its cluster of retail stores served the whole area.

Mutton Hollow, on the other hand, was stuck well back in the nineteenth century. Never a town, it was no more than a collection of houses, cabins, and subsistence farms. The people there would probably have conformed exactly to the popular notion of "hillbillies," a term that was then just coming into use. Uneducated, many of them illiterate, they kept apart from the townspeople, their only contact on occasional trips into Branson to buy what they couldn't make or grow on their own. They lived just about as their people had lived, two and three generations before. These were the people that Harold Bell Wright stayed with and later described so attractively in *The Shepherd of the Hills*. And these were the people that so fascinated his readers that they felt compelled to come and meet them from as far away as Chicago, Des Moines, Kansas City, Dallas, Memphis, Louisville, Indianapolis, and St. Louis. This is just about the radius that provides the big-city weekenders for 76 Country Boulevard today.

You can still get a full, if not necessarily perfectly accurate, idea of what life was like in Mutton Hollow around the turn of the century. Two places located precisely where Harold Bell Wright set his novel do a good deal to keep alive the spirit of the place, and they have made it a lot more fun to visit than it was in the first decade of the twentieth century.

Mutton Hollow Craft Village

Driving west on Missouri State Highway 76, you pass out of Branson at the crossroads where the Ray Stevens Theatre is located. Nearly at the corner, just beyond it on the left, the turn for Mutton Hollow Craft Village is well marked. Turn in, and you will find a family theme park that seeks to re-create the atmosphere of that remote time in the Ozarks when Harold Bell Wright first came and discovered it all so unspoiled and innocent.

Today's Mutton Hollow may be more commercially aware than the one he knew, but its attractions are many and all quite innocent. It offers Ozark life minus the dirt and barnyard smells. For a modest admission, families, couples, or singles may wander through the park's streets and get an idealized, slightly glamorized picture of the past. The author of *The Shepherd of the Hills* couldn't help but be pleased to discover that Mutton Hollow Craft Village maintains a Harold Bell Wright Museum containing all manner of souvenirs and memorabilia from the writer's life, including the original, hand-written manuscript of the novel that made the original Mutton Hollow internationally famous. A half-hour film shown there gives the details of his life.

The six hundred-acre tract of land on which the theme park is situated is owned and was developed by the Cushman family. On it is the site of the original "Jim Lane" cabin, where the originals of Baldknobber Jim Lane and his daughter, Sammy, lived. Their lives were at moral cross-purposes in the novel.

"The Craft Village started," I was told by Leslie Wyman, a spokeswoman for Mutton Hollow, "when Amanda Cushman decided she would like a quilt shop right next to the old cabin."

After that, the new Mutton Hollow just mushroomed. The entire family—mother Amanda and kids Jerry, David, and Vicki—became deeply involved in the creation of the theme park. Yet it had the advantage of being created by a family that had at least some memory of life in the original Mutton Hollow.

"My family's house was the last residence on 76 in Branson," said Vicki Cushman. "There was no electricity when we moved here. My grandfather moved the family to this area fifty years ago form Ncosho, just west of here. At one time he had twelve hundred acres, all the way down to Roark Creek. He was hunting for a cave."

The limestone caves were and still are big tourist attractions in the Ozarks. The very successful Silver Dollar City took shape at the mouth of Marvel Cave.

"When we first came here," she said, "the best crops here were tomatoes and moonshine."

Vicki Cushman, who oversees day-to-day operations at Mutton Hollow, makes certain there is no moonshine or bottled-in-bond on the premises. It is a family attraction, if there ever was one, and she means to keep it that way.

A walk through Mutton Hollow Craft Village, as it is today, reveals thirty-five specialty shops, most of them offering Ozark crafts of various kinds. (Pizza, though offered, is *not* an Ozark speciality.) There is a pottery shop, a jewelry shop, an antique shop, a candlemaker, a cedar woodworks where visitors can come in and watch furniture being made, a leather shop, a coppersmith, and of course there is also Amanda Cushman's original quilt shop.

A million-dollar expansion for the 1992 season provided, among other things, for the opening of the County Fair area that features the kinds of rides that don't scare kids and are completely in keeping with the turn-of-the-century period of the park. The recently installed carousel, for instance, is an antique example of its kind, rebuilt and renovated for smooth operation to old-fashioned calliope music. There is a Ferris wheel, a water ride, and a kid-sized train ride that circles a large section of the park.

A ticket of admission to Mutton Hollow will get you a seat at the new Cedar Mountain Music Hall, a 300-seat, open-air theater (it has a roof but no walls). Native bluegrass and gospel music are featured, along with Ozark vaudeville and comedy. With five shows a day, entertainment is more or less continuous.

Also part of the expansion is the new Mutton Hollow Revue Dinner Theater. You have to pay something extra for admission, but for your money, you get to eat Ozark style and enjoy a ninety-minute country music show. Harold Bell Wright never had it so good.

Shepherd of the Hills

Farther west on 76, less than a mile out of Branson, is the Shepherd of the Hills Homestead and Outdoor Theater. You're still well within the bounds of what the novelist knew as Mutton Hollow when he came during summers in the first decade of this century. You know you are, for on these grounds is situated the old Ross family cabin, the home of John and Anna Ross, with whom Wright first summered in 1903. He actually roughed it a bit, pitching a tent at a point on their property that overlooked the most breathtaking view for miles. He called it Inspiration Point, and the name stuck. When he came to write the book, the Rosses served as the inspiration for his characters, Old Matt and Aunt Mollie, the moral pillars of the community.

Shepherd of the Hills is a dual-purpose attraction. At night, it offers a two-hour dramatization of the novel in a big amphitheater underneath the stars. By day, it functions modestly as a theme park recreating the same turn-of-the-century ambience as Mutton Hollow Craft Village down the road (and, for that matter, Silver Dollar City farther up the road).

Although more modest in dimension, what is offered there at Shepherd of the Hills seems somehow more authentic. Ed Marshall, whose title is director of daytime entertainment there, wants to be sure that people who pass through the homestead come away with some sense of the significance of this place and learn a little of the history of the Ozark region. Though there are souvenir shops, a flag museum, a restaurant, and various other spots where visitors are welcome to spend money, the main feature of a daytime visit is a guided tour of the grounds.

Ed Marshall explained his goals. "We want history given to them as entertainment in the daytime. As much as possible what we expect from our tour guides is that they get in certain facts and figures but develop their own story for the tours—choose their anecdotes, make it interesting.''

On a couple of occasions I have cited Marshall as an authority on local history, and for a good reason. He knows it well. It is not just that he is well-read, though he certainly is that, but he is also in close touch with the stories of the region, the local lineage, the very feeling of this distinct corner of the world they call the Ozarks.

Ed is all but a native of the Branson area. Born forty miles to the south in the Arkansas Ozarks, he moved here with his family when he was two years old. A big man, massive in appearance, Marshall is bearded and wears his sandy hair long in the authentic style of turn-of-the-century Ozarks. It seems to suit him; it's as though he were so steeped in the lore of a hundred and a hundred fifty years ago that he had adopted a guise and created a persona for himself that is pure Ozark.

Ed Marshall took me first to the old Ross cabin. It stands below and back from the highway, four walls of ancient history with a wood-shingled roof and a weathered look that makes it seem even older than it really is. He took me inside, and I found the interior pretty well matched what I'd already seen. The handmade furniture was simple and utilitarian. The fireplace was purely functional.

''John Ross built this himself, of course,'' said Marshall. ''Some of the insides have been replaced, because at one time this place was in pretty sorry shape. The logs are all original, though. Look here, you can see the axe hews.'' He bent down and pointed and yes, you could see the rough tracks of the axe there in the wood.

I asked how old the place was. ''Well,'' he said, ''this first room here, the main part of the cabin, went up in 1884. They built out and a little up from here, as you can see. I don't know quite when. But they lived pretty close, as you can tell. There's elements of the covered wagon here, real pioneer stuff. They had a lot of gumption.'' These were Marshall's people. He seemed proud of them.

On the way to Inspiration Point, he pointed out an old-fashioned country church, small but big enough to have a bell tower. It fit perfectly into the Mutton Hollow setting. Had it always been there? "No, we found this old church in Morgan, Missouri, run-down, unused. We brought it here and restored it. Looks new, doesn't it?"

A gazebo marks the site where Harold Bell Wright pitched his tent and beheld the view. The point is high enough that looking southward, you can see miles and miles into Arkansas. Yet from nearby Inspiration Tower you can see much, much farther. At 230 feet tall, it is a landmark in the area, easily visible from spots along the 76 entertainment strip. Two glass-walled elevators take visitors to the observation deck that provides a 360-degree panorama of the surrounding country. Northward, you can see Springfield with no difficulty, for the country flattens out considerably and a bit uninterestingly. The view to the south is still best, made better by the great height at which we stand to study it. At this level we can easily see across the Ozark hills of Arkansas, all the way to the Boston Mountains.

"Some of the old-timers in the area had some animosity when we wanted to put the tower up," said Ed Marshall. "But when it went up, they liked it, and we're glad about that because we respect this area, and we want folks' support. See, there's been a great influx of people who've come into this area and started businesses in the last years. Fine. We don't have enough local business here—or we didn't. But I have to say that some of the people who've come in don't have a sense of the place that we want to keep. The values are different, I guess."

He drove me down to the 1,840-seat outdoor theater, a regular stop on the daytime tour, before the show in the evening. Viewed in full light from the stage area, the place seems pretty vast. The rows of seats march steeply uphill, giving it the aspect of a football stadium. Not surprising, for the stage area itself, at eighty yards, is nearly the size of a football field.

It has to be wide enough to contain a barn, sawmill and gristmill, a store, and the shepherd's cabin (which "burns down" every night about ten o'clock)—not to mention the herd of sheep, the many horses and mules, and the antique auto with which the actors share the sandy stage.

How can actors make themselves heard in such a vast space? Why, by electronic amplification, of course. All the twenty-four players who have speaking parts are miked. Their words go out through five speakers arranged to reach each of the seats that are tiered up to the top of the hill.

For a presentation that doesn't spare on spectacle, the most impressive bit in the *Shepherd of the Hills* show is the burning of the shepherd's cabin. It may come under the heading of special effects, but the fire is real all right. "You bet it is," said Marshall. "I lost my beard one night, slapping the fire out with burlap. It just got singed right off."

But how do they manage to burn it night after night? "Well, we built it with green wood, see, and in between the logs there are strips of burlap soaked in kerosene. That makes for a good burn without getting out of hand. It's the kerosene that catches and not the wood."

Ed Marshall's regular role in the show is that of Buck Thompson, which he describes as "comic relief," but he also understudies the John Ross role—Old Matt. In a pinch he could probably play six others. Everybody understudies everybody else. "It's a family here," he said. "I know you hear that a lot, but it really is true. There's very little turnover in the cast from year to year. Most of those who do go are younger ones who are going off to try their wings. I've left to see other places. I'd summer here and winter someplace else, but I always came back. I've had eight years in the show this stretch and there were some years before that, too.

"Yeah, I always come back." He gestured at the green hills surrounding us. "You look around here, and often you take this for granted. But you get away from it, and you miss it. Being here can work wonders on people. I see them come here from the city, and they don't look you in the eye. They're just amazed at you, that you're real friendly. If I could get the whole country to spend a week here, I could change everybody's attitude, get them real friendly. Hell, bring the whole Middle East over here, and they'd start smiling at each other after a while."

He wanted me to know that there were other stops made

along the way on the daytime Homestead tour (which, by the way, is ordinarily undertaken in a Jeep-drawn caravan). The stops include: a country music show at the Parlor Theatre; a working blacksmith shop; and the big fellas that keep the blacksmith busy pounding out horseshoes—a whole stable full of Clydesdales, available for surrey jaunts.

But most of all Ed Marshall wanted me there for the nighttime show. He promised that the crickets, locusts, katydids, and tree frogs would provide "ambient noise" that would get me right in the mood. "Really," he said, "there's nothing like outdoor theater. Anything else is just . . . oh, I don't know, too confining, I guess."

The Show

Anytime that a full-length novel is adapted for two-hour dramatic presentation on a single set (no matter how big the set), you can be darned sure that some liberties have been taken. The *Shepherd of the Hills* show is no exception. But Shad Heller, who was associated with Silver Dollar City for much of his life, did a remarkable job of cutting and shaping the Harold Bell Wright text. He may have lost nuances of character and a few of the more subtle plot points, but every ounce of melodrama and violence that was there between hard covers has been faithfully translated to the outdoor stage. According to Ed Marshall, the Shad Heller adaptation was first performed in Branson "down on the lakefront." For thirty-four years, however, they've been doing it at the big amphitheater just below Old Matt's Cabin.

Although "curtain" is not until 8:30, it is just about mandatory that you arrive a half-hour before that time, for you have to get down to the outdoor theater by means of the same Jeeps and vans that haul passengers around on the daytime tour. If too many arrive late for the Jeeps and vans, they will most likely miss the opening "curtain."

And if you get there late you're liable to miss Ed Marshall at his best. It is his job to warm up the crowd (sometimes not so easy on cool spring evenings). But he does it with all the style and good humor of a natural-born Ed McMahon. He had referred to the warm-up as "*my* genre. Most of it's ad-lib, of course. I might take a jab at someone in the crowd, kidding them, and if he comes back at me, we ad-lib back and forth for a while. The idea is to get audience participation and make them feel at home—they love it. But of course it's a different crowd every time. So you have to be alert and listen for what's different about them. Keeps you on your toes."

What was different about the audience that night was that it was kind of damp. Rain had fallen earlier and threatened again. On nights like that the show sends its own weatherman up to the top of Inspiration Tower to eyeball the thunderclouds and lightning and judge their position and course. There was rain out there, all right, but the word was that it was about twenty miles away and headed away from the Shepherd of the Hills Outdoor Theatre. So although somewhat delayed, the show would go on.

Ed Marshall, already in his Buck Thompson getup of pinafore overalls and long john shirt, challenged the crowd to complain about a little "Missouri dew," joshing the many Minnesotans there about the snowfall they had escaped on this May night. It was all done in good humor, and although abbreviated because of the delay, it got them in the mood for the show.

Action began with a small herd of sheep driven across the wide stage area by the mysterious but well-liked shepherd. Cast members arrive on horseback. Mules are tethered in front of the little barn next to the sawmill. You don't get that kind of realism on Broadway.

And then the conflicts arise as the plot begins to spin out. Wash Gibbs, the bully of Mutton Hollow and a sure-enough villain, tries to force himself on pretty little Sammy Lane. Young Matt, who pines for Sammy, forces Wash to leave off his impolite overtures. And so it goes until the postmaster arrives in his horse and buggy with big news: President McKinley has been assassinated, Teddy Roosevelt is the new president, and the bank down in Branson has just been robbed.

Well, Wash Gibbs may not have killed President McKinley,

but we find out soon enough that he and his gang of renegade Baldknobbers robbed the bank. But before he gathers them in the second act for more villainy, all the good folks of Mutton Hollow get together for a good, old-time square dance in the barn. Buck Thompson calls it out and invites people from the audience to join in with them. A few brave souls march down from the audience. Some of the rest wander up toward the refreshment stand. This is intermission. The square dancing will continue unabated all through it with music provided by a little three-piece hoedown combo. So in a sense the show never stops, and there's audience participation throughout the intermission.

There's lots of action, all kinds of action—and most of it in the second act. By the time you've witnessed a fierce fist-fight that we know had to come between Young Matt and Wash Gibbs; after we've seen the Baldknobbers ride in, looking fierce in their authentic black flour sack masks; once the inevitable shoot-out is over; once the cabin fire has been put out—after you've seen all this, you have the feeling that you've been watching a new form of entertainment, something like a movie with live actors. Seats up front are a little more expensive, but the closer you get to the action, the more realistic it seems.

And somehow or other, the story gets sorted out, too. Pretty little Sammy Lane chooses correctly among the three suitors who pursue her. We learn the identity of the mysterious but ever-so-spiritual shepherd of the hills, and we learn that the ghost that haunts Mutton Hollow is not really a ghost at all, but . . . Well, never mind. Just trust me that all the loose ends are tied together; good is rewarded, and evil is punished.

As Ed Marshall described it, ''The *Shepherd* is basically a western with a little bit of everything in it—shoot-outs, a love story—and in a lot of ways it resembles a soap opera, too.'' That about sums it up.

But you don't go to a show like this expecting great art, or art at any level. No, you go to be entertained, and *The Shepherd of the Hills* is eminently entertaining in all the old-fashioned ways. It provides convincing spectacle, offers a high

Missouri Route 76 in Branson—Country Music Boulevard

The beginning—Presley show opens on Highway 76 in 1967

The class of 1992 on opening day, May 1, 1992. From left to right: Boxcar Willie; Steve Presley; Shoji Tabuchi; Lloyd Presley; Johnny Cash; Gary Presley; Moe Bandy; Andy Williams. *(Kathy Oechsle)*

Mel Tillis

Shoji Tabuchi

Live action at the Shepherd of the Hills outdoor drama

POET KNIFEMAKER: A man as tough as the Ol' West, yet Ray Johnson's poetry can bring a tear to anyone's eye. Johnson recites his poetry while demonstrating his art to guests of Silver Dollar City.

TISKET, TASKET, A MAN WHO WEAVES A STERLING SILVER BASKET: Donnie Ellison, a native of the Ozark lakelands, came straight from high school graduation to an apprenticeship in basketry at Silver Dollar City in 1973. Donnie's apprenticeship lasted four years; now he has apprentices of his own, and his shop displays hundreds of handmade baskets, including some made of fine metals such as sterling silver.

PARDON ME BOYS, IS THAT THE SILVER DOLLAR CHOO CHOO? Authentic 1930s German steam trains whistle through the turn-of-the-century theme park daily.

Boxcar Willie

Roy Clark

Andy Williams

Glen Campbell

Willie Nelson (*Mark Jenkinson*)

level of professionalism in all production details, and gives you just enough drama and story to hold the whole package together. And Ed Marshall was right: all that "ambient noise" from the surrounding woods did contribute somehow to the enjoyment of it all.

I saw him afterward just long enough to tell him how much I liked the show. He was there with all the other cast members at the point where the Jeep-drawn vans stopped to haul everyone back to the parking lot. Actors, actresses, and audience mingled freely. A few autographs were signed. It reminded me a little of Shoji Tabuchi's long good-byes to the bus people.

11

A Local Marvel

According to local legend, Marvel Cave, which became the site for one of the Branson area's grandest attractions, was discovered by the Osage Indians in the course of a bear hunt.

Their hunting dogs pursued a scent all the way up to the top of what is now called Roark Mountain, where the Osage hunting party found that the dogs had cornered a black bear on a limestone ledge just above a gaping hole in the ground. The problem for them was that the ledge was hollowed out against the mountain, and the bear had shrunk back against the wall and was protected from a clear arrow shot. One of the hunting party bravely volunteered and, armed only with a knife, swung down onto the ledge, with the bear and the dogs. He made a lunge at the bear with his knife. The bear leaped at him and both tumbled off the ledge with one of the dogs, and all disappeared down the gaping hole. The hunting party rushed to it and looked—there was nothing to see. They listened—there was no sound. It was as if the bear, the brave, and the dog had simply been swallowed up by the earth, as indeed they had been. The Osage notched the trees around the spot to indicate danger and thereafter called the place the Devil's Den.

Early white settlers in the region heard of it from the Indians. And although before the Civil War none was brave enough to descend into it and explore, there it was, the Devil's Den, an entrance to hell.

The first exploration of the cave had probably taken place by 1869. Miners prospecting for lead lowered themselves down on a rope, carrying lanterns. They found the floor of the great room beneath the sinkhole to be more than two hundred feet from the surface. In three hours down there, they found passages leading off in a number of different directions, a huge quantity of bat guano, but no sign that there was lead to be mined anywhere in the cave. Henry T. Blow, the mining engineer who headed the expedition, however, came out with the conviction that there was marble to be mined within it. As it turned out, he was wrong. Nevertheless, it eventually came to be known as Marble Cave, and only the locals called it the Devil's Den.

By the time Blow's error had been discovered, the cave property had been bought by the Marble Cave Mining and Manufacturing Company. Some were still convinced that there must be lead down there. But beginning about 1884, all that was ever mined from it was bat guano. It was not unprofitable, for the stuff was rich in nitrate and was used in the manufacture of gunpowder; in those days it brought $700 a ton. Guano mining continued until 1889 when the great quantities that were readily accessible had been exhausted.

In that year, the mined-out cave was sold to a Canadian, William H. Lynch, who eventually opened it up to visitors. Well, at that time there weren't many visitors to the Ozarks. But he and his daughters, Genevieve and Miriam, explored the cave thoroughly and established its present, recognized limits. There is, however, an underground river that flows through and out of the cave whose source and mouth is unknown. William Lynch died in 1927, and in 1950, his two daughters, who felt they could no longer take an active role in operating it as a tourist attraction, leased it to Hugo and Mary Herschend.

The Birth of Silver Dollar City

By the early fifties, Marble Cave had become Marvel Cave. The Herschends first learned of it when they began traveling down to the area with their two sons, Peter and Jack, from their home in the Chicago suburbs in 1946. What attracted them to this out-of-the-way corner of the Ozarks?

"They loved wildflowers," Jack Herschend told me. "They loved to hunt wildflowers, and this was where they did it. I'd love to tell you that we did this intensive study and decided this was exactly the right place to locate a theme park like Silver Dollar City, but it all came about because my dad, actually my stepdad, worked hard in the city—he was a branch manager for Electrolux—and loved to get away from it all."

And this corner of Stone County, Missouri, just across the line from Taney County, was about as far from the bustle of the business world as he could get. They liked it so well that they kept coming back summer after summer. Inevitably, they toured Marvel Cave and came to know Miriam and Genevieve Lynch quite well. By this time the Lynch sisters were quite elderly. By 1949 they had reached the point where they decided that they could no longer guide visitors through the cave. Hugo and Mary Herschend leased the cave from them for ninety-nine years and began operating it themselves as a tourist attraction. A couple of years later, when they discovered that the parking lot for the cave was about to be sold out from under them, they bought the property surrounding the cave outright.

"My dad, Hugo, was really kind of a visionary," said Jack Herschend. "My brother Peter is very much like him in that way. Anyway, way back at the beginning Hugo talked about building a little village where people could stop along the highway to see these Ozark people at work at their native crafts."

Hugo Herschend never lived to see that idea brought to fruition, dying of a heart attack in 1957 at the age of fifty-six. But, as his widow and two sons continued to operate Marvel Cave as an attraction just off Missouri State Highway 76, his idea came to them again. Originally, the village was thought of as just a way to keep people interested and occupied while waiting to take the cave tour. And in just that modest way Silver Dollar City was born. That was in 1960.

It seemed proper to bring visitors back in time to the nineteenth century, for in this way they would be reminded of the history of the area and the cave. "This had been a stage stop between Springfield and Berryville, Arkansas," said Herschend. "I remember the day when the history of it all was brought home to us. It was in 1957, the year my father died, a man named Charlie Sullivan drove up in a 1937 Buick. Now, he was eighty-seven, and yes, he was right there behind the wheel. He told us he had been born in Marmoros, the original Marble City. That's where the miners lived. But there was another Marmoros about four miles away. You can find both of them in early atlases. The second one burned down about 1894. What's left is now just a ghost town. But I'll tell you, seeing him and hearing about what was here before, really made me think, gave me a sense of all that had gone on here in the past—the mining and just everything."

They might have reestablished it as Marble City, or named it Marvel City, after the cave. But Don Richardson, an active publicist who entered into the enterprise, came up with Silver Dollar City—and a gimmick. They would hand out silver dollars in change. Although not as scarce as they are today, they were rare enough to elicit comment whenever they were spent.

"Where'd you get this? Don't see many silver dollars anymore."

"Little place down in Missouri, call it Silver Dollar City. There's a big cave there that's really something to see, and some little shops where the local people sell things they make right on the spot. My wife got a quilt there she just loves, and I got these in change."

And that was the way word spread around the Midwest and mid-South area. Here was a place out in the middle of some of the prettiest country in America, situated near three lakes where the fishing was just great—and you could go there and spend a lot or a little, but you'd come away with beautifully made things you couldn't get in places like Dallas or Chicago. Not a bad reputation for a theme park to have. And it was enhanced considerably when Silver Dollar City held its National Crafts Festival in 1963.

"We're much less ride-oriented than other theme parks," said Herschend. "I guess that's because almost half of our visitors come here without kids. We have crafts and music shows, that are of interest to a couple twenty-five years old or a couple sixty-five years old. Music's always been a part of Silver Dollar City. I guess you know the Baldknobbers down on the strip started here with us.

"But look, I'm not going to sit here and tell you about it when you could go out and take a look for yourself. Why don't you do that? If you've got any questions after that, come back, and we'll talk some more."

And so I left Jack Herschend's comfortable executive office—comfortable, not luxurious—for the actual tourist attraction itself.

Silver Dollar City is about seven miles outside Branson on Missouri 76. You might say that it's a straight shot, except in that stretch the road winds up and down and all around through the Ozark hills. It is indeed beautiful country but until comparatively recently it was isolated and undeveloped. Jack Herschend told me that when they moved here back in the early fifties, there was no electricity, no telephone, and no running water. They did what they could to change all that. His mother, Mary, had the first indoor plumbing in Stone County.

You can't miss the entrance to Silver Dollar City—it is well marked. Hang a left off 76, and follow the signs. The same tour buses that have made Shoji Tabuchi the local star he is, also assure the continuing success of Silver Dollar City. They were parked in a specially designated area of a huge parking lot, row upon row of them. Later in the day they would move on to Branson.

Inside the park, there really is a kind of late–nineteenth century flavor achieved through cobblestoned streets and walkways and the weathered frame construction of all the buildings along the way. Silver Dollar City is a good deal larger than Mutton Hollow. More important, there is a greater emphasis on the performance and execution of the separate crafts whose products are put on sale in the little shops. There is more of a workshop atmosphere to the place, exactly the sort of thing that Hugo Herschend must have had in mind when he envisioned the crafts village by the side of the road—but on a grander and more complete scale.

Walk down the street that runs through the park, and you will be surprised at the workshop activity all through the place.

There is glassblowing, fascinating to see, done just about the same way it was in Venice centuries ago. There are the candymakers who prepare their wares right there before you; you can watch them make the peanut brittle, then come back and sample "our" batch after it has come out of the oven and cooled. And then there's Violet Hensley, "an Ozark legend," who makes fiddles and plays them; she has been a guest on national television, as welcome for her bubbling, though slightly cantankerous, personality as for her craftsmanship. There are wood-carvers. There are quiltmakers. There is an old-fashioned nineteenth century furniture factory, where furniture is built the way it was done way back when. And it's important to note that these people work the year round, even when Silver Dollar City is closed to visitors during the winter months, in order to fill orders that have come in from all over the country, some from all over the world.

Knife maker Ray Johnson is certainly one with an international reputation as a craftsman. He forges and tempers his knives to incredible strength, and he is more than willing to demonstrate that strength by banging on blades with a hammer, or by using his knives to punch holes in an empty 55-gallon oil drum.

He paused at his forge to talk a little about his work. "Well, you know," he said, "people come in trying to learn how it's done. Just like that. But it's taken me nearly twenty-five years to find that out. I started with steel as a hobby, something our folks had done. I was in welding and knife making is related to that. The way it started with me, I was a supervisor of a welding crew. There was a union strike, and I couldn't do anything while it was going on, so I ground out a knife, and it just went on from there. So when people ask, 'What would it take for me to do that?' And I tell them, 'Twenty-five years.' "

Born in Alton, Missouri, Ray Johnson grew up in the Ozarks. A part-time poet, he has the gift of gab—no doubt about that—and he puts that, too, at the service of his craft. He calls knife making "an addiction," and explains, "All of us are getting ready to make Excalibur. There really aren't many of us full-time knife makers around, and it's easy to get obsessed.''

Does he work all through the year? You bet he does. ''This year I'll build one hundred fifty blades, working here and at home. I've got another shop at home just like this, and I work ten hours a day, wherever I'm working. I can sell more product than I can make basically because my product is more valuable. Just when it says 'Ray Johnson' on the blade—they know they're getting something.

''But what I am really is a toolmaker. A knife may look dangerous, but it's a tool. Now, you can spend $1,500 and get a Weatherby rifle, and it'll fire a projectile whose only purpose is to kill. But this knife here''—and he hefted the big Bowie knife he was working on—''it'll be put to a hundred different uses. It'll open oil cans, pork and bean cans, might be used to skin an elk. But if you get right down to it 90 percent of a knife's life will be used for prying, and only 10 percent of it for cutting.''

Ray Johnson said he started full-time at knife making in 1983. ''I'd worked for one outfit for twenty-six years,'' as he told it, ''and my future was secure. I had a family to feed, but I knew how to build a knife. This will be my fifth season with Silver Dollar City. They treat me well. They give me free rein, and leave it to my imagination, and I do the best I can for them. I'm probably the luckiest man in the world because I'm doing what I wanted to do and making a living at it.''

And he means it. I left him reluctantly. Ray Johnson gives quite a demonstration.

There's music all around at Silver Dollar City. Each street seems to have its own little music hall—the Dockside Theatre, the Riverfront Playhouse, and the much larger Echo Hollow Amphitheatre. You can hear country and Ozark-style country, gospel, even a little Dixieland.

And although Jack Herschend played down the number of rides available in the park, those they offer are imaginative. They include ''Fire in the Hole,'' a roller coaster, and water rides—the Waterboggan Flooded Mine, and the Lost River Raft ride—and a full-sized steam train that will carry visitors in a wide circuit around the park. The train runs on the somewhat narrower European-gauge track, for it was brought over from Germany, but it looks authentically nineteenth century American as it chugs along. (Riders should be forewarned that they may find themselves prey to Ozark train robbers on the trip—and they put on a good show!)

Backing onto the water and close by the Riverfront Playhouse is the basket-weaving workshop. Donnie Ellison is the master craftsman there. I'd been urged to talk to him because he had done his apprenticeship in that same workshop. He was proof that the Ozark crafts are being passed on right there in Silver Dollar City.

A quiet man, youthful in spite of the gray in his hair and beard, he was born and raised over the line in Lead Hill, Arkansas, but then toward the end of the sixties he moved up to Lampe, Missouri, not far from Branson. It was there in 1973 that he heard that Leslie Jones, Silver Dollar City's basket weaver, was looking for an apprentice. Jones, who could neither read nor write, had worked at the craft for fifty years and was acknowledged to be just about the best at it in the Ozarks. He was also acknowledged to be rather cantankerous and had a reputation for running through apprentices rather quickly.

"My grandfather wove baskets," said Donnie Ellison, "and he taught me a little of it before he died. So I went to Leslie Jones and applied for an apprenticeship. He looked me over and seemed kind of leery, said something like, 'You're not too big, are you?' Then he told me that apprentices find out soon enough that splitting logs wasn't much fun and let me know that's what I'd be doing.

"And that's what I did, all right—I split logs for six months. Here was one of the greatest craftsmen I'd ever met, and he would let me do nothin' but split logs. No wonder so many apprentices quit on him. But you know, you can't go just anyplace and learn this craft, and this was his way of teaching it. The first year I spent splitting logs. The second year I spent splitting strips. I worked with white oak logs, which grow around here. You can use ash or willow or hickory. But white oak makes the best baskets because it's the hardest. It's also the hardest to work with."

Was Leslie Jones hard to work for? "Yes, but when he

finally let you do some weaving, you knew just what to do. I remember when he let me make my first basket. I worked hard over it, and when I finished it, I said, 'How's this?' He looked at it and didn't say anything, just shook his head three times. 'What's the matter with it?' I asked him. 'Nothin',' he said, and he just kept on with what he was doing.''

Donnie Ellison worked an apprenticeship of four years. In order to become a journeyman, he had to duplicate all fifty of the basket styles woven by Jones. He did that and eventually added styles of his own. ''My title now is master craftsman,'' said Ellison. ''But to me a master craftsman is Leslie Jones. He raised eight kids making baskets. He was quite a man.''

I was introduced to Ellison's apprentice, Patsy Stengley—''a man or woman can both do this job''—and then taken on a mini-tour of the shop in front. The variety of baskets seemed endless—and not quite all, as it turned out, had come from their workship. They also offered Indian-made pieces from Cherokee, North Carolina. ''They work with their ash just the same way I do with our white oak,'' he said. In what they called the Appalachian Room, there were samples from Kentucky and Tennessee. ''This is the same country where the Missouri basket makers came from. You can see the similarities, but some of their shapes are different.'' In the Shaker Room, there were pieces from the Nantucket area, all out of ash, and they included woven furniture. All beautiful stuff.

There is strength and a kind of purity to these handmade products. Donnie Ellison acknowledges that some baskets can be manufactured mechanically. ''But a white oak basket will last because you follow the grain of the wood,'' he said. ''What attracted me to learning the craft was the challenge. It wasn't a factory job. The product is unusual, really an heirloom product. It'll last.''

The Underground City

Silver Dollar City is the best-attended theme park in the entire Midwest. Each year 1.7 million visitors pass through its gates. The crafts village, rides, restaurants, and music theaters are laid out over forty acres. An additional two hundred acres are given over for parking. And all around it there is a wide zone of green—two thousand acres of woods and meadows kept undeveloped so that the park will retain its unspoiled nineteenth century look.

All this is above ground. Beneath it, of course, is Marvel Cave, without which there might well have been no Silver Dollar City. To visit this underground labyrinth is to move into another world entirely. This cave tour requires more hiking and climbing than most, and once undertaken it can't be broken off at any point along the way. And so visitors are warned beforehand not to undertake it if they have a history of heart problems or respiratory difficulties.

They mean it. The tour of Marvel Cave, if not exhausting, is challenging at some points. Once you have completed it, you will know you've taken a good, long walk and climbed a few stairs.

It begins, of course, with a long descent into what may seem to some to be the most impressive part of the entire cave complex—the Cathedral Room, the largest entrance room of any cave in America. It is 210 feet from ceiling to floor—a 20-story drop that Ed Marshall had described, with a width to match a building of such proportions. In the 1950s, square dances were held there on the floor of the Cathedral Room; and as a stunt, a few underground balloon ascents have been successfully undertaken there, the first in 1963 by Don Piccard, one of the famous family of French balloonists.

Although it is indeed awesome, the Cathedral Room does not provide a premature climax to the tour. What follows is like nothing you've ever seen before, and as you trail the guide through the narrow passages and begin to explore the rest of the cave, you feel like you're really spelunking. There is a series of rooms and subterranean overlooks—the Egyptian Room, the Cloud Room, Lost River Canyon—each more impressive than the last. All the while, as you continue to descend, you might keep an eye out for cave fauna along the way. They are not intrusive; many are blind and on the endangered species list. All you are likely to see are a few bats, tiny animals hugging the cave walls where they hang. There are 100,000 of them in the cave, most of them in great colonies secluded in rooms that are closed to the public. In Lost River Canyon you just might see some sudden, swift movement along the banks of the Mystic River that leads out of the known area of the cave into nowhere. If you do, you will have glimpsed a very rare creature indeed—the Ozark Blind Cave Salamander, only about four or five inches long and virtually colorless.

You will continue to descend, past the Waterfall Room, in which the Mystic River drops some fifty feet in a natural waterfall, and move on at about the same level toward the Mystic Pool. This is the deepest part of the cave tour—505 feet down.

There are parts of Marvel Cave still unexplored. There are a couple of underground lakes that are believed to have a depth of two hundred feet. There is the Mystic River-of-no-return that has them all baffled (they've dropped dye into it and waited for it to come out in one of the streams or rivers in the nearby Ozark area, but it hasn't been spotted yet). There are, in short, about as many mysteries as marvels in the cave.

Jack Herschend's life is intimately connected with Marvel Cave. He was married there, in the Cathedral Room. "My wife and I courted there," he had told me, "so it seemed appropriate." And his life almost ended there at the age of twenty-eight.

It had been planned for a while to provide a "cave train," so that visitors would not have to make the full ascent of 505 feet at tour's end in order to make their exit. To make this possible, a tunnel was dug diagonally through the clay and limestone to a cave room known as the Elves Chamber. Jack Herschend designed, engineered, and oversaw the project— the excavation of the tunnel, the laying of the track, and the installation of the cable mechanism that would haul cars out of the cave and back up to the top of Roark Mountain to a point near where they had started.

Then, as now, he practiced hands-on management. He climbed into a car to make the first trip down through the tunnel—and make it very slowly, so that he might check clearances along the way. But just as the car started moving down, the cable slipped, and, with Jack Herschend inside, the car plummeted 238 feet and hit solid rock at the bottom of the tunnel at sixty miles an hour. Because he had been thrown clear by the impact, he was still alive, but three discs in his spinal cord had been crushed, and a leg was broken in five places. Told he would never walk again, he walks today with a limp.

In the thirty-five years since, the cable has not slipped once. The cave train is safe, and it returns visitors to Marvel Cave on an easy uphill ride to a comfortable landing at the souvenir shop marking the entrance to the cave, right where they started out.

The Herschend Organization

When I later resumed my conversation with Jack Herschend in his Branson office, we didn't talk about his brush with death, but rather about the Herschends' plans for the future in the area—and about Dollywood.

That's right, the Herschend organization is in partnership with Dolly Parton in what has proven to be the most lively and entertaining complex in the Gatlinburg/Great Smoky area. Jack Herschend is proud to say that at both Silver Dollar City and Dollywood the emphasis is on "crafts and local activities." He makes the point, too, that Dollywood is a bit more music-oriented.

"It's fascinating," he said. "Celebrities play there, of course, but there's equal interest in her kinfolk. They play at what's called the Kinfolk Backporch Theatre. Altogether there are thirty of them who work at the park, including eleven brothers and sisters.

"But I have to say that Dolly herself has been unbelievably delightful to work with." He said it as though he meant it. "To be honest, I'd heard the opposite. But when we asked to meet to negotiate, she just said, 'Meet me in Denver.' We went there to the Holiday Inn where she was staying. She met us at her suite, gave us hugs and said, 'I want to be in business with you.' It was that kind of positive spirit right from the start. And let me tell you, when she talks about an idea for Dollywood, I listen.

"She has a sense of what the public—her public—wants. As an example, she told me, 'We really have to have a Dolly Parton Museum.' I told her, 'I *hate* museums.' But she said, 'I know, but we really need to have it. You don't understand my fans.' And believe me, she was absolutely right. Her Dolly Parton Museum is one of the biggest attractions in Dollywood. It's got little videos, a lot of her early songs. People line up all through the day to go through it. She really knows what the public wants—her and her kinfolk. There's Aunt Granny's Restaurant, backwoods, Smoky Mountains stuff, and they give out recipes!

"And she performs—a lot. It's not just Dollywood in name only. And that woman has a great heart for helping people. There's a real literacy problem in that area, and she raises $300,000 every spring for the Sevier County Literacy Program. Reba McEntire and Burt Reynolds are going to help her out this year."

I asked about the Herschends' own plans for the future. "Well," he said, "we've got the showboat planned for 1995, and it's the Grand Palace this year, and next year the Grand Village right next door. We plan that as a real shopping experience—Ozark Mountain–style. There are statistics that say that 94 percent of the people who come here shop as part of the vacation experience. In the first phase, it will be our attempt to build truly unique shops—shopping and dining different from what you have at home. After all, you've got a Wal-Mart at home. We hope to take people out of the present and bring them back in time. It will be more of a Gay Nineties experience than Silver Dollar City, which is really a little further back in time."

But what about the showboat? "Well," he said, "we hope to build a 1,000-passenger showboat that will operate on Table Rock Lake. The entire complex will be known as White River Junction. We may have a big announcement about that later."

They did. It turned out that the old "gambler" himself, Kenny Rogers, would work as a partner in the showboat enterprise, both as a performer and, well, a presence. Shortly after the announcement on his partnership with the Herschends, Kenny Rogers had this to say to *USA Today*: "The

Grand Canyon has four million visitors a year . . . Five million people will come to Branson this year."

All of which brings me back to Jack Herschend's words on Branson's future: "I'm optimistic about the whole Ozark Mountain Country. But it has less to do with whether Branson will go boom or bust than with the value system here. People have tried a little off-color entertainment here, and they've found it doesn't go. They say, 'Why, I believe I'm going to capture the blue humor market here,' and they've found it does not work. There's a G-rated aspect to it all here. You can bring your grandmother or your grandchildren anyplace around here. There's a foundation we don't talk about much—but it's here.

"Are we experiencing more growth than we can sustain? No question about it. But I've been here forty years, and I have faith in this part of the country."

12

Rival Pioneers

Al Brumley, Jr., son of the great gospel composer ("I'll Fly Away," "Turn Your Radio On") and an Ozark native, put it directly when asked just how Branson came to be. "I'd say it was the *Shepherd of the Hills* Show, Silver Dollar City, the Baldknobbers, and the Presleys," he said. "All that combined gradually started the ball rolling. Somebody had to start it, and I'd say it was them."

The Baldknobbers and the Presleys—both claim to be first, and both have some right to make that claim. According to the Presleys, they were "first on the strip." Well, true enough. Gary Presley, Lloyd Presley, and company had been performing at the Underground Theater, fifteen miles away in Kimberling City, pulling in about 125 paying customers a night at an auditorium which, as the name implies, was located in a limestone cave.

But then, in 1967, they put up one of those tobacco-barn theaters on Highway 76 at a point that was then located two or three miles outside the Branson town limits. Ed Marshall, who recalls the occasion well, remembers, "Everyone thought the Presleys were crazy for building that far out of town." Well, today, of course, their theater is one of the closest to what they now call "downtown Branson." The strip, as such, stretches out a few miles to the west of the Presleys. All of it,

146

of course, is now in Branson. The town has leaped out to the end of the strip to encompass it all.

But what about the Baldknobbers? Their claim is simple. "First in Branson." Again, true enough. The Mabes had been around for years. You've heard Jim Mabe, "Droopy Drawers" in the Baldknobbers show, explain that they settled on their name because they had played Baldknobbers in the *Shepherd of the Hills* show. But prior to that, they were also present at the very press conference announcing the opening of Silver Dollar City in 1960. The Mabe brothers played the first season there, giving forth with that old-time Ozark sound and managed to chase a Nashville contingent that shared the bill right back to Nashville. Finally, the Mabes opened up in a tent theater in Branson right down on the Lake Taneycomo shore. It was there they first called themselves the Baldknobbers. They got by there for seven years but couldn't claim to have changed the entertainment climate in town, nor could they boast that they did great business down on the lakefront. And so what did they do? They moved out onto Highway 76 to a spot across the road from the Presleys and perhaps a quarter of a mile closer to town. This was in 1968. And so the Mabe brothers—Bob, Lyle, Jim, and Bill—opened as the Baldknobbers there, offering an old-fashioned Ozark music show. They were first in Branson but second on the strip.

There has always been a rivalry between the Presleys and the Mabes, in the beginning a bit contentious but now quite friendly. There is, after all, more than enough business to go around. The two theaters stand within sight of each other and are roughly the same size, capacities right around two thousand—big, modern showhouses that give no hint of their humble beginnings. Each has its own shops and restaurant beside it. Both offer big, fast-paced, country revues that retain something of the Ozark flavor.

There developed a bit of friction within the Mabe family during the Baldknobbers Theatre's early years of operation— enough so that Bob Mabe left the show and struck off on his own in 1977. He opened the Bob-O-Links Theatre. His show, the Country Hoe-Down, then became the fifth in town. Always an active performer, he had sung and picked his banjo on a live radio program from Springfield as early as the fifties. He put together a package that for years gave stiff competition to the Presleys and the Baldknobbers. But he also became active as a businessman, saw the future of entertainment in Branson, bought land, and built on it. In 1988, he closed down his show and retired, retaining ownership of his theater and leasing it out. The Bob-O-Links Theatre is now known as the Celebration Theatre, a venue for touring acts in gospel and country— Marilyn McCoo, Paul Overstreet, the Talleys, the Cathedrals, the Whites. Bob Mabe just collects the rent.

The Baldknobbers

The Baldknobbers show—or, to call it by its rightful name, the Baldknobbers Hillbilly Jamboree Show—was one of the early openers in Branson. On a weekend in mid-March they threw open their doors and began their season. (The Presley show opened the same weekend.) Starting that early, they couldn't expect much of the tourist trade, nor did they get it. But it's become a kind of local custom in Branson and surrounding towns all the way up to Springfield to come and catch the Baldknobbers and the Presleys just as soon as they open. People know about the rivalry. Some have even chosen sides. And in downtown Branson, in the drugstore or the Show Biz Cafe, you'll hear people arguing about which of the two had the better show. Although unique, Branson is in many ways just like any other small town. Along with the local high school football team, they talk about the local shows. Exactly to the point, for the enthusiasm here for the Baldknobbers and the Presleys stems from the fact that both have a strong identification with the town and with the Ozark region. The fact that they do just fine, thank you, competing with the big names of country music, like Mel Tillis and Willie Nelson, is a point of pride in Branson.

The refreshment stands at the Baldknobbers Theatre were doing land-office business when I got there and it seemed that just about everyone who went inside the auditorium was loaded down with a bucket of popcorn, a soft drink, and some sort of candy. They found, when they entered, that the "warm-up show" was already in progress. At seat level, off at one corner of the stage, there was a sign marking "Joe's Ragtime Piano Parlor," and beneath it Joe Griffin held forth on an upright piano. It was a long set of piano music played at that ricky-ticky tempo that is meant to approximate turn-of-the-century ragtime. Although, with the possible exception of "The Darktown Strutters' Ball," not a single real rag was played, and in spite of the fact that the tempos were not true ragtime (check Joshua Rifkin's Nonesuch recordings), the time spent by Griffin at the piano provided a pleasant prelude to the main action. It was certainly preferable to the preshow videos I later saw at some of the other theaters. The reason for this was chiefly Griffin himself who, with his line of patter, jokes, and wisecracks, kept the arriving crowd entertained and attentive. He's a lot like an old-fashioned Jewish *tummler*, the man who mixes it up, gets people talking to the strangers beside them. It fell to him to do the routine geographical survey. "Any of you folks from Texas? Let's hear it for Texas!" The barest smattering of applause greeted that exhortation. Not that the Texans were shy—they never are—but there just weren't many of them there. It was, as I had been forewarned, a local audience that night.

What surprised me about the Baldknobbers Hillbilly Jamboree was the extent to which it is still a family show. By that I don't mean just a show suitable for the whole family—though it is certainly that. No, it is still, after all these years, largely a production of the Mabe family. Although Jim Mabe, who does his comic turn as Droopy Drawers, is the only one of the four brothers who can be seen onstage, the show is produced, and mostly directed by Bill Mabe. A son—Dennis Mabe—and a granddaughter—Joy Blue—are in the cast as featured singers. But just so you don't suppose that the show is completely parochial, there is also fiddler Mike Ito, who is introduced as "a young man from Tokyo, Japan," and was a Baldknobber well before Shoji Tabuchi hit 76 Country Boulevard.

It's extremely fast moving, and I'm willing to bet that with the exception of the intermissionless Willie Nelson show, more songs are sung and played during the course of the Bald-knobbers revue than in any other show in town. For the most part, selections favored current hits—Garth Brooks's "Against the Grain," Vince Gill's "Look at Us" (Dennis Mabe in a duet with Joy Blue), and Trisha Yearwood's big one, "That's What I Like About You" (Joy Blue really belted it). But there was a cowboy medley that was just as inclusive. And of course there were Mike Ito's specialties, too—singing as well as playing the Bob Wills tunes and red-lining "Orange Blossom Special" at rpms to match Shoji Tabuchi's.

What was it Bill Mabe said? That people wanted a "whole show" with comedy, singing and dancing"—something like that. Anyway, they got it that night with clog dancing, comedy bits by the toothless Stub Meadows and in pantomime by Jim ("Droopy Drawers") Mabe. The whole cast was onstage for the finale, a patriotic number that ended with "The Star Spangled Banner."

There could be no encores after that. Send them out humming Francis Scott Key and you've put a swell in their chests and a spring in their step. That, in any case, was how the audience seemed to leave the theater on that opening night—in an elevated state, a kind of moral glow suffusing the mass of men and women as they marched toward the exits.

One thing Bill Mabe wanted understood right from the start: the Baldknobbers were there first. "By about eight years!" he declared. "It wasn't easy. There were nights when hardly anybody showed up at all. Finally, we made a rule that if we didn't have at least fifteen in the audience, we wouldn't do the show. That was in the beginning."

"That was the four of us brothers and a couple of other fellas," put in Jim Mabe. "Bill and I and two brothers who're now kind of semiretired. But we started out in a little town about thirty-five miles north of here, played all the funerals and picnics around home, had a radio show, then all over in this area—Shepherd of the Hills, Silver Dollar City, then down in Branson."

They had settled me down in the empty theater auditorium. It was right around noon. There had been some rehearsing that morning, a few rough spots in the opening night show that they wanted to smooth out. Bill and Jim Mabe were across from me in the front row of seats. Joy Blue, Dennis Mabe, and Mike Ito were seated up on the stage, their blue-jeaned legs dangling from the apron.

Jim gestured up at them. "These three up there are going to take my and Bill's place in the business."

One by one, they declared their satisfaction with the Bald-knobbers and Branson.

Mike Ito: "We like it here just the way it is."

Dennis Mabe: "When the show ends in the fall, I do some recording. That takes care of my extracurricular activities."

Joy Blue: "I'm very content to be here."

(All three have talent enough to take them to Nashville.)

"So when me and Bill have to retire, the future of the show will all be solved," said Jim.

Bill agreed: "Right now they're the stars of the show, and we're doing good business. Last year we averaged between 70 and 80 percent capacity, with 20 percent repeats. A lot of nights we fill up and have to turn them away."

Dennis laughed and gestured down at the two seniors. "Yeah," he said, "and we got thirty-three years of experience sitting right there to tell us how to do it right."

Dennis and Joy grew up with the show. When they were kids, 76 Country Boulevard was just plain old Missouri State Highway 76. They used to go to the roadside and hold up signs, "COME TO THE SHOW!" as cars barreled by at seventy miles an hour. A lot has changed since then. Now they're *in* the show as mainstays—and traffic has slowed down considerably.

With Mike Ito, of course, it's an altogether different story. "I grew up in Tokyo, concrete and crowds. When I was a kid everybody was listening to Peter, Paul, and Mary—except me. For me, it was Roy Acuff. I used to listen to him on the AFN live broadcasts of the 'Grand Ole Opry,' then I'd get my fiddle out and try to do it just like him."

He got good enough at it that when he came to America he found a job with a good band in Dallas, the Side of the Road

Gang. They toured, played Nashville and as far afield as Saudi
Arabia.

"We heard Mike in Texas," said Jim. "We told him if he
ever came up to Branson, he had a job."

Bill nodded. "That was in the Whiskey River Club in Dallas. And he didn't waste any time getting here."

"I joined in 1979. Branson's quite a contrast to Dallas and
completely different from Tokyo—all this green and the lakes.
I like it here."

They all do, it seems. And they all seem certain that Branson will keep right on booming for a while.

"Oh, it's going to reach its peak someday," said Jim Mabe.

"Looking down the road," said Dennis.

"But you know it's amazing," said Bill Mabe, "when you
think how many towns have tried this—had a few shows in
town but never built up to what we've got here. Why has
Branson been successful? Two things, I think. First of all, it's
centrally located, easy to get to. And second, it's family oriented—and that's real important."

Ozark Comedy at Presleys'

Let's talk about country comedy. It's certainly not to everyone's taste. It's simple, often silly, and at its most risqué it
is PG-rated. Yet within those limits you may hear a good deal
of social and political commentary from country comedians,
even a bit of sharp wit and genuine wisdom. Remember that
whatever else Will Rogers was, he was fundamentally a country comedian.

There are certainly stand-up comics in country. Jerry Clower
is the best known today and perhaps also the best of the bunch.
He's big enough to be booked into the 4,000-seat Grand Palace,
makes frequent appearances on TNN, and has had guest shots
on the major networks. That's not, however, to overlook the
grande dame of country comedy, Sarah Ophelia Colley, aka
Cousin Minnie Pearl. Yet what she does is not so much stand-up
comedy as it is storytelling, a different and older (some might
say, a more honorable) tradition. Jim Stafford? Well, it's true he

appears up there on the stage all alone, but he's got his own tradition going—call it off-the-wall country.

But the kind of comedy you get in Ozark shows like the Baldknobbers Hillbilly Jamboree Show, the Presleys' Mountain Music Jubilee, and the Brumley Show at the 76 Music Hall, is essentially two-character comedy—straight man and funnyman. This didn't just happen. It comes from another very specific tradition. It pits the country bumpkin against the sophisticated outsider—guess who gets all the laughs. And guess, too, who wins out in the end, who shows himself ultimately wittier and wiser. Same guy. In fact, it's an Ozark tradition that harks back to a series of two-line jokes about the bumpkin and the city slicker. In the nineteenth century they were cobbled together into a sort of play that was called *The Arkansaw Traveler*.

A little outdoor theater in Hardy, Arkansas, has performed that play for years. It is entertaining in a corny, antique, country way. I speak with some vague authority in this because I sat under the stars one night years ago in the Arkansas Ozarks and saw it from start to finish. To tell you the truth, I don't remember much about the plot (there couldn't have been much to begin with), just that through most of the play—right up until the end in fact—all the jokes were on the bumpkin and turned on his ignorance and naïveté. But then, the tables were turned, and he showed himself to be a whole lot smarter than that city slicker thought he was. It was fun. We Americans love to see pomposity deflated, pretension brought down.

This is Ozark comedy. Now, admittedly, a couple of Branson comedians play the bumpkin as a fool, pure and simple. This is how Harley Worthit (Perry Edenburg) of the Presley show and Chester Drawers (Eddie Bowman) of the Brumley show do it—but even fools get in their licks now and then. And Gary Presley's Herkimer may act pretty foolish, but by the end of his show you can bet he's deflated his straight man Sid Sharp (Windy Luttrell), who is inclined to be a bit pompous when not acting plain silly.

Baldknobber Jim Mabe pulled off the best sight gag I saw in Branson. All he did was suddenly march across the stage in the middle of a musical number wearing a pair of bunny ears and beating a big bass drum—the Energizer rabbit.

Nevertheless, the award for Best Ozark Comedy goes to . . . May I have the envelope, please? *Presley's Mountain Music Jubilee*!

They had me going right from the preshow warm-up. Easing into it in the auditorium, Harley Worthit comes on as an usher on his first night at the job. His straight man tells him what to do and scolds him when he does it wrong. Both of them, of course, are miked.

Harley actually does show a few people to their seats— among them a couple of newlyweds. "Marriage is like a phone call in the night," he tells them. "First you get the ring, then you wake up."

"Where you from?" he asks another couple. It turns out they're from Arkansas. "Oh," he says, sounding truly solicitous. "I'm sorry." (They have a lot of fun in Branson with their friendly neighbors to the south.)

To a party that has come all the way from California: "Livin' in California is just like livin' in granola—them that ain't fruits or nuts are flaky."

The straight man criticizes Harley's style with theater patrons and demands to know his employment history. "Oh, I was selling fertilizer," Harley tells him. "I was number one at selling number two. (Pause) 'Course I had a part-time job on weekends as a speed bump in a parking lot . . . That takes a lot out of you! (Pause) But I also been goin' to night school up in Springfield. I'm takin' Italian. I'm studyin' up to be a foreigner." The straight man challenges him to say something in Italian. Harley thinks a moment and says, "Innuendo." What's that mean? the straight man want to know. Harley: "That's Italian for Preparation H."

Well, just remember that reading a joke is not the same as hearing it. Perry Edenburg (pronounced like the city in Scotland), a tall, blond string bean of a fellow, has wonderful timing. His Harley Worthit is a true Ozark creation, just the kind of good-natured half-wit who might have welcomed Harold Bell on the latter's first visit to Mutton Hollow.

And once the show itself begins, Gary Presley, as Herkimer,

proves he can match Harley silliness for silliness. A couple of samples:

Herkimer: "My wife's on a rotation diet."

Sid Sharp: "Yeah? What's that?"

Herkimer: "She eats every time she turns around."

Or how about this:

Herkimer: "I got fired from my job at the pork and beans factory."

Sid Sharp: "Oh, my, what'd you do now?"

Herkimer: "I was puttin' the beans in upside-down. (Pause) Gave everybody the hiccups."

But some of the exchanges have some bite to them. This, for instance, during the primary season of 1992:

Herkimer: "I've decided to run for president."

Sid Sharp: "Honestly?"

Herkimer: " 'Course not. You can't win that way!"

But ah yes, music. You might get the mistaken idea that the Presley show is just one comedy routine after another. Far from it. There are three featured singers, Paula Wilhite, Sue-Ann O'Neill, and Stu Wayman. They do mostly current country hits, but they do them with real style and frequent changes of costume. The pace of the production seems as fast as the Baldknobbers with just a shade more glitz and polish.

Although the band is generic country, they gave a straight nod to the real, old-fashioned Ozark style when Lloyd Presley, Gary's father, stepped forward with his big upright bass and sang, "You Get a Line and I'll Get a Pole." There were other more or less traditional tunes done in a medley—"Old Joe Clark" and "Orange Blossom Special" among them. Sid Sharp also did a couple of old-time numbers—"White Lightnin' " and Jimmie Rodgers's "Mule Skinner Blues"—but in parody, garbling out the words just about incomprehensibly in imitation of the backcountry balladeer who hid away in the hollows and created the hillbilly style.

So there was music, and there was comedy-with-music. Scott and Greg, Gary's kids, did a harmonica and fiddle duet. Cecil and drummer Steve Presley (Gary's brother) did "Come a Little Bit Closer." And it all climaxed when Herkimer appeared in gold lamé pants to realize his ambition to become a "rock star." He does what he announces as "a little Ozark boogie-woogie" and demonstrates that he can really pick that Fender guitar. This is his locally famous "machine-gun act," when he wanders the near-reaches of the auditorium, aiming the neck of the instrument here and there, letting loose with bursts of hot notes that knock the patrons dead. It's the show's finale. More than half of those present had probably seen it before, but they love it every time.

Herkimer Speaks

There are two houses behind Presleys' Theatre, just at the far edge of the parking lot. One of them belongs to Gary Presley and wife Pat, and the other to Lloyd and Bessie, his father and mother. They are modest, middle-class houses that fit the people who live in them pretty well. As Gary Presley led me into his, the only hint there that he might be doing better than average was the top-of-the-line Lexus that stood in his driveway.

Gary as Herkimer may be swaggering and sort of dim, but Gary as Gary is intelligent and direct, a remarkable combination of businessman and performer. He brought me into the living room, sat me down and poured a couple of Cokes for us, and made it clear that the Baldknobbers were here first. "But we were the first to go to a bank and say we want to build a theater out here three miles from town."

It wasn't such a crazy move, as he explained it, because Silver Dollar City was growing and Table Rock Lake had plenty of tourists. This was the highway—Missouri 76—between the two.

"We had an individual out of Springfield loan us some money, and we went to the Security Bank in Branson for the rest. We bought a little bit of land—ten acres. It was $15,000 then. We all went to the bank—my father and mother, my wife and I—and signed papers. We're equal partners. I've been president of the corporation, and my father is vice-president. I guess you know he plays bass and banjo in the show, and in the business end, he offers wise words when it comes time to making decisions.

"We put up the original theater, which was actually from a boathouse plan, and had folding chairs inside. We lived in a farmhouse that was behind there. People had to knock on the door to buy tickets. In the beginning it was kind of tough. I remember one night playing to thirteen people, but we gave them a full two-hour show, eight of us then. We figured that if we're going to stay in business, we had to honor the paying customers. It was tough enough so that in the beginning we all worked daytime jobs. I worked in a typewriter factory up in Springfield, had an eighty-mile commute. My wife worked for Security Bank, my mom was a secretary at the gas company, and my dad was a fishing guide on the lakes."

But gradually things changed? "Oh, yeah," said Gary. "The Baldknobbers built across from us on the strip, then the motels started. But the growth here has really been amazing. I thought there might be room for four or five shows along here. I had no inkling it'd develop the way it did. It's scary what's happened. I'm anxious to see if it'll last. I don't see the town going out of business, but I wonder how it can go on the way it is. Of course it's been good for the town. There's been a labor shortage here in Branson for a long time. And the money that comes in, well . . . "

But Gary Presley doesn't want to see the town change *too* much from what it was. "It's that Ozark flavor I talk about," he said, "more of a simple way of life. We don't want to come across as real simple or anything, but we'd like to hold on to what we have. You know—the humor, it's simple and ancient, and gospel songs—man, this is the Bible Belt! This is the kind of thing I mean. The basic town here shares attitudes with most of the people who come to visit—family values, no drugs. That's going to change, I'm sure. Success, publicity and all that, will bring in elements we don't want—the price of success, I guess.

"When you've seen this develop the way I have, it kind of pains you to see elements come in who are here to make a fast buck. We've always had competition here between the theaters and the shows, but we work together. It's been an important thing in the development of this whole situation here.

"But we've come a long way here, we really have. Let me show you something." He led me over to the window and pointed across the empty parking lot to the rear of the theater. "See that part there that doesn't match up with the rest of the building? Well, that's all that's left of the original theater. We've built onto it six times, and now that's all that's left. Put in a balcony to bring it up to 1,500, and then brought it up to 2,000 when we added wings. For a while it was the biggest theater in town.

"My dad's over there now. Why don't you go talk to him? He's got more experience in the business than anybody else in town, and he's always got something to say."

Lloyd Presley is a big comfortable man, friendly, and characteristically Ozark in style. I knew somehow that he would tolerate from me the question he must have been asked thousands of times already. However, I knew I had to put it to him. "Are you Presleys any relation to Elvis?"

He smiled and shrugged. "Not that I know of," he said. "Some of his people wondered the same thing. But he was from Mississippi, and our people were from Tennessee—originally. Grew up here, though."

Although Lloyd grew up with a keen interest in music, he was largely self-taught. He saw to it that his own kids learned to play and sing as they were growing up. As a result, there are six Presleys, three generations, in the current show.

"My younger son, Steve, is in there as the drummer," said Lloyd, "and he's pretty good, all right. And Gary, he plays lead guitar and different instruments, and he's good, too, but he got so involved in doing this Herkimer bit that nobody really appreciates how good he is. And the women in the family, well, they contribute plenty in the business end."

Lloyd and I were sitting side by side in the empty auditorium. He had his feet up on the seat in front of him, a vice-president's privilege, and he seemed just about ready to answer any question. So I asked him how he saw Branson's development—meaning, the future—and I got an interesting answer about Branson in the present.

"I compare it to the 'Grand Ole Opry' thirty or forty years ago, the way it used to be, when the Duke of Paducah and Minnie Pearl were on all the time. The comedians keep this show of ours rollin', and I think they're real important to all the shows. I think that's the difference between Branson and Nashville. Nashville's lost the flavor of what the Opry was all about. Nashville's kind of lost sight of it. What's happened, or what's going to happen here, well, I'm afraid to say."

13

The Little Town and How It Grew

Why Branson? After all, at the end of the sixties, there were just two music shows, the Presleys and the Bald-knobbers, sitting out there on the highway beyond what were then the town limits. What was it that accounts for the growth from that beginning to its present preeminence as a perform-ance showcase for country music?

Other locations in the area offered music. Lampe, right there in Taney County, had an amphitheater where big stars in coun-try played touring dates. And long before the Presleys set up shop on Missouri 76 there had been a flurry of show activity at Lake of the Ozarks, begun when Lee Mace opened up his Ozark Opry in the fifties; it continued strong through the six-ties but faded fast in the seventies—just as Branson began to build up steam. Maybe there's only room for one big music town in the Ozarks. Why should it be Branson?

Donna Moon of local Table Rock Realty declares that the reason is the town itself. "We came here twenty-one years ago and bought a small resort," she says. "So there was the couple we bought it from, the attorney we used for the deal, and the insurance man we went to—and oh yes, the man at the hardware store where we bought some things. The next time we went into town, which was two days later, those five people said hello to us on the street and called us by our first names. That's what makes Branson different. If we ever lose that, then we've blown it.''

That may sound like rank boosterism, but there's something to what she says. In the memory of virtually everyone living in the town, Branson has been a vacation spot. They have learned to be welcoming and helpful, learned it so well that it seems to come naturally to everyone, from the chief of police to the waitress at Starvin' Marvin's who pours you that third cup of coffee without making you ask for it.

The town also gave hometown support to the shows that gathered out there along Highway 76. The initiative shown by the Presleys was widely admired. And once out of their lake-shore tent location, the Baldknobbers were given more enthusiastic backing than before; Branson made sure the Mabe boys got bigger audiences. As anticipated, the two shows drew from vacationers who had come to fish and relax along the lakes and from tourists visiting Silver Dollar City and Shepherd of the Hills. When Mutton Hollow opened up, they pulled them down from there, too. They never felt in competition with those larger attractions in the area, but rather believed that they were there to give visitors a little something extra to do, a reason to stay around Branson a little longer.

That highway location proved so advantageous that other theaters opened up around them, as well as motels and restaurants. There turned out to be two distinct cycles in the growth of the entertainment strip. The first went through the seventies and continued into the early eighties. The music shows of that era all featured more or less local Ozark talent. Most of them were family shows—certainly in their G-rated appeal, but also like the Mabes and the Presleys in the way that they were basically single-family enterprises. Gospel was even bigger along 76 in those days than it is today.

Jimmy Lancaster, entertainment editor of the thrice-weekly *Branson Beacon*, came to town in 1981. He is frank to say that he got his job because his father bought the paper the year before. ''My dad told me I'd like it because there were a lot of music shows here. 'What kind?' I asked him. 'Rock?' When he said they were country, I wasn't so sure. I didn't even like country music when I came. But I'm a convert now.

"And that happened just about immediately. I went to see the Foggy River Boys when I got here, and it was one of the greatest shows of any kind I'd ever seen. I'd done rock reviews and interviews, and I could tell there'd be a lot to write about here."

The Foggy River Boys continue in their own theater on 76 Country Boulevard, since 1974 one of the longest-running shows in town. Built around the close harmony singing group, the production puts strong emphasis on gospel, yet it is fast moving and doesn't take itself too seriously. They do a lot of country and old-fashioned barbershop harmonizing too. A show like theirs, without a national reputation to support it, has to have been dependably good for a long, long time. The Foggy River Boys, having established a reputation in the area, get strong local backing and a lot of repeat business as visitors return to the area. Many come to Branson two and three weekends a year from cities comparatively close by, places like St. Louis, Kansas City, and Tulsa.

The Lowe Sisters is another act that has had a long run in the Branson area. Originally located out on Indian Point, just two hundred yards south of Silver Dollar City, Lowe's Ozark Mountain Country Music Show began in 1981. They opened the Lowes Theatre on 76 at its present location. The Lowes—Sheila, Kathy, Sandy, and Teresa—have a good local reputation and in 1986 were the first from Branson to play the "Grand Ole Opry." Their theater became a venue for touring single acts, but the sisters, who sing harmony and step out to do solos, continue to open for the stars. Loretta Lynn has become a strong presence there. During the 1992 season Lowes was "her" theater.

In 1982, the year before the entertainment strip's second cycle of growth began, there were thirteen theaters going on what was then simply called West Highway 76. Most of them offered Ozark shows—Cousin Zeke at Banjo's Dinner Theatre, the Plummer Family at their own theater, the Wilkinson Brothers Country Music Show, Shad and Molly Heller at the Corn Crib Theatre, and so on. But a few provided temporary homes for touring stars and their shows, like the Starlite Theatre, Bob Mabe's Bob-O-Links, and one they called the Hee-

Haw Theatre. The odd thing was that the shows featuring local Ozark talent generally did better than those that booked in big-name talent from Nashville. That's what makes what happened in 1983 so remarkable.

Dawn Erickson of the Branson/Lakes Chamber of Commerce says, "I generally measure the growth of Branson as an entertainment mecca from the arrival of Roy Clark in—what was it? 1983?"

Yes, it was. And what was different about his arrival was that he put down roots, the first nationally known country music performer to do so. He opened the Roy Clark Celebrity Theatre right on the strip. He didn't play a whole season there; in fact he doesn't do it today, but it has continued to be his home away from home (in Tulsa) right up to the present. And local identification has remained strong and steady: just last year he was voted Branson's Entertainer of the Year—perhaps a belated thank-you for settling down in Branson in the first place.

Born in 1933 in Virginia, Roy Clark first won distinction for himself as a winner of the National Country Music Banjo championship, then showed up on Jimmy Dean's nationally syndicated TV show. He went with Marvin Rainwater, then got fired for outshining the headliner. There was another TV stint with George Hamilton IV and another featured spot on tour with Wanda Jackson. Finally, in 1959, he went out as a single.

In a car and a trailer, out on the road, Roy played 345 dates in a single year. His first hit single on Capitol, "Tips of My Fingers," in 1963, gave him a leg up. His next, in 1969, "Yesterday When I Was Young," (maybe not quite country but a beautiful rendition of a beautiful song) propelled him into a continuing cohost role on "*Hee-Haw*," the successful and long-running country television show broadcast out of Nashville.

There were only a handful of other recorded hits—"I Never Picked Cotton," "Thank God and Greyhound," "A Simple Thing Called Love," "Come Live with Me," "Honeymoon Feeling," and "If I Had It to Do All Over Again." They were all in the seventies, as were his CMA awards—Entertainer of the ear, Instrumentalist of the Year, and so on. Nevertheless, his continued identification with television through "*Hee-Haw*," as well as the fiendish performing energy of the man, kept him in demand as a live entertainer. And not just in Branson.

He plays Vegas frequently and was, in fact, the first country music artist inducted into the Las Vegas Entertainers Hall of Fame (as a charter member). He plays state fairs and county fairs, and twice a year he goes off to shoot half a season's worth of "*Hee-Haw*" shows.

Those who played Roy Clark's Branson theater in his absence make up a roster of stars who have played, play, or will play in theaters of their own on 76 Country Boulevard—performers like Mickey Gilley, Louise Mandrell, Mel Tillis, Conway Twitty, Ray Stevens, Boxcar Willie, the Gatlin Brothers, and Ray Price. Like Mel Tillis, they took a look around and came away saying, "Boys and girls, there's gold in them there Ozark Hills." And they came back to pan a mint for themselves.

This, then, was the second cycle of growth; when Roy Clark opened the Roy Clark Celebrity Theatre in 1983. His name, his "*Hee-Haw*" connection, and his personality attracted other stars of his magnitude to the theater. When they played dates there they couldn't help but notice the steady crowds, the enthusiasm, and the favorable logistical support offered by motels and restaurants up and down the strip. This wasn't just a place to play a one-nighter, or a two- or three-day engagement. A performer could settle in here for a season, maybe years, do some fishing, play some golf; the people would come and keep right on coming.

Boxcar Willie was the first of Roy Clark's guest celebrities to set up shop permanently in Branson; that was in 1987. Ray Price came on board the following year. Mel Tillis and Mickey Gilley opened theaters of their own in 1990—and the race was on. It's created the boomtown situation that exists today. Since Roy Clark opened his own location the number of theaters has more than doubled. The big names in those theaters have gotten bigger and bigger.

In 1986, the Ozark Mountain Amphitheater opened just off

Highway 76 on the Shepherd of the Hills Expressway (located now just beyond the Shoji Tabuchi Theatre). Its huge, 8,000-seat capacity made it the biggest theater of any kind in town—and it still is. Its location in a natural bowl on a sloping hillside gives it good sightlines, and its excellent sound system put those in the back rows right up on the stage. But the Ozark Mountain Amphitheater is used strictly as a venue for the big names who come there for single-night engagements. In 1992, shows were scattered through the spring and summer—only one in May, none in June, most in July and August. Yet the season lineup included Patti Loveless, Lee Greenwood, Barbara Mandrell, Alan Jackson, the Bellamy Brothers, Ray Charles, and Ricky Van Shelton.

The TV Connection

Television has played a more important role in the growth of Branson than you might suppose. Although the "*60 Minutes*" segment on "the live country music capital of the entire universe," which was broadcast on December 18, 1991, was what really put it in the national spotlight, "*Good Morning America*" had been there first. As early as 1987 the ABC show had done hookups with Silver Dollar City, Presleys, and the Baldknobbers and given the little town in the Ozarks its first national television exposure. There will be a good deal more, particularly when the planned Branson cable television network is on-line in a year or two.

There is another television connection operating here in town that may not be immediately apparent. But if you go down the list of stars who have settled in Branson, you see that most of them have had some strong identification with the television medium. Just consider them: Roy Clark, "*Hee-Haw*," of course; Andy Williams, a long-running variety show; Johnny Cash, a country-biased variety show; Louise Mandrell, her sister Barbara's variety show; Glen Campbell, a variety show; Jim Stafford, summer replacement show and a regular on "*The Smothers Brothers Comedy Hour*"; Ray Stevens, summer replacement show; and Mel Tillis, countless guest appearances on network prime-time and late-night shows.

What this tells us is not just that the electronic medium has great star-making power, which, of course, we already knew, but also that such stardom, once conferred, is far more lasting than we may have supposed. Most of those named are drawing upon fame accrued from the tube a decade or two back. And although all have years of recording and personal appearances behind them as well, it seems to be their appearances on television that make them truly special in the eyes of their Branson audiences.

What effect has this infusion of star power had upon the professional scene in town? Well, for one thing, it has upgraded the musical quality of the shows tremendously. Some of the shows back in the seventies were admittedly pretty amateurish. People in town remember them as having a certain goofy charm but nothing like the slick, fast-moving shows on 76 Country Boulevard today.

The Brumley Show at the 76 Music Hall is in many ways like those old Ozark shows—old-time comedy, strong gospel content, and so on. Yet it differs in a very important way. Musically, it is first-rate. In Tom Brumley, the show has one of the best pedal steel guitar men in the business. And in Barry Bales, they have a lead guitar who could play in any show on the strip—or on any session in Nashville. As Bales says it, "You have to be good to be in this town anymore."

But there is some resentment up and down 76 among those who have been in Branson longest. Jimmy Lancaster of the *Branson Beacon* put it this way: "There are complaints by local musicians that they are being put aside as the stars come in with their own bands. There's some bad feeling about this."

Some of the long-time local headliners also wonder how long they can compete against Andy Williams and the kind of stars who are booked in regularly at the Grand Palace. It's that question that keeps coming up again and again: How long can Branson and the entertainment it offers keep their old-time Ozark flavor?

14

A Long Journey by Boxcar

In Nashville, they talk of "country" as if it were quantitative. "So-and-so?" they used to say. "Oh, he's too country." Or maybe at a recording session, "Could you give us a little less country on that?" These days, with the resurgence of the hardscrabble sound among New Traditionalists like Randy Travis and Alan Jackson, you're likely to hear those selfsame Music Row executives say that "So-and-so isn't country enough."

You'd think they had some exact standard in mind. It's as if they had all agreed that there was a specific voice that had just the right amount of twang and catch in it—a little more and it was sort of primitive and a little less and it was getting into pop. Who could they be thinking of? Jimmie Rodgers? Hank Williams? No, all those dead guys are *too* country; that's one thing they're sure of. Or maybe it's George Jones. After all, the new guys all like him—Alan Jackson seems to adulate him—so maybe he's Nashville's idea of pure country. But no, it's hard to imagine that the executives who sit in those glass towers just off Broadway would choose "No-Show" George as their standard. Or Waylon. Or Merle. Or Willie Nelson. For the awful truth of it is that if you brought in those decision makers one by one and hooked them up to a polygraph, you'd probably find that some of them don't even *like* country music.

167

They only like what happens to be on the Hot Hundred in any given week. Whatever it may be.

Is there a pure country sound? Sure, there are several of them. All of those nominated above certainly have it. And it's not a question of region, either. There are many southern accents, after all. And Hank Snow's nasal Nova Scotia tenor is no less country than Johnny Cash's faltering Arkansas baritone.

Just take Boxcar Willie. His voice, his phrasing, his whole style is about as country as you can get. When he lets loose with such authority on old country standards like Jimmie Rodgers's "He's in the Jailhouse Now" or Bill Monroe's "Blue Moon of Kentucky," there can be no doubt that he grew up on the music and that he's been singing it a long, long time. That's why it surprised everybody when he came on the scene, a full-blown talent with a developed style that was, well . . . pure country. This was no kid. Where had he been all these years?

That's a long story.

Texas-born, Lecil Travis Martin (aka Boxcar Willie) hails from Red Oak, a town about the size of Branson south of Dallas. He was, he says, named after a hobo. His father knew a lot of them back in the Depression when Lecil was born. "He was a track foreman on the Katy."

(You remember the old blues line, "She took the Katy and left me the mule to ride?" That's the railroad he's talking about—the Missouri, Kansas & Western.)

"And my dad was a darned good country fiddle player. So yes, I was brought up listening to Bob Wills, Hank Thompson, and Spade Cooley."

We were talking in Box's office backstage. Not much to it, really—just a desk, a couple of chairs, a clock on the wall, and a nice big comfortable sofa where he often stretches out to take a preshow nap. He'd volunteered his nap time to talk to me, but he kept his eye on the clock because he always had plenty to do before curtain time at eight o'clock.

He told how his father had given him two big things in his life—a love for country music and a love for the railroads.

But Box spent a good part of his life in the Air Force. "Twenty-two years," he said. "But it spanned almost thirty years because I was in the Air Guard part of the time—1949 to 1976, all told.

"I went in during the Korean War, but I spent that in Spain. I was a flight engineer, and I flew B-36 Peacemakers, old B-29 Superfortresses, KC-97 flying tankers, and C-5 transports. And wherever we went I carried my guitar with me. I was the entertainment. We went all over the world on those flights, some of them. We could see the sights, but we didn't have money to burn. So, like I said, I was the entertainment."

No, he didn't have money to burn. Married to Lloene—Mrs. Box—he had four children by the time he finished that last stretch in the Air Force during the Vietnam War. But finish it he did, and he decided to make what he called "a heck of a long jump" and try for a professional career in country music. Taking his Air Force retirement pay (it would have been more if he had stayed in longer), he moved his family to Nashville, created the character Boxcar Willie, and began trying to sell him around town. The persona came from the little hoboing he had done when he was sixteen and seventeen. "It was easy," he said, "my dad had all the train schedules in his pocket." But he'd fooled around with Boxcar Willie in the Air Force, too, donning striped bib overalls he bought back in Nebraska, rubbing on a greasepaint beard, and singing at the base clubs.

"When I got out and started this crazy business, I gave Box three years," he said. "I swore that if something hadn't happened by then, I'd look for gainful employment. Well, nothing started to happen until 1978. I guess it all dates from then."

That was the first year that he went to Great Britain. An agent from the U.K. came to Nashville looking for low-priced, high-quality talent. He found Box playing at one of the showcase spots in town, the Possum Hollow Club, and promptly booked him for his first tour. Box made a couple of circuits of the small clubs where British blue-collar types went to listen to country. He went over just fine, built up a bit of a following there, and got himself booked on the bill for the 1979 Wembley International Country Music Festival, an annual country music weekend held just outside London and attended by vast numbers. And they're still talking about what happened when he appeared there. He'd received a grand reception during his set, terrific hands from the crowd. But then, when he raised his hands high above his head to show that he was done . . .

"Well," said Box, "it was the damndest thing you ever seen in your life. They just stood up there and applauded there for ninety seconds, a minute and a half. Somebody timed it. I know exactly how long it was. Now let's just look at that clock up there."

Box pointed up at it, made me look, wouldn't say a word. We waited together as fifteen seconds ticked off. It seemed a very long time.

"Now, see?" he said at last. "That's just fifteen seconds, only one-sixth of the time they were applauding. And this was 150,000 people. Let me tell you, you can't even imagine it."

As it happened, Wesley Rose was in the audience that day at the Wembley Football Stadium. (That's Wesley, as in A-cuff-Rose, perhaps the biggest music publishing house in Nashville.) His connections with the "Grand Ole Opry" were pretty good through Roy Acuff. He went back and told Acuff, "You gotta have this man on the "Grand Ole Opry." And since old Roy was such a power on the Opry he could have just about anyone on it he wished to, and once he himself had heard him, Roy wished to have Box. He liked what this ex–Air Force man was up to because it was real, certifiable country—and if there was anyone who was a good judge of that, it was Roy Acuff, the "Wabash Cannonball" man.

Box went on. The audience, both studio and radio, just loved this guy with his romance-of-the-rails and the authentic-sounding train whistle he coaxed up from his throat. And so he was invited back—again and again. In record time he was made an official member of the Grand Ole Opry family.

He could hardly believe the way he went over. "I feel very humble about it," he said. "And I thank the good Lord for it. But you know, when I came up, it was the most terrible time for country. Everyone was trying the outlaw scene, or everyone was trying to be a pop star—Bill Anderson with strings, everybody with strings. Nobody was doing plain country anymore. All those other people made a star out of me. It was like all the fish in the stream jumped out except one—and that's me. Pop is fine. It's got a place. But they were calling it country. You know who the big 'country' stars were then? Olivia Newton-John and John Denver! I couldn't believe what they were putting out then." He sighed. "Oh, well, Nashville shoots itself in the foot just about every year.

"It pleases me no end to see these young fellas today playing real country. Ricky Skaggs got off on a tangent—and it may ruin him. It's very seldom you can make that combination of pop and country click in any real, good way. They get country music from me—not the cowboy image but the lure of the rails—music from the forties and fifties and some of the thirties."

They love it in Branson. He was a comparatively early visitor to this part of the Ozarks. Box first played the Sawmill Theatre, out by itself in Taney County, then returned to play the amphitheater in nearby Lampe. "The third time," he told me, "it was right here to Branson, where I played the Roy Clark Theater when Roy was away. That time I saw this theater we're in now standing empty, and it was just too tempting. I hocked everything, bought it in 1986 and opened it in 1987, bought a home here, too. I did it so I could be with my family. Kids are grown now, but three of the four are still here—Larry's in the show, and his twin sister is going to college at Springfield, and Tammy, she works in the office. So it was a good move for them."

He gave one final frown at the clock and said, "Now, you go on, get out of here. I've got a show to do. Come on back tomorrow, and we'll talk some more, if you want to."

I wanted to. As I headed for the door, he called after me, "Go see my museum next door. There's stuff about me in it but a lot of other things that are just plain interesting, mostly about railroads."

Boxcar Willie's Railroad Museum stands next to his theater, a good-sized building on its own. It's about half souvenir store—the first half. They sell the usual items—Boxcar Willie T-shirts and sweatshirts, *tchatchkes* of every conceivable kind—and one unusual item, perhaps unique—a big, deep whistle made to duplicate the locomotive wail that Box produces unaided.

A ticket to the show gives the holder admission to the rear of the building, perhaps a little more than half of it, which contains the museum of which Box is justifiably proud; otherwise, admission is two dollars. The part of it devoted to the railroads contained many artifacts, photographs and models, assembled (I suspect) to explain to younger visitors—younger than forty—what American railroads were all about in their heyday, when they moved passengers, as well as freight, from one end of the country to the other, when there really was romance in train travel.

I needed no such education. My father had worked as a station agent, telegrapher, and finally train dispatcher on the Burlington, the Chicago & Northwestern, and the Southern Pacific. I knew all about railroads, but I didn't know all about Box, so I wandered through the section devoted to him. Again, there were pictures, plenty of clippings (including some detailing his Wembley triumph), the certificate making him an official member of the Grand Ole Opry, and so on—quite a lot, really, for one whose professional career in music spans only fifteen years or so.

But Box had memorabilia from his Air Force career, as well. In fact, the most impressive piece in the entire museum had to do very specifically with his Air Force career. It was the cockpit of the KC-97 flying tanker in which he had flown for years in the Strategic Air Command. This was the real thing, let me assure you—not a mock-up. I leaned in and took a good look. The instruments were there, the controls, and seats for the pilot, copilot, navigator, and flight engineer—all crammed and cramped together. It is always remarkable just how tiny the business end of these huge aircraft really is. Why, this one was small enough to be cut from the fuselage and tucked into a space in a building that was once a single-story house. I wondered how Box had made away with it.

It was soon time to go over and claim my seat next door. The Boxcar Willie Theatre is up near the west end of the strip, next door to the Jim Stafford Theatre and not far from Lowes, where Loretta Lynn appears off and on through a good part of the season. It's on the small side, as Branson theaters go, and probably seats no more than eight hundred. "I make a living," he had said—and he probably makes a good one, for at this midweek evening performance, well before the height of the season, the place was filled. Video is big in Branson this year, and the assembling audience was watching some choice clips of Box in performance on a screen up above the closed curtains.

Then the screen went dark, the houselights went down, and a voice boomed out over the speakers, "Box will be the first person you see when these curtains open and the last person you see when you leave the theater." Translation: He'll be available to sign autographs as long as anyone wants him to. Then the music kicks up, the curtains part, and there is Box in the middle of it all, right where the pitchman said he'd be.

"Orange Blossom Special"—a train song, in case you hadn't realized it, all about one of those flyers down to Florida that used to amaze folks in the little towns along the right-of-way as it shot through at fifty miles an hour or more. And Box makes sure the audience knows it's a train song as he crowds into the microphone and lets go with his famous train whistle sound. How does he do it? It rises up from deep within his throat, something between a howl and a wail, and Lord, yes, it sure does sound authentic. There's something defiant in it, too, expressing the man, sort of his version of the Rebel yell. He sings the song. That's right, it isn't just a fiddle tune, but one of those I-wonder-where-all-those-people-are-going-and-ain't-it-grand-they-can-get-there-so-fast kind of songs, of which there were many in the Thirties. But yes, it's a fiddle tune, too, and after Box has had his turn at the microphone his young fiddle player steps up and acquits himself admirably.

At the beginning of all this there was something that seemed odd to me. The screen above the stage was suddenly again alive with close-up images of Box and his musicians. It took a moment or two for me to figure out that what we were getting was live projection from a camera placed above and trained down on the microphone. In this way, even those in

the back rows of the theater had a good view of what was
going on centerstage.

They finished with a flourish and got a good welcoming
hand from the crowd. Box stepped up and said, "It's good to
be here with you tonight. 'Course at my age, it's good to be
anywhere. I want you to just sit back, put your hand in your
neighbor's pocket and listen while we do 'The Boxcar Blues.'"
It's a signature tune for Box, and he belts it out in that strong,
unashamed way that singers used to use when microphones
weren't so sensitive. Have no doubt about it: he sings *loud*.
There were some take-your-turn solos, and when the piano
player started on his, Box shouted out, "That's David Byrd
on that piano. It's a Kimball piano, made in America!" There
was rising applause at that, and not for David Byrd, nor for
Kimball.

You have to be prepared for Boxcar Willie's show, and
maybe a little indulgent. It's not weird or anything like the
Jim Stafford Show next door. And it's certainly not Vegas-
slick like Shoji's, Andy Williams's, or even Mel's. The band
is small and country all the way, no fancy arrangements, and
there are no onstage special effects. No, Box's show is loose,
rowdy, and downright goofy by turns. There is a wonderful
ad-lib quality to it that makes you wonder what will happen
next—and if the performers even know themselves. But the
music is sinewy and sincere, and they sure seem to be having
a good time playing it. Those interested in how the world was
before television might do well to study this show. It's about
as close as anyone could find today to old-time country entertainment, the kind that generations past feasted upon.

It's not all Box. He shares the stage with a young singer
named Mary Lou Turner, with his son Larry, and with a ven-
triloquist, Patti Davidson (she got off one of the best lines of
the evening when she threw open her arms and said, "Welcome to Branson, home of country hospitality and New York
traffic"). And then there was Box's pedal steel guitar player,
Harland Powell. He had proved himself earlier on that rather
intractable instrument with something called "Roadside Rag."
But then in the second half of the show he and Box staged a
quarrel so that he could return later, supposedly inebriated.

Using Box as his straight man, he then put on what has to stand as the classic drunk act of all time. Nobody, but nobody, has captured the slightly repulsive foolishness of the barely mobile *borracho* as has Harland Powell—and he probably repeats it two shows a day, six days a week.

Box's big comedy turn was a series of impressions of various singers—Bill Anderson, Waylon Jennings, Willie Nelson, and Johnny Cash. The best of them was Box's Willie Nelson—not because he put on a silly pigtailed wig to do it but because the two have a lot in common, mainly their intonation, the basic sound of their voices. But he caricatured them all with equal ruthlessness.

After a hell-for-leather "Wabash Cannonball" and a sweet, solemn "Danny Boy," he sent the audience out of the theater with a patriotic finale, "The Spirit of America." Or he sent about half of them out, for it seemed all the rest stayed to form an orderly line seeking his autograph on whatever they had bought at the gift shop or any spare piece of paper they might happen to have in their pockets. Just put it in front of him, and old Box would sign it.

Next day I showed up a little earlier, not wanting to cut into his nap time, as I had before. He was in fine shape, grinning about last night's show but apparently unwilling to be in the least bit analytical about it. "Look," said Box, "I go back to the basics. I'm a showman, an entertainer, so I don't take myself seriously. I make them smile, even cry, if they want to. The whole show is ad-libbed in one way or another. I mean, anybody can say anything that pops into his head, and then I have to respond. Now, you take that drunk bit of Harland's. That's right out of the top of his head. I don't know about you, but I think it's the best drunk act in the world, and I think we're the best two-man comedy act in the world. When you see me break up with him, it's genuine laughter from me. The man just destroys me."

Box asked me if I'd visited the museum, what I thought of it. I sort of waffled around on that until I finally got to the question that had me baffled. "Now," I asked him, "was that the cockpit of the very KC-97 you flew in, just like it says?"

"The very one," he said.

"Well, how in the world did you get it away from the Air Force?"

He looked kind of sheepish then and said, "Ah, well . . ." Then he raised his eyes and began studying the paint job on the ceiling. Thereby hung a tale, one he had no intention of telling.

We finished up just after that, but as I rose to go, he mentioned that he was writing a book, too. "You know," he said, "kind of a self biography. My story."

He pulled a loose-leaf binder down from a shelf on the wall and opened it up on the desk. There was a good-sized chunk of manuscript there, neatly typed, held together in the three-ring clasp.

"I been working on it a while," he said. "When I get it finished, Janet Dailey's going to help me get it published."

"You've got a lot to write about, haven't you?"

"Well," said Box, "there's a lot of interesting things in it. I've seen a lot and accomplished a lot. Not as much as some and maybe not as much as I wanted, but I've accomplished some things."

15

Your Time in Town

The circus had come to Branson.

It was a media circus, one of those occasions when television, radio, newspaper, and magazine reporters descend in force upon a town and turn it upside down. The occasion for all the attention was that May 1, 1992, had been designated the official opening day of the music season. Never mind that a number of the shows—including the Baldknobbers, the Presleys, and Jim Stafford—had been doing business for over a month, this was a genuine, bona fide pseudoevent, the kind that the media thrive on.

The hot ticket that day was one to the CBS taping of its "This Morning" show—and it was free. The only drawback was that the show began at five-thirty in the morning. Nevertheless, two thousand early risers were settled in their seats when weatherman and second-string host Mark McEwen began warming them up for the taping which was to begin at six. They knew that, national television exposure or not, they were in for a good show. And they got one—thanks partly to McEwen, who kept things moving very well indeed, even managing to humor the audience successfully through retakes. But thanks went mostly to the assemblage of talent that had turned out at that ungodly hour. There were casual early morning TV–style interviews, but the focus was on music in Branson, just as it should have been. The biggest stars in town were there, along with some others who had been around longer and were just as deserving of recognition.

Among the latter was the whole cast of the Presley show, who did their own numbers and provided band accompaniment and backup vocals for all the rest. And all the rest included Mel and daughter Pam Tillis duetting on the Alan Jackson hit, "Don't Rock the Juke Box," Andy Williams doing his specialty number, "Highway 76," a song-promo for every act in Branson, and Willie Nelson singing what may be everybody's all-time favorite, "Blue Eyes Crying in the Rain."

Also on hand for a duet were Johnny Cash and June Carter. They proved what troupers they were just by showing up. Probably every soul who had come to the Ray Stevens for that earliest of early morning shows knew that Johnny and June had big trouble. For days the Johnny Cash Country Music Theatre had been doing big business at the box office—refunding tickets. His name alone had been enough to stimulate a brisk preseason ticket sale. Orders came in from far and wide.

But not too many orders came in from the immediate area. It had been known for at least a couple of months that there were problems at the construction site. Way back on May 1 of the previous year, David Green, a shopping mall developer from California, had announced his plans to build a theme park on 76 Country Boulevard. The Johnny Cash Country Music Theatre would stand as the centerpiece to the $35 million project, which would open, he promised, one year from that date.

But then, on March 1, two months before the announced opening, the Killian Construction Company of Springfield walked off the job. Although no public finger pointing was done, and no reason given, it was obvious that Green's problems were major league. Killian had worked on a number of projects in Branson and had a good local reputation. Work halted—temporarily?

That's how things stood on the official opening day, May 1. The theater manager bravely declared that it would be opening May 15. That was the line that Johnny Cash took there at the CBS "This Morning" taping and later that day when he appeared on Larry King's radio talk show, which was broadcast from Branson. Refunds were given on an option of cash-back, or two tickets for a future performance for every ticket purchased.

May 15 came and went, and the nearly completed theater was still not open. Then on May 28, a subcontractor on the project, Smith Mechanical, said that it was owed $28,000 and began an action to force David Green's company into involuntary bankruptcy. When the matter came before the U.S. Bankruptcy Court in Springfield, the case was decided in Green's favor, leaving him free to go out and search for the additional financing he needs to finish the job. He hasn't found it at this writing.

Now, Johnny Cash himself is not an investor in the theater, but he gave his good name to the enterprise. When its continuing financial woes are discussed in the press, it's not the David Green Music Theatre they talk about. So Cash has lost something in the deal already—credibility, trust, reputation. Add to that the blocks of time in his schedule that he left open to perform at the theater that would carry his name. That's not just time lost; for a performer, it's money lost. But he's still saying he intends to open the theater whenever it's finished.

If it's ever finished.

Go with the Flow

It's true that traffic got a lot heavier in May, right after the official opening of the season. But I found out a couple of things. First of all, drivers are a lot more courteous and generous here than those in, say, Los Angeles. They'll hold back and allow you to join the traffic flow, even let you make that left turn when you fear you may be marooned there in the middle lane. Secondly, there *are* some side road shortcuts that will help out a lot. Check that map that the Chamber of Commerce provides and watch for the colored signs that show the way.

Maybe the best way to handle the traffic is to summon the proper attitude. Give yourself plenty of time to get where you're going. Turn on KRZK, and you'll get a radio sample of the music you came to hear. Enjoy it. Take note of what there is to see along the way. Just take a look at that red pickup truck ahead of you. What is that scrawled in whitewash across the back window? "Greg 'n' Kim just got hitched." They turn in at Mickey Gilley's Family Theater, and you lose sight of them. Then you notice that the little Suzuki Samurai you let in just ahead of you carries a carefully lettered sign taped on the back: "Just married/Starring/Jim and Suzann." And the two of them seem to be taking proper advantage of the pauses in traffic, playing kissy-face every chance they get. Branson seems to be popular with newlyweds—a bargain honeymoon, yet kind of special.

Perhaps you're hungry. Yet there are so many places to eat along the way—how can you possibly choose one from the rest? Well, most of them feature standard Ozark fare with all-you-can-eat as today's special with hush puppies on the side. If that's what you have in mind, you can do no better than Starvin' Marvin's, up near the top of the strip, Penelope's (with locations on 76 and in downtown Branson), or the Ozark Family Restaurant.

But having hung around Branson for a while, I can report that there are plenty of options available. Remarkable, isn't it, that a town this size can offer you not just a choice of restaurants but a choice of cuisines? What follows is wholly subjective and incomplete, yet it does have behind it the value of personal experience—mine.

Branson has two "best" restaurants. The Candlestick Inn is not really in town but across Lake Taneycomo on a hill above it and has the kind of great view you might expect from such a location; the menu is American, with lake fish well prepared and desserts spectacularly good. The other, Dimitri's, is on the other side of Roark Creek at the Roark Motor Lodge and offers a Continental menu. Both of these are well away from the clutter and traffic of the entertainment strip but are worth the trip.

A guy I knew back in Chicago once gave me very good advice on choosing a restaurant and ordering from the menu. How was it he put it? He said, "Never order against the house." If you're going to a Chinese restaurant, order Chinese—and not the hamburger they may have on the menu for the kids and less adventurous adults. When you go to a Mexican restaurant, don't order pizza just because they offer it (if you wanted pizza, you should have gone to Luigi's down the block). In both instances, you're sure to be disappointed; cooks do best what they do most often. Make your commitment when you pull into the parking lot. Never order against the house.

That understood, here are a few recommendations.

Mr. Lou's & T. C.'s is a Cajun specialty restaurant near Starvin' Marvin's on West 76. Actually, they offer two different menus on the same card. Mr. Lou's side is standard American—nothing exceptional there, but the local lake catfish is dependably good. But just try it *blackened*! Whoever T. C. is, he sure knows how to cook Cajun. Not only are the blackened specialties done to a taste that would satisfy Paul Prudhomme himself, all the traditional dishes—jambalaya, gumbo, red beans and rice (with sausage here)—are also done with (spicy) élan.

The Koi Garden and Mary's (up on the strip) both call themselves "Oriental restaurants"; both are basically Chinese. Maybe they offer teriyaki, I forget, but what you get in both places is a mild menu that features Mandarin and American compromises, dependably well prepared.

I know good Mexican food when I eat it, and I know I've eaten it at Manny's. What they offer would probably come under the heading of "Tex-Mex"—the usual enchiladas, tamales, tacos, and chimichangas, but there's probably a *mamacita* back there in the kitchen who's been at it all her life because somebody obviously knows how it's done. Compromises to mid-American tastes are not made on the Mexican side of the menu but rather in the column marked "American Food." Manny's also features an outdoor veranda where they serve margaritas and a full range of Mexican beers. You can sit there and watch the traffic go by on 76 Country Boulevard and remember you're on vacation. It's only fair to say that I know I've also eaten good Mexican food at Tres Lagos, but it's a bit out of town in Branson West, out beyond Silver

Dollar City. If you find yourself out that way around lunchtime
or dinner, it is certainly worth a shot.

And now we get very subjective indeed. The place I went
to most often was The Outback Steak and Oyster Bar. I practically set up shop there in the daytime, using their pay phone
as my office, encouraged to do so by Allan Obermayer and
Dee-Ray behind the bar, slurping up Virgin Mary after Virgin
Mary (a very healthy drink, lots of vitamin C). And of course
I ate there, too. As you may gather, The Outback is an Australian theme restaurant. I'm told that there is at least one other
along the same lines in this country but the owner Steve
Woods thought Branson's up all by himself. After a trip down
under in 1988, he came back convinced that what Branson
needed was a one-of-a-kind Australian restaurant, just about
as genuine as he could make it. Well, the decor seems genuine
enough. The building itself is outback Victorian with a blue
tin roof capping the big eat out porches; and inside, the rough
wood walls are covered with everything from a crocodile skin
to antique posters and a collection of rusty license plates from
exotic places like Queensland and New South Wales. As for
the menu, Australians have a reputation as hearty eaters, and
so quantity counts. Beef is featured (mutton, an Australian
staple, is unaccountably absent), and although I've had as good
at the Copper Penny across the way, what is offered at The
Outback is every bit as good as it needs to be. Specialties
include oysters, raw and fried, an alligator sandwich (that's
right, and it tastes just like chicken), and the Outbackburger—
really something memorable as it comes topped off with a
fried egg and a slice of ham; the french fries are, as they say,
out of this world. The Outback is a big, noisy place, usually
crowded but always friendly.

And finally, Rocky's. You've heard me talk about it before
and sing the praises of its owner, Chuck Barnes, and so you
may suppose me to be compromised. You may think what you
like, but ain't it grand to find a good Italian restaurant in a
town this size out in the middle of the Ozark hill country?
Remarkably, the chef himself, Dwain Hertz, is no more Italian
than his name may indicate. Yet he apprenticed to a talented
cook named Charlie Guitea at the latter's restaurant in the St.

Louis Italian section known as the Hill. His pastas, particularly his spaghetti carbonara, tortellini, and canneloni, are very good—not to mention his linguini with clam sauce; chicken dishes include chicken picata and one new to me, chicken San Marino; and choice veal—Marsala, Piccata, and Parmesan. All of it well served in a nice, quiet, dark atmosphere that is good for conversation.

Quiet, that is, until later in the evening when the music starts up next door in the bar. (Even then the sound level does not preclude talk.) Rocky's bar is really a small club. A few tourists manage to find it, tucked away by the tracks downtown, yet it has a steady clientele made up of permanent residents and some of the seasonal sort (that is, a lot of musicians around town who drop by after their shows are over.) It's the hippest crowd in Branson. They come to listen. And they hear a group that would fill a club in Kansas City or St. Louis. The leader, Dock Butler, plays a very commanding tenor sax and, surprisingly, doubles on trombone. Singer Brenda Severson keeps her place on the stand even when the band swings into up-tempo instrumentals, for she plays very respectable jazz flute. It goes on like that well into the night. In Branson, Rocky's is the most fun you can have in public after eleven o'clock at night.

But what do you do during the day? For about half a week it would probably be possible to go to breakfast shows, matinees, and evening performances at the music theaters in town and barely have time to squeeze in time for lunch and dinner. Yet nobody can keep that up indefinitely. First of all, there aren't that many breakfast shows in town; you'd soon find your mornings free. But then, if you tried to keep it up, you might experience Entertainment-Overload Syndrome; those discovered in such a state—wandering along the side of Highway 76, eyes glazed, a foolish smile on their faces, unable to do more than hum "The Orange Blossom Special" when asked direct questions—are immediately carted off to Skaggs Community Hospital for observation. So really, you can see you're better off taking a little time off from the shows every now and then.

Shopping can provide a reasonably healthful diversion. I

know! I know! It, too, has its unhealthful side. Obsessive behavior of this kind—the Shop-Till-You-Drop Syndrome—is just as dangerous, but in Branson there aren't a great many places to go crazy on high-priced items. That said, I'll do the irresponsible thing and tell you about a couple of places where you can. Just show a little restraint.

The Engler Block, located on 76 Country Boulevard just across from the Holiday Inn, is a sort of Ozark crafts department store—or perhaps better put, a collection of Ozark boutiques under a single roof. The old brick building from which the frame additions sprawl out on either side was originally a general store operated by the Engler family from 1876 onward. Peter Engler, grandson of the original proprietor, has had a grand reputation as a wood-carver for years; he collaborated with the Herschends on the mounting of the 1963 National Crafts Festival at Silver Dollar City. He conceived the Engler Block as a permanent in-town location for himself and other Ozark craftsmen to show their wares. There are demonstrations, too, though nothing on the scale of what you will find at Mutton Hollow or Silver Dollar City. Still, the exhibits are well worth a careful browse and the location is extremely convenient to Branson visitors putting up at motels and hotels up and down the strip. You may do more than browse. You may be tempted by items you see in the Pottery Shop, the Antique Gallery, the Heirloom Lace Shop, at Beers Custom Rods & Tackle. Most tempting to me were things I saw at Englers Woodcarvers and at Mountain Rockers (where they sell more than rockers—a wide variety of old-fashioned, handmade Ozark furniture).

The large, red-roofed complex plainly visible from the upper end of the entertainment strip is the Factory Merchants Outlet Mall. It is on Gretna Road only about a quarter of a mile from Highway 76. Anyone who has traveled anywhere in this country has probably seen and shopped at ''factory outlet'' malls. Branson's is surely one of the best.

How would you judge good, better, and best among them? Why, by the size and variety of the stores they house, by the quality of the brand names represented there. According to this standard, the Factory Merchants Outlet Mall would surely rate high. Just to cite a few outlets that are housed there, you would find Bugle Boy, Evan-Picone, Geoffrey Beene, London Fog, American Tourister, Bass Shoes, Florsheim, Oneida furniture, and Corning (by no means a complete list). I can't guarantee that you will save money shopping there, but I can promise wide and complete selections in brand lines.

Accessibility, parking, and mall design count for something, too, and here Branson's also gets high marks. Built on two separate levels, it is a pleasant place to amble through. But if you are in a hurry and are looking for a specific outlet, you will find maps of the mall posted at convenient locations with all stores plainly marked. One thing that sets the Branson mall apart from many is the presence of a bookstore, the Book Warehouse. Consistent with the nature of the mall, it is a remainder operation, offering a wonderful hodgepodge of books, hardback and paperback, from publishers in the United States, Canada, and Great Britain at discount prices. Some of them are no more than a season or two out of date. None are used.

Of course there are many, many places to shop in Branson, probably half a hundred gift and souvenir shops and flea markets up and down the strip. In the downtown area, you'll find the kind of stores you would hope to find in any small town—a full-line drug store; an office supply store; Dick's five-and-dime that announces to visitors, "We got what you forgot"; and special to Branson, the Mountain Music Shop that offers just about every variety of stringed instrument known to the Ozarks, including dulcimers, banjos, dobros, and "over 100 old fiddles." And there's always the local Wal-Mart; it's complete, user-friendly, and the prices are low.

According to the Branson/Lakes Chamber of Commerce, over half of those coming to town will arrive with children of various ages. Traveling with children means keeping them interested and entertained—right up to college age. And let's face it: sometimes a successful adult vacation means letting down your hair and acting like a kid. And so this list of attractions to be found in and around Branson—again subjective and incomplete—may appeal to children of all ages.

The Ozark Zoological Park and Petting Zoo, located on Shepherd of the Hills Expressway just half a mile south of 76, features monkeys, baboons, apes, reptiles, ponies, and farm animals that are fully grown. There are also lion, tiger, and leopard cubs that may be touched and petted. Picture taking is encouraged.

There are at least four miniature golf courses up and down the strip—one of them, Story Book Land, specifically designed to appeal to younger children, with holes running through Mother Goose territory. Old King Cole, Humpty-Dumpty, and the Old Woman's shoe house are right there along the short fairways. The 76 Mall offers miniature golf indoors as a rainy day alternative.

There are a number of water attractions, the most spectacular of which, the White Water ride, features the 505-foot Tropical Twister, a downhill splash in a sturdy, inflatable raft. White Water is one of a chain masterminded by the Herschend organization. It is well known throughout the Midwest, South, and Southwest.

There are water attractions of another kind, too—the Ducks, for example. These are World War II amphibious vehicles that carry a full load of parents and children on a seventy-minute ride along the strip, then off into the Ozark countryside, and for a dip down and a brief cruise on Table Rock Lake. There are longer lake cruises available on Lake Taneycomo. Two boats, the larger stern-wheeler *Lake Queen* and the *Sammy Lane* leave from a dock in downtown Branson. (A little extra drama is offered on the *Sammy Lane*'s seventy-minute cruise; it seems that each time out, as regular as clockwork, it is overtaken along the way and raided by a band of lake pirates.)

Older children—though usually not quite old enough to possess a valid driver's license—seem to love zooming around the track in Go-Karts. They get the sensation of speed without the risk; some adults like it, too, for the very same reasons. Kids and their parents can give it a try at two tracks on 76 Country Boulevard—Kids Kountry and The Track.

And finally, another driving thrill—this one from an earlier era: adult drivers may rent vintage Model A Ford roadsters for an hour or a whole day, plying the strip or taking off into the countryside for "traffic free scenic routes." Although the roadsters are two-seaters, all have rumble seats—kids in back; a few Coupe de Ville (convertible sedan) Model A's are also available for larger parties. Roadsters-U-Drive is located near the corner of Highways 76 and 165.

16

The Grand Palace

The Grand Palace held its official opening on May 1, along with the rest of Branson's entertainment network. It had been operating a week or so in a kind of dress rehearsal situation. There had been snafus, jinxes, and breakdowns, all certainly quite normal for a new theater. For one as grand as this one they were to be expected. The sound system needed work; there were no malfunctions, but it turned out there was an acoustical "dead" spot in one section of the auditorium. And it was decided, too, that in order to give patrons the sort of access and comfort intended for the entire theater, the first row of balcony seats would have to be removed.

Yet none of this was to mar the official opening, for the Herschends know how to throw a party. It was a big affair, upwards of two hundred invited guests. Probably the majority of those were members of the press, electronic and print, for it was first and foremost a media event. But there were others: Missouri's governor, John Ashcroft was present, as were Springfield real estate developer John Q. Hammons, and performers from other theaters on 76 Country Boulevard like Moe Bandy and the apprentice-Liberace, pianist Dino Kartsonakis.

All seemed to be having a fine time. True, Silver Dollar City's no alcoholic beverages policy prevailed, but food was plentiful—everything from quiche for the ladies to beef tenderloin for the gents. And the setting was right. To say the reception was held in the lobby does no justice to either the party or the place, for the lobby of the Grand Palace is like no other in Branson, perhaps none in the country. It is, of course, very large, as befits a theater with a 4,000-seat capacity. And its layout and details are in keeping with the antebellum Southern mansion exterior. There are two wide staircases leading up to a balcony landing that must be about ten feet across, then on up to the upper level seating.

From that balcony landing the assembled crowd was welcomed by Louise Mandrell and Glen Campbell, who play opening act hosts to the touring acts at the Grand Palace. Not surprisingly, they had nothing but praise for the big theater, and they promised that the glitches that had marred earlier performances would be taken care of soon. (Then they disappeared to get ready for their official opening show; Randy Travis was the featured act.) Governor Ashcroft said a few words—he would later read a proclamation from the theater stage declaring this to be "Country Music and Gospel Week" in the State of Missouri. And the officers of the Herschend organization—Jack Herschend, president; Peter Herschend, executive vice-president; and Rick Todd, vice-president for development—made the welcome very official.

There were forty-five tour buses in the huge parking lot of the Grand Palace for that night's performance.

Rick Todd was the hands-on overseer of the Grand Palace project. He had probably been by the construction site every day—and sometimes for whole days—since ground was broken for it over a year before. An organization man in the best sense, he began as a parking lot attendant at Silver Dollar City when he was fifteen. He kept working summers as he attended the College of the Ozarks, thinking it would be just a part-time job until he finished his education. Well, it took him a long time to do that, because after graduating, he began taking management courses at night at Southwest Missouri State. He estimates he must have taken three hundred plus hours of management training, and he now teaches it. And in the meantime he had joined the Silver Dollar City organization.

"They kept bringing me up in the organization," he told me, as we talked in the Herschend suite of offices. "It seems to me I've worked in all the various aspects—personnel, financial—I'm in planning now. I guess you'd say I'm the director of planning."

He recalls that his first big project was helping to negotiate the purchase of the Tennessee theme park that eventually became Dollywood from the Cleveland Browns.

That's right, the Cleveland Browns. The owner of the football team, Art Modell, had felt the urge to diversify in the late sixties and had bought a not very successful amusement park just outside of Gatlinburg and had run it with no greater success as Gold Rush Junction.

"If we at Silver Dollar City were to take over a football team, we would probably have done about as well as they did with that park," said Rick Todd. "They had 109,000 attendance the year before we bought it.

"I remember the day we signed the contract with Modell's lawyer. Modell himself was in Los Angeles negotiating with the ballplayer Paul Warfield. They were talking back and forth away from us, but when the deal was made and the contracts signed, the lawyer called Modell and told him that it was wrapped up. That left him free to make the deal with Warfield. So just think about it. We bought a park that now employs over a thousand people. We changed the lives of people in that area. And what did they buy? They bought a wide receiver."

From 1976 to 1986, the park was operated as Silver Dollar City/Tennessee. Then came their very successful negotiations with Dolly Parton, the necessary alterations to the park, and its rebirth in 1987 as Dollywood.

But what about the Grand Palace? "Well," said Todd, "we're proud of it. It's come out to be what we intended. It's a concept that was born out of what was going on in the music industry today and a way for Silver Dollar City to get involved in what was happening right in Branson. People had come to us over the years with various proposals, but we had no reason to diversify in that direction until the Grand Palace idea came along.

"Basically, the idea was this—to build a theater that had the capability—enough lights and sound—to produce any kind of show, not just concerts. And if we built a big enough house, we could also bring in current popular stars. We'd build a theater that would attract television specials, award shows, one that could be adapted for television like Opryland. There are big advantages to that—actually, Opryland is a little bigger. What we've done with the Grand Palace—well, if Branson is the live country music capital, what we've done is give it a capitol building. We've built a landmark.

"Once we had that, a unique concept of what we wanted to do, we went out and found two hosts, people who could entertain and do a production for whoever came into the theater. We took a good hard run at Glen Campbell and Louise Mandrell—and we got them!"

But why *two* hosts? "Well," he replied, "it's to alternate them. If either of them had to do it day after day, week in and week out, they'd get tired. We want them to be fresh. This way we'll have some of the top names in country music—*assisted* by Glen Campbell and Louise Mandrell, who are big names themselves. We've booked people like Reba McEntire, Kenny Rogers, Ricky Skaggs, Waylon Jennings, Randy Travis—oh, it's a pretty long list.

"We're booking the top talent in country music, but we've got riders in the contract we offer that set out two specific things we expect from them. First of all, we expect a family show. And second, that there will be no alcohol or drugs on the premises of the Grand Palace. Some of the people we've talked to won't book because of this.

"But since we were planning and building the theater while we were booking, we went to the entertainers, and we asked them to tell us from their point of view just what should be here. For instance, what should be the height of the stage? What did they want in the way of a green room? How far from the stage should the first row of seats be? What about the temperature of the theater? We listened to them. We took to heart what they had to say. They helped design it."

Rick Todd went on to talk enthusiastically about other uses to which a theater of the size of the Grand Palace might be put. "We're going to have the best gospel in America on Sundays at two o'clock in the afternoon," he promised. "And we'd like to try some other entertainment offerings there. I'm talking about symphony orchestras on tour, and Broadway productions. My hope is that we can come up with clean comedy acts that are nationally known. We'll try all these and see what happens."

He ended by urging me to take a look at the theater. Even though at the time we talked it was in the late stages of completion and not yet open to the public, he said it would give me an idea of the size and scope of what they were up to. The chances were good that he would be there himself, he said, because he was spending a lot of time there in these last days. But if not, he would leave my name at the door, and I could just walk around and take a look for myself.

Inside the Palace

I had seen the place from the outside, of course. There was no missing it as you went up or down Highway 76. Especially from the west, driving from the top of the strip toward downtown Branson, the Grand Palace seems to loom up at you from a distance. The large outer building, the style and size of a plantation house along the Natchez Trace, looks almost tiny against the huge, bulbous blue-painted auditorium to which it is attached. How to describe that auditorium section? Well, if you've ever seen a blimp hangar—that is roughly the shape of it, but as for size, the Grand Palace would surely be larger.

Yet entering from the front, down the walkway that leads from 76 Country Boulevard to the mansion facade, you get no sense of gigantism from the auditorium behind. What your eye takes in is a handsome colonnaded exterior, large, but of human proportions—against a blue background. Or backdrop, perhaps, for there is something about it all that suggests a beautifully designed, carefully constructed movie set.

As it happened, Rick Todd was not around when I stopped by. But, as good as his word, he had left instructions that I was to be let in and given the freedom to ramble around on my own. And so I rambled.

Although it was a few weeks before the opening, the lobby seemed virtually complete and looked just about as it would opening night. What I admired most during that tour were the many points that exceeded the mark. The thick pile carpet, for instance—they could have made do with tile floors, couldn't they? And what about that chandelier? Was it real crystal? Probably. You had the sense that they had not spared cost to make the Grand Palace truly grand. I climbed up the stairs, past the ministage landing, and on up to the second level, a kind of mezzanine that runs around the entire lobby area and from which various rooms and offices open. But that second level (accessible also by elevator, by the way) also provided entry to the auditorium balcony. One door to it was already propped open, and that was the one through which I entered.

Well, there I did get the sense of vastness, for standing just inside the balcony of the theater, I looked out and down at the stage below. It seemed hundreds of feet away—and probably was. I found myself wondering how it would look from the reverse angle, and so I went downstairs to find out.

There was plenty of work activity down below. There must have been three separate crews at work—installing seats, checking the sound wiring and working their way across the stage, doing something to it with a machine that was pretty noisy. As I made my way down the aisle, I worked my way over to the left side of the stage and found a few stairs that would later be curtained over, that led up to the stage. It turned out that the crew working up there was sanding the floor. A fine saw dust sifted under my feet as I made my way to the center of the stage and looked out and up across that great expanse. The auditorium was indeed capacious; huge, vast—all those adjectives that denote the sort of space that, in its size, seems almost unreal. Its 4,000-seat capacity makes it nearly twice the size of even the biggest Branson theaters, like Mel Tillis's new one that seats exactly 2,101. What must it be like to play on a stage like this? Even with the houselights down, you had to be aware of its immense size. What was it like to know that all those people were out there, looking at you, listening to every word you said, every note you sang?

Glen Campbell

Glen Campbell had told a reporter from the *Springfield News-Leader* that the Grand Palace "has the same look to it as some of the theaters we've been to in England, except those are 2,000-seaters and that's what you put downstairs here." He was discreet enough to make no comparison to the Opryland Theatre, which Rick Todd had admitted was slightly larger, but he was clearly glad to be a part of a new venture such as this one, especially one on so large a scale.

He may have felt himself lucky, but then, as the seventh son of a seventh son, he has had his share of good luck all his life.

Born not far south of Branson in Delight, Arkansas, in 1936, he took up the guitar early and was reasonably proficient on the instrument by the age of six, which made him something of a prodigy. As a teenager, he went out to New Mexico to play with his uncle Dick Bills's band, then took off at the age of twenty-four for Los Angeles where he found a career for himself as a session guitarist.

For years he was kept busy as an instrumentalist, backing singers as varied as Nat ("King") Cole, Frank Sinatra, the Beach Boys, Ricky Nelson, and Elvis Presley on their hit records. And for years singing was something Glen Campbell himself did in the shower. But when he did venture out as a solo singer on a small label, Crest, he got a hit with "Turn Around, Look at Me," which was really more of a pop ballad than a country song. He signed with Capitol Records, and not long after that, the hits really started coming.

In many ways, Glen Campbell was the perfect embodiment of the pop-country style that dominated Nashville in the late sixties and seventies and all the way into the eighties. Significantly, Campbell himself never made his home base in Nashville; he was always a West Coaster (and today makes his permanent home in Phoenix). His first big hit, John Hartford's "Gentle on My Mind," was folk-rock in style and could just as easily have come from Arlo Guthrie or Gordon Lightfoot. His Jim Webb songs, "By the Time I Get to Phoenix" and "Wichita Lineman," were essentially Jim Webb songs—neither country nor pop, but (the former especially) infused with Webb's personal, autobiographical spirit. And "Galveston"? That's the title song for a Broadway musical that was never written, an anthem, the kind of number that wouldn't sound right without full orchestral backing.

The only thing really country about any of these was Campbell himself. And it wasn't just a matter of where he was from. He had a pleasant, soft-edged manner that translated well to the screen in his two movies, *True Grit* and *Norwood*, and made him a big hit on television on "The Glen Campbell Goodtime Hour." His was the face and style that country music put to the world in the seventies—this at a time when Willie Nelson, Merle Haggard, and Waylon Jennings were an embarrassment to many in the industry.

In choosing Glen Campbell as cohost for the Grand Palace, the Herschend organization had clearly chosen a middle-of-the-road course. Certainly his name alone and his TV fame would bring in many visitors to Branson who were not up on the current stars of country moving through for runs that seemed to average out at two and three days at a time. A sweet guy like Glen would provide a nice balance to performers like Waylon and Randy Travis.

Louise Mandrell

Something of the same thinking must have led to the choice of Louise Mandrell. She also carried the cachet of regular television exposure. Although never as big a name as her sister, Barbara, she had begun, and successfully maintained, a separate career before coming in on their television show (with the third sister, Irlene), "Barbara Mandrell and the Mandrell Sisters." That early eighties run on TV has given quite a boost to Louise's career, while Barbara's, stalled for a while by se-

vere injuries she suffered in an auto accident in 1984, has gone
into a slight decline.

Although born in Corpus Christi, Texas, Louise grew up,
as did her sisters, mostly in southern California. All three
live in Nashville today. None of the three has had much
experience of life outside of the show business careers toward
which their father pushed them very early on. They're not
a coal miner's daughters. Not one of them had a coat of
many colors sewn up for her from patches and remnants.
They're just musically talented, middle-class girls who happened to connect in country; rock or pop would probably
have suited them just as well.

This is not to minimize their gifts, nor what they have done
with them. Louise Mandrell, especially, is proficient on an
almost dizzying number of instruments—fiddle, piano, banjo,
synthesizer, bass, accordion, drums, mandolin, clarinet—as
she demonstrates in the course of her show. And quite honestly, I've never seen a performer work harder than she does
up there on the stage. The self-proclaimed "Queen of the Palace" takes very seriously her role as cohost at Branson's biggest theater. But a warning to all those country performers for
whom she is scheduled to open: Louise Mandrell is a hard act
to follow.

And hers is essentially a Las Vegas act. I mean, any show
that begins with the first bars of Richard Strauss's *Also
Sprach Zarathustra* (the music from *2001*), then follows that
up with "The Star Spangled Banner" had better have a lot
to back it up. Well, she delivers—as well as the line of chorus boys and chorus girls who dance and sing their way
through a series of production numbers. She does both—si-
multaneously—no lip synching for her; she pounds vigorously on a grand piano, thumbs out a solo on the electric
bass, then picks up the fiddle and jams out a hoedown tune.
If she sounds busy, that's just what she is. Her show moves
with meteoric swiftness. Even her gospel medley begins up-
tempo with "I Saw the Light" and "When the Saints Go
Marching In," and only slows down when a church window
is illuminated behind her and she renders soulful versions of
"What a Friend We Have in Jesus," "The Old Rugged

Cross," and "Amazing Grace." Then from that into a fifties medley in which she shares solo vocals with members of the chorus. It has its quiet moments—"Love Me Tender," "Unchained Melody"—but it ends hell-for-leather with "La Bamba," "Great Balls of Fire" (which she does Jerry Lee Lewis–style, sending special effects fire shooting out from the piano), then "Johnny B. Goode" and "Rock It Up." Mind you, they're dancing their way through these numbers as they sing them.

That was the finale. With a flag-waving finish like that, you know there's got to be an encore—and of course there was. Country? Well, something like that. Louise Mandrell picked up her fiddle and did "Orange Blossom Special" (that one again!). On this, she managed to outdo even Shoji Tabuchi—not on pure speed alone but by playing it very, very fast while *skipping* across the stage. That, surely, is showboating in the grand tradition!

After the intermission, she reappeared before the closed curtain and introduced Larry Gatlin and the Gatlin Brothers, who were at least nominally the stars of the show. The curtains parted to reveal the three of them with if-looks-could-kill grins on their faces. As she bounced off toward the wings, Larry gestured toward her and called out to the audience, "Isn't Louise wonderful?" and led them in a round of applause for her. (I tell you, those show business folks are *so* sincere!) But then the band picked right up with a heavy rock beat, and the Gatlins began their show with a hit of theirs, "Never Want to Be Set Free."

And Now . . . Larry Gatlin and the Gatlin Brothers

Jack Hurst, a knowledgeable and intelligent critic of country music, has written of Larry Gatlin that he "possesses probably the most beautiful voice in contemporary country music." As the group's songwriter, he has also composed some songs that were not just hits but strong, memorable pieces, like "Broken

Lady'' and ''All the Gold in California,'' that deservedly remain in their performing repertoire; they are songs that will always be Gatlin Brothers songs.

Nevertheless, Larry has caused a lot of trouble for the group and for himself. Even when Larry Gatlin and the Gatlin Brothers were riding high back in the late seventies, he had earned a reputation for himself as something of a flake, an arrogant kind of guy who hadn't much respect for audiences, the press, or radio deejays. Then, later, after he had undergone treatment in 1984 at the Careunit Hospital in the city of Orange, in southern California, it was revealed that a lot of that so-called arrogance was just that old devil cocaine working inside of him, pumping up his ego.

But not all of it. Larry has been clean for a lot of years now, but the fundamental personality remains. He is who he is. The Gatlins hadn't a prayer of matching the energy generated during the first half of the Grand Palace show by Louise Mandrell. What they offered instead was a kind of negative energy of their own. There was a slightly mean edge to Larry's repartee with the audience. He kept putting down Wisconsin and people from Wisconsin. They did a bit about posing for pictures—shooting photos is not just permitted, it is officially encouraged—that sneered at those gathered below the stage with cameras. And so on. Had that can-you-top-this dare by Louise Mandrell provoked this response from them?

Nevertheless, once they settled into their groove, the music that Larry and his brothers, Steve and Rudy, put out was quality stuff. Larry introduced ''my favorite all-time country song by my favorite country writer'' (cute—he was referring to himself), and he did a memorable rendition of ''Broken Lady.'' There were others—''A Star-Spangled Broken Heart,'' ''Houston,'' the very reliable ''All the Gold in California,'' and a tribute to Roy Orbison with ''Only the Lonely.''

In introducing one of his songs, ''So Easily Hurt,'' he made reference to throat surgery he had had for cysts the year before and thanked God that he was able to sing a song that night that he hadn't been able to sing for four or five years. It's true Larry's throat problems kept the group out of action for just about a year. They were on the road again, but, they announced, it was for the last time. Come 1993, they will have locations in Dallas, suburban Minneapolis, and—Branson. Yes, they had already broken ground for a development that included a hotel, a restaurant and *two* theaters that would be located just about across the street from the Grand Palace.

Did Larry Gatlin mention that? No. Although it might have put Louise Mandrell in her place, it would have been rude to his true hosts, the Herschends.

17

Ladies' Choice

The women who comprise half the country music audience today, no less than women everywhere, must work their way through a labyrinth of choices, countering demands, and competing responsibilities. Can you see yourself with this guy or that one for life? Is a marriage like your mother's what you want? Must marriage mean children? Must children mean full-time motherhood? Do you take a job or try for a career? What happens if love leaves a marriage? Drinking? Cheating? Are they symptoms, or are they the disease?

On and on. Even for the women of Middle America—or perhaps especially for them—life is a balancing act. Are they going to listen to blandishments of a bad boy like David Allen Coe, inviting them to lie with him in a field of stone? Or applaud a Hank Williams, Jr., who licks his chops over women he's never had? Will they pity George Jones and his "hurtin' "? Or will they respond to the mooning style of a Vince Gill as he urges them to "Look at Us" and sings the quiet joys of long-lasting relationships? Is the "real man" image so vigorously put forth in country music now out of date? It's pretty clear from the male singers who are now most popular that women want something more, if not something different. The songs they sing today, those that their female fans put up there in the top ten, are enough to tell us that.

But the question now, barely touched on before, is just how female country singers address this changed and changing female audience. Tammy Wynette proved that something was different out there among them all when she notched a big hit in 1968 with "D-I-V-O-R-C-E," but then, covering herself, that same year she released the very traditional "Stand By Your Man"—another big hit, which indicated a conflict of some sort. Loretta Lynn, more venturesome, had had her dukes up as early as 1966 when she warned, "Don't Come Home a-Drinkin'." And gradually, through the seventies, she became country music's spokeswoman, if not for feminism, then for the response it stirred in women of Middle America. Loretta registered a complaint about the woman's lot as broodmare in "One's on the Way." She took an even stronger position with "The Pill" in 1975, in which she made it clear she was all for birth control; her fans proved they were all for it, too, by making the record a hit.

It was evident by the mid-seventies that things were no longer quite the same among the women who listened to country music on the radio and bought the records at K-Mart. Yet they were not perhaps so very different, either, as Melba Montgomery showed when her recitation and song, "No Charge," became a number one hit. In it, a boy brings his mother an itemized bill in which he charges her for each of the chores he performs; she counters with a bill of her own—for the nine months she carried him, the nights she sat up with him, etc., "no charge"—and then, shamed, the boy writes "paid in full" across his own accounting and tells his mother he loves her. Well, sure—what mother could resist such sentiments? There were some feelings that neither prevailing social currents nor the Pill could alter.

The sexual revolution never got much further in country music than miniskirted Jeannie C. Riley and her "Harper Valley PTA." The story of the divorcée who is accused of loose behavior and then makes a few accusations of her own, it went over big with women who found themselves in similar situations or were afraid sometime they might. It was sassy.

But the sexy girl image and sexy lyrics never really caught on with the female country audience. More than one career sputtered and stalled during the pop country era when women in the audience perceived that the woman at the microphone was not singing to them or for them, but rather aiming straight at their men. Bold, brassy, takeover, sexy has never played well in country. Tanya Tucker's Lolita appeal was tolerated, but her affair with Glen Campbell did neither any good; though both survived it, their careers suffered. Right now, Trisha Yearwood seems to speak to and for the conflicting desires of the womenfolk with her song, "I Want a Man," in which she sets forth contradictory criteria in her description of her/their ideal.

It's interesting to note that "Harper Valley PTA" directly mirrored a Biblical situation—Susannah and the elders—and it should be remembered that country music abounds with such Biblical subtexts and references. There are Bible readers and Bible quoters on both sides of the curtain. Occasionally, because of the diversity and changing nature of the country audience, that same Susannah and the elders scenario is played out for real, and performers (almost invariably female) are forced to defend themselves against charges of immorality onstage; usually that means they're just being too darned sexy.

It happened in Branson just about that way last year.

Remember I described Louise Mandrell's opener for Larry Gatlin and the Gatlin Brothers at the Grand Palace as a high-energy, Vegas-type show? Well, I didn't mean to imply that there was any nudity involved. Certainly not! Louise was completely clothed from her throat to her ankles through most of the show. Of course it *was* Lycra Spandex she wore, and it fit her muscular body like a second skin, accentuating every hump, bump, and declivity. And it's true, too, that when she danced, particularly during the "Let's Give Them Something to Talk About" number, she agitated her pelvis and other parts in a manner that thirty or forty years ago might have been considered provocative. Yet there was nothing in her half of the show that went beyond what might be seen today on prime-time TV.

But—what do you know? She gave them something to talk about.

John Bowers, president of the Branson/Lakes Chamber of Commerce, received complaints from a few—"just two or three, nothing to be concerned about"—who objected to the dancing in Louise Mandrell's show at the Grand Palace.

"It was in the early part of the year," said Bowers. "And I guess that the people who complained are just accustomed to more traditional fare. Now, understand that we work hard to maintain our reputation as a family destination here in Branson," he went on. "And anything that would deviate from that we would be concerned about. But I've seen her show myself, and it's just a high-energy act with a little more pizzazz."

Case closed, as far as he was concerned.

For her part, Louise Mandrell declared that she was a Christian first and wouldn't have done any number that she felt was offensive.

There were reports that the Grand Palace management had also received complaints about her act. When asked if they had asked her to tone it down, she didn't actually say yes or no, but began talking effusively about how perfect the situation at the Palace is for her, how great the people are to work for, how good the staff is, and how she thinks God meant for her to work there. "I think it's God's gift," she said.

Ladies Sing Sacred

The frequent invocation of God's name and the attribution to Him of a directing role in their lives and careers is particularly common among female country music performers. One of the roles they play in the music directly reflects the role chosen by the women in the greater community of listeners and fans—that of the stabilizing influence, the enforcers of morality. This is probably why Madonna will never make it in Nashville—or Branson. Unless, of course, she were born again.

Take the case of Jeannie C. Riley, the "Harper Valley PTA" girl. That crossover hit sold the album so well that it brought her a gold record and a Grammy award. Yet she hadn't much, if any, performing experience behind her when she hit it big and because of that faded swiftly during the seventies. Or perhaps she became a victim of her own sexy image. But it was about that time that she had a personal religious experience that led her to announce she had been born again and would no longer sing in places where alcohol was served. She did some recording after that, but it was all in the gospel field.

Female singers have had great success in gospel. Males in the field seem to seek safety in numbers, bonding together in quartets—from the Blackwood Brothers in the thirties, to the Jordanaires in the fifties and sixties, and many more today like the Talleys and the Cathedrals. A couple of the big male country groups—the Oak Ridge Boys and Larry Gatlin and the Gatlin Brothers—began in gospel and had considerable success before they began singing "secular." So while you can't say that women dominate the gospel field, they certainly show greater strength there than in straight country music.

Country music's women are also expected to program gospel or gospel-tinged material, right along with their songs of love, desertion, and protest. Some may mix in a few tracks on an otherwise secular album. (Sometimes, as on Wynonna Judd's first album as a single, the contrast can be rather jarring.) Others, when well established, may make an all-gospel album—and such albums sell surprisingly well. Yet, after all, why should it be surprising? For in preaching, giving thanks, and witnessing in song, they simply give voice to the higher yearnings and feelings of the women in their audience. It's all between them and God.

Cristy Lane Takes It "One Day at a Time"

Women are no better represented in the Branson shows than in country music generally. Certainly the younger headliners pass through town—Patti Loveless at the Ozark Amphitheatre, Tanya Tucker, Trisha Yearwood, and some others at the Grand Palace. But for the most part, the names there on the theaters are male—Moe Bandy, Mickey Gilley, Jim Stafford, Mel Tillis. All but Willie Nelson feature female singers—and it is usually the ladies who perform the requisite gospel set.

Cristy Lane is an exception in one sense—the obvious one, as she has a theater of her own. Although she shares it part of the time with Ray Price, the doleful, deep-voiced Texas troubadour, she is the big draw, the name that pulls them in. Except for one huge crossover hit, she is not well known outside the country field. Nevertheless, to watchers of cable and late-night TV, and even to readers of the *National Enquirer*, she is well known for the ads that continue to sell her albums and cassettes.

Born in Peoria, Illinois, in 1940, Cristy Lane married Lee Stoller, a country music fan who was certain that his young (nineteen) bride had a singing career ahead of her and was determined to make it happen. Under his driving direction, she became a name in central and southern Illinois, cut a single in Nashville, "Janie Took My Place," that became a local hit, and signed on as a USO entertainer in Vietnam. There, entertaining the troops, she actually came under fire; in one ambush situation, the driver of her jeep was killed. Husband and wife moved to Nashville in 1972, where she got her first national hit in 1977 on LS Records—the label Lee Stoller had set up for her—"Tryin' to Forget You." Others followed, but Stoller got in deep trouble in Nashville for promoting her records a little too aggressively. Cristy Lane created a persona for herself with her songs during the seventies. She presented herself in the role of the woman-as-victim, with hits such as the ones named and others—"Let Me Down Easy," "I Just Can't Stay Married to You," and so on. Nevertheless, she first topped the country charts and made a crossover to pop with a gospel number, "One Day at a Time." It became "her" song, the one for which she is known and remembered to this day. The gospel album on which it appears, *One Day at a Time*, is claimed (by Lee Stoller) to be the biggest seller of all time in the field; he may well be right.

She, of course, headlines her own show at the Cristy Lane Theatre. Lee Stoller is there, too, serving as pitchman and master of ceremonies. (The two live during the season in an apartment above the theater.) The second-liner was a young

Irish tenor named John McNally, who has attracted some attention in town since he makes no attempt to present himself as a real country singer; what he offers is quite off the beaten track for Branson. It blends well, however, with what the star of the show offers; she—or should it be Lee Stoller?—deserves credit for a smart bit of casting. For her part, Cristy Lane does long sets of her hits and favorites, the longest of all, her gospel set which features, of course, "One Day at a Time."

Barbara Fairchild: God Willing

Barbara Fairchild's situation in the Mel Tillis show is much more representative of women in country—certainly of those in Branson. Though she had headlined her own show here in the past for short engagements at venues such as Lowes Theatre, she is second-lined at the Mel Tillis Theatre in a very full show that features a lot of Mel and the Statesiders, the singing of prodigy Levi Hare, and in a few production numbers, the Melody Greenwood Dancers.

With a show as well packed as this one, Barbara Fairchild has a rather short set—just three songs. Still, she makes the most of them and has great impact on the audience, due in no small measure to her just-us-folks style onstage. Oh, she is beautifully coifed and prettily gowned and certainly looks every inch the star up there, but her manner is familiar and her speech pure (Arkansas) country. She joshes with the audience and even tells jokes.

She does not, however, come on timid. Her opener is one to go to the hearts of a whole lot of women—"I'll Walk [i.e., leave] Before I'll Crawl," and the audience—in the majority, female—eats it up and demonstrates with long, loud applause.

There is a kind of performance tradition in Branson, and perhaps elsewhere too. It has to do with the show's female vocalist choosing a man at random out of the audience, getting him up on stage, then singing a love song to him—maybe even getting him to join in. Well, Barbara Fairchild chose a tall, beefy guy named Ed, talked him up there in front of everybody, and hugging him close, sang her biggest hit, "The Teddy Bear Song," to him. And yes, she even got that big, old teddy bear of a guy to join in and sing it with her. He didn't sound bad.

In fact: "That was good, Ed," she told him. "You sound as good as Andy Williams!"

Ed: "Well, don't tell him!"

Then she let him go and got serious, announcing the tour to the Holy Land she would be conducting this coming winter and how easy it was to sign up for it. And then she used that as an entry to her "current hit in gospel"—she only did the one song—"Could You Walk a Mile in That Man's Shoes?" It's a nice number, one that urges us to put Christian love to the service of the homeless, the unloved, the lonely—good advice, and the crowd at the Mel Tillis Theatre accepted it with warm applause.

Some years ago, Barbara Fairchild did something almost unheard of in the competitive world of country music: she dropped out. She didn't just take an extended vacation. A few years after hitting the top of the country charts and bounding over to the pop charts with "The Teddy Bear Song,"—and landing hits afterward—she left Nashville for Texas, not knowing when she would come back—or *if* she would come back. During a conversation after the Mel Tillis show she talked about what brought her to that point and what led her to return.

It had to wait, however, for a good half hour, as she dutifully (no, *cheerfully*) signed autographs after the show and had her picture taken ten or twelve times with that many different people. But eventually, there in the lobby of the theater, the end finally came. The last of her fans had left. Still dressed in the blue, sequined gown she had worn onstage, she led the way back to her large, star-sized dressing room. There was a whole closetful of similar (though not identical) sequined dresses and a teddy bear needlepoint on one wall sent to her by a fan. We sat down and talked in this room of mirrors.

She told me what led to her departure from Nashville back in the seventies and admitted, "Career-wise it was probably the worst thing I ever did—but for me personally, I needed it."

She had been in Nashville, making records, since she was

sixteen years old. It began for her, as it does for most singers there, singing on demo tapes that are used to audition new songs. She recorded "Love Is a Gentle Thing" on Kapp, and that brought her to the attention of Columbia who signed her when she was just eighteen years old. Then the hits started, and her career took off. It kept her running until well into the eighties.

"All these years being in it," she said, "and I had a lot of stress and stuff. And I just come to a place where I didn't know if that's really what I wanted to do, so I took off and went to Texas. My contract was up. It gave me a chance to really get my perspective."

She had remarried—an evangelist singer and songwriter, Milton Carroll—and she was happy. "But then one day," she continued, "my husband said, 'How do you feel about not singing? Because I think God has really given you a gift to communicate.' And he told me if I never wanted to do that again, that would be fine, but he said he wanted to be sure that we weren't wasting what God gave me. So I started praying about it and said, 'Show me if You want me back there.' And doors kind of started opening. I thought I was going to go back to Nashville and write gospel music, and so we moved back there, and I called Don Williams just to let him know I was back in town, and his manager got on the phone, and he said he'd help me. I'd told God I'd go through the doors he opened, so I don't set goals or make plans."

So, without quite intending it, she found herself in the business again, out on the road, singing the songs she had made hits, and back in Nashville writing and recording gospel. "My records in gospel are very, very successful," she said proudly.

She first began coming to Branson five years before settling into the Mel Tillis show. "And people would come up and say, 'God is going to do something here in Branson, and we really feel like you're supposed to be part of it.' And I would say, 'You know, I'm here, and I'm available to Him.' And then I got the call from Mel and Judy to come work here which puts me here all the time. And I think God wants to do something with music all across the country, not just here. There's a music coming out of all this called Christian country music.

It moves people. And Branson is a place that's very open to God. More and more shows include gospel. I'm not saying that everyone here is sent out to evangelize the world for Christ, but there's not a negative attitude in the shows that are here. And to most of the people who come here, traditional family values are important.''

Does she think this will change as Branson gets bigger? ''I hope it doesn't,'' she said. ''I have a little prayer group started on Tuesday mornings at my home, and we pray that it won't change. I think if you look at it from the natural standpoint, it's inevitable that you're going to have other folks come in here that don't hold to the same [values], unless they understand that that's why this place is successful and decide to go along with what works here. People don't want off-color stuff.''

Right now, she owns two houses— one in Nashville and one in Branson. (''I had to buy a home here because I couldn't find anything to rent, and now I'm glad I did.'') Two of her children, still in high school, remain in Nashville, with ''a house-sitting, kid-sitting couple.'' Another, nineteen, is here with her. Her parents live just four and a half hours away in Arkansas, and her husband, who travels a lot in his ministry, finds Branson's central location good for him.

And what does she think about the competition between Nashville and Branson? ''Well, the media likes to sensationalize things because it makes a better story,'' she said, ''but I don't think there's a question that when you're talking about country music, this place is going to have an impact on Nashville because it's tourism. I think Nashville is going to be the recording capital of country music. I'd be real surprised to see that change because they've got such great studios. But the funny thing is that in living in Nashville—Nashville as a city—I don't think it ever embraced country music. It's been like this little thing in the middle of it, but it's not like the whole town says, 'Yeah, we're the big music city.' I think they're separated. And in Branson the whole town revolves around this music thing.''

I asked her what she thinks when they talk about Branson as a town for country music's has-beens. ''Sounds kind of like sour grapes, doesn't it?'' she said. ''But there's no question but that the record company powers that be view someone who's had a career—they view us as has-beens. But it's kind of like throwing the baby out with the bathwater. You look here at Mel Tillis, and he has thousands and thousands of fans, and they want to see Mel, and they want to buy Mel's products, and that doesn't make him a has-been. He's a very happening fellow. And I think there's plenty of room for the young artists that are here.

"I think the thing that's happening [in country music] is very much like rock and roll used to be years ago. Now there are short-term careers for people that they're running through the music mill. Many aren't talented enough to have long-term careers. But I think the way the industry's handling it, it will be here and gone with a lot of them, and that's unfortunate because many of these older fans are loyal. When you appeal to a younger market, that's great, but kids are fickle in what they like. Here, the fans that we have are loyal, they're dedicated, and they like you. They like you, and they want to know about your family, what you like, and they care about your hobbies—they care about *you*."

And would she like to have her own theater in Branson? "No. I'm not saying that wouldn't change, but very realistically it wouldn't make any sense at all to have my own theater. It's competitive here just by virtue of the amount of theaters there are. The town can only handle so many, and I'm realistic about where I'm at. . . . Even in my booking I've tried to be very realistic about what I'm worth to the guy 'cause I want the guy who books me to make money. I don't think I could fill a theater. I think I'm an asset to Mel's show, but I wouldn't want the responsibility of filling a theater this size."

And about her age. She's forty-two, a baby boomer: "It's a good time in my life. You know, I think you gain a little wisdom in life. I feel great, and I just like it. I wouldn't have thought I'd like being forty as much as I do."

And if you saw her, caught her act, you'd know that Barbara Fairchild has many more onstage years ahead of her.

God willing.

18

And Direct from
Las Vegas...

There it was on 76 Country Boulevard, just east of the Grand Palace—a building site below road level that stubbornly refused to reveal any hint of what it might become. There was a dark part, and there was a light part, and in between there was a sculptured cement, ridged and layered in the style of the local limestone. What, really, was it going to look like when it was finally finished?

And would they get it finished before the announced opening date of May 1? I must have passed it at least a couple of times every day, just making the rounds—but it never seemed to change. It was just that great muddy lump out there on the strip, and it must have seemed to some that they hadn't a chance of completing it on time.

This was the Andy Williams Moon River Theatre.

There were those in town who would just as soon it never opened. For one thing, here was this fella from Los Angeles, or Hollywood, or wherever he was from, who'd been a big star on TV a while ago, and the kind of music he was known for just had nothing at all to do with country. "Moon River"? "The Days of Wine and Roses"? "The Village of St. Bernadette"? You call those Andy Williams hits country?

But there was resentment that went even deeper. Evidently when Andy announced he was coming to Branson and building a theater there, he had some things to say about the kind of entertainment offered there that offended a lot of people in town. Now, I don't know what he said because I wasn't present when he said it. And afterward he insisted that he had been misquoted. I won't quote the misquotation here. I will say, though, that he was widely perceived as having denigrated Branson and its brand of music.

But why would he have done that? After all, Andy Williams had come into town as an outsider, a performer identified with television, with Las Vegas, and never really with country music. He had obviously seen considerable potential for himself as a performer with a permanent presence in Branson. If he meant to stay, what would be the point in angering those already established? And anyway, did this really sound like Andrew, the squire of Camelot, friend of the Kennedys, and prince of players? No, it did not. He had always been a class act.

On-Site Inspection

Tennyson Flowers was the man I was supposed to talk to. I knew nothing about him except that he had a rather florid name, the name of a poet—and that, as far as I was concerned, was a mark in his favor. He had agreed to meet and talk with me. Where? Right at the construction site. His office was in the trailer.

So there I was, my car pulled up behind a pickup truck, the mysterious muddy lump about fifty yards away, with workmen all around it, moving purposefully up and down the scaffolding and in and out of the gaping entryways. I knocked on the door of the trailer. But that seemed sort of timid, and so I opened the door and walked right in.

There was a secretary. She told me Tennyson was out for a minute, and if I'd just take a seat and wait, he'd be right back. It wasn't long until he was there.

He burst into the trailer, an impressive figure—tall, longhaired, dressed in dusty jeans and plaid shirt. There is a hurried conference with the secretary. Listening (not eavesdropping—

we're crammed too close inside for that), I can tell he's upset about something. I can also tell he's from nowhere near Branson; he could be from either coast, but he sounded sort of, well, preppy to me.

Then he turned to me, asking, with his raised eyebrows, who I was. I identified myself, and he said, "I need ten minutes," and swept past me into his office.

He took those ten minutes on the telephone. It was evidently a call to the architect, or the interior designer of the theater, and it all had to do with the placement and lighting of the onstage moon. He was excited, insistent, and perhaps just a little bit angry because he seemed to feel that he had been left out of the loop. If things were done according to spec, he insisted, the Moon River Theatre moon would be quite invisible. He stated his case forcefully. They had a frank exchange of views. Finally, he jammed down the telephone receiver, left his office in a rush, and slammed out of the trailer.

Curious, I followed Flowers out after a moment or two and saw that he was over at the building, standing close to the scaffolding, engaged in a shouting match with a foreman. Then, throwing up his hands, he left the man looking after him and headed across toward the open entrance. But before he disappeared, the secretary leaped out of the trailer. "Tennyson!" she called loudly. "Tennyson! Andy is on the phone!"

"Tell him I'll be right there," he yelled, then he began trudging back up the hill.

I turned to the secretary. "Look," I said to her, "I can tell this isn't a good time for him to talk."

"It really isn't."

"We can do it another time."

"Why don't you come back tomorrow?"

The situation was obviously pretty hectic there at the Moon River Theatre construction site. The pressure was on Tennyson Flowers, but he seemed determined to deliver. As I backed my car up then turned around to head up the dusty, unpaved roadway to 76, I had to wonder if perhaps Andy Williams's ill-wishers might not have it right: it looked doubtful to me then that the theater would open on the day that had been announced. Why, it was just a month away!

But I went back the next day, as I'd been invited to do. The man I had come to see was waiting for me in his trailer office this time, just as calm and in command as he had seemed frazzled and fractious the day before. The transformation was impressive.

Although he was obviously in charge, I still hadn't a clue as to his actual position there. And so I asked him—rudely, I suppose—just who he was and what his job might be.

"I'm Andy's manager," said Tennyson Flowers. "I represent him here directly. It's up to me to see that the job gets done the way he wants it done. To tell the truth, it's been a great experience—nuts sometimes, but . . . "

If Andy Williams's manager had come out to Branson to oversee construction personally, then that bespoke a strong commitment to the project by the singer himself. I was impressed.

So we talked. Flowers told me that Andy's brother, who manages Ray Stevens, first told him about Branson. "Andy told me to take a look at it, and so I came and then went back and brought him—and that was it. He was in. He had me here every other week in 1991 looking for the right location, and I found it. These parcels of land are right next to the Thousand Hills development they're now building and the Grand Palace with its Grand Inn, opening this year and Grand Village, which is under construction. The Gatlin Brothers' hotel and theater is going to be right up the road across from Wal-Mart. This one is in all ways the best location."

There was nothing smug about the way he told this. Just the facts, ma'am. He was equally straightforward when I asked him if Andy Williams might not be taking a chance in bringing his kind of music to a town so strongly oriented toward country. "Well, in a way he is, and in a way he isn't," said Flowers. "After all, Ray Stevens, Roy Clark, Shoji Tabuchi, Jim Stafford—they're all country people but they're more pop-oriented. And Andy, Willie Nelson, Stevens, and Stafford are all performers who have played in Vegas. And this is just my opinion, but I've yet to see a tourist who has come to

Branson who is a hard-core country fan. I think the people have gone to the country shows because that was what was available.''

Then, putting it to him delicately, I brought up the matter of the theater's design. That *is* supposed to be limestone around the entrance? . . .

''Oh yeah, the limestone.'' He nodded. ''We knew what the inside of the theater should be from the start, but we struggled with the outside, trying to visualize it, for a long time. Andy wanted the Dorothy Chandler Pavilion—you know, the big theater in Los Angeles. But then while we were down here trying to work this out, Andy and I happened to be driving along Highway 65 one day. You know how it is, those spectacular limestone cliffs. And suddenly he had me pull over, and he got out of the car and made me take a look. 'The entrance to the theater could be there,' he said 'between the limestone formations.'

''The idea, you see, was to take these natural cliffs and have an urban building rising out of it. Using the natural thing, this is the concept—that we're combining the urban with country.''

So Andy Williams was very deeply and specifically involved: ''Listen, I've known him for seventeen years, and I've never seen him like this. He's excited at having his own place, doing his own thing. I'll tell you something. I and a couple of other people tried to talk him out of this—not because we were against it but because we were testing his commitment. But we couldn't budge him. He's throwing his life into it.''

I went out of town for a while then—to Nashville and points south and west. Nobody had told me, but I was in for a surprise when I came back. Driving up 76 Country Boulevard, I glimpsed something that called for a closer look. Swinging into the left turn lane, I swooped down into a long drive next to the Grand Palace, stopped, and stared.

The muddy lump had vanished. The scaffolding had been removed. The building stood alone, looking sturdy and substantial. Then I glanced around me and realized that the blacktop drive I was on had been the same dusty construction road

I had parked on before. The trailer was gone. Down beyond the theater was a parking lot that stretched just about to Thousand Hills Road, neatly curbed with spaces marked. Not only that, but trees had been planted just about everywhere they could be set out. It was an amazing transformation. There could be no doubt that the Andy Williams Moon River Theatre would open right on schedule.

The biggest surprise, though, was the theater itself. What had seemed questionable in the design, disjointed and arbitrary, now appeared well integrated. The cement piling on each side of the entrance had been lightened and colored slightly so that it really did look like limestone. The ''natural'' and artificial had come together in a convincing style. Distinctive and well thought-out, it was, in its exterior at least, the best-looking theater in town.

May 1 was the official opening day of the Branson music theater season. Andy Williams was present, and of course made no negative remarks to the press, to bystanders, and certainly not to the other entertainers who had gathered to pose for a big group portrait, sort of the Class of '92. He conducted himself like the gentleman he most certainly is and made no enemies that day. In fact, he made some friends. His opening night performance was a benefit for College of the Ozarks' Camp Lookout, a summer camp for the needy children of Taney County. With tickets at prices inflated for that show only, Williams raised $40,000 for the program. Missouri Governor John Ashcroft was in the audience, and composer Henry Mancini was onstage with Andy: the event won front-page coverage in the *Springfield News-Leader*. It was apparent that Andy Williams was well on his way there in Branson.

Andy Onstage

Midweek, midday. There was a considerable cluster of cars in close to the Moon River Theatre belonging to advanced ticket buyers. Orderly ticket lines moved along swiftly, evidencing a smoother box office operation than some of Branson's theaters could claim. In no time at all then, I had my ticket tucked in my pocket and was free to roam the lobby, looking it over.

What was it Tennyson Flowers had said? That they had known what the inside would look like right from the start. Well, here it was. And if this was the lobby of the best-looking theater in town, it more than met the claim made by the handsome exterior. There was a kind of understated elegance to it that I hoped the ticket buyers appreciated. It was the use of light-stained wood and the gentle inclines (just right, by the way, for wheelchairs) that made it different and right. And yes, I think those who had come in, as I had, to buy tickets for later performances sensed that there was something special here, for I found a few of them wandering around with me looking at the art on the walls. I remember particularly a piece of primitive art woven in a vague animal shape, and a big charcoal sketch of a female nude (bold for Branson). I learned later that all the art in the lobby was from Andy Williams's own collection. That seemed right, too, for if this was truly his own place, then the lobby was his living room. He had made it so with things that were his.

When I returned for the performance, I was also impressed by the auditorium. Again, I'm no expert. All I ask is a comfortable seat and a good sightline, but I did notice that the sightline was practically guaranteed because the Moon River Theatre has more of a rake (incline) to it than other Branson theaters. Was the stage then below ground level? No, because the theater was built on the downhill, and the auditorium follows that general line. Everything, it seemed, had worked out in Andy's favor.

The show? Well, it began with the band playing that perennial opener, "Strike Up the Band," and when a screen descended, we were treated to a whole series of clips from Andy Williams's sixties TV show—unnecessary, to my mind, but not everyone has a memory as long as mine. There were the Osmond Brothers, when Donny was just a little kid; Bob Newhart; Woody Allen; Roy Clark; and Willie Nelson. Then, with an on-screen accompaniment of "September Song," we were given glimpses of the dear departed—Bette Davis; Pearl Bailey; Bing Crosby; Jack Benny; Jimmy Durante; Tennessee Ernie; Liberace; and Judy Garland. Then, upbeat once again, as the band swung into "L-O-V-E" spelled out across it. And out comes Andy to sing the song for us.

He looks great. Unabashedly gray-haired—no Grecian Formula for him—he bounces out to center stage dressed in a white suit, looking trim and tan. He really belts the number out, too, making it clear that his pipes are still strong, and he means to use them. The man came to sing.

But not *just* to sing, for between every couple of songs he talks to the audience. Chatter? No, he comes across as too warm and personable for the standard onstage blather. He tells them, for instance, that until a year ago he didn't know where Branson was or what it was—he's up-front about it. Then he adds that he spent two whole days in traffic, but he noticed that nobody got angry, nobody honked. A little later he tells them where he's from—"Wall Lake, Iowa, population 749, including the cemetery." All these little conversational riffs are intended to break down any barrier between him and the audience. And you can tell it's working, for with each song he sings, the applause swells louder. There are some of his old hits, like "This Place Called Lonely Street" and "The Hawaiian Parting Song," and "Born Free," and others, like "MacArthur Park," that hadn't before been his.

The show is well paced, relaxed but not slow-moving. Andy seems always to know just what the next move should be—even when the next move is to get offstage, which he does artfully. Before he goes, though, he introduces Philip Welford, who proves to be the perfect contrast. What to call him? Comedian? Juggler? He manages to be both—brilliantly—reminding us (well, me, anyway) that the great W. C. Fields started out as a skillful juggler and attributed his famed verbal timing to the physical demands put upon him as he told jokes while at the same time keeping balls, apples, oranges, or whatever, up in the air. Wellborn was physically funny, too, juggling as a dyslexic, then as a schizophrenic. (Kind of hard to describe and probably not funny if explained in detail on paper, anyway.) At any rate, during the 20 minutes or so he was onstage, Philip Welford held the audience just as completely as Andy had. There was no letup whatever.

There was no intermission, either. Usually Branson shows, shows anyplace, will break after an hour or so. It's considered taxing to the audience to keep them in their seats much longer than that—and difficult, too, to keep them focused and enthusiastic. But Andy Williams took the chance—and pulled it off. He led with a medley of Academy Award songs that included two of his biggest hits, "Charade" and "The Days of Wine and Roses." He had sung all of them on Oscar telecasts in the past.

A word about Andy's band. It was big—eleven or twelve pieces—but had a rather unusual instrumentation, with three keyboard players and a single violin (in this case *not* fiddle). Of more interest was the fact that it included five women even a female drummer! And when a back curtain came up to reveal a choir, the Moon River Singers, ready to join him on the obligatory religious set, it also revealed the only black face to be seen onstage in town—a young lady front and center. Altogether, Andy's second half was even fuller than the first. There was a patriotic medley that included "Dixie" (slow and sentimental). And as a finale—what else could it be but "Moon River"? Well, he brought the crowd to their feet with that. It was a really emotional outpouring from them, spontaneous and personal, nearly a minute of applause. It was as though the people there felt that they had been present at some special occasion.

And in a way they had. Sure, this was essentially a pop music program in a country town. Andy Williams, a self-described "middle-of-the-road singer," had given them all his hits, as any performer would do. But he had given them something more—about forty years of show business experience that had begun when he was the youngest of the Williams Brothers backing the hip, hardy Kay Thompson. No headliner in Branson can boast a longer career. And when you concentrate all that experience into two hours, without intermission, the result is bound to be something special—twice a day, every day but Monday.

Andy Offstage

I had an appointment to talk with him after the show. It wasn't hard finding my way backstage. I was passed from one usher to the next until I found myself among musicians packing up their instruments and was then left in the care of Tennyson Flowers, who saw me the last bit of the way to Andy Williams's dressing room. He knocked. Andy's valet answered, then stepped aside to let me in.

Andy Williams seemed remarkably relaxed for someone who had just brought the crowd to its feet with two long sets. But then, he had seemed pretty relaxed onstage, too. Dressed in a dark, checked, terrycloth robe that looked about as thick as a rug, he sat down after our handshake and said he was holding up just fine. "I like doing these shows," he went on. "A lot of people, performers, make it look hard. It's part of some people's act. But Bing, Perry, some others made it look easy. I guess I'm with them."

But it must be hard to be easy, given his style of singing. He's a tenor. He hits the high ones, song after song. And I did notice as he talked on that he seemed to be saving his voice. He kept it quiet, only a little above a whisper, during the entire conversation.

How is what he does in Branson different, say, from Las Vegas? "People come to Branson to see shows. You can be much more informal in Vegas. Nightclubs, supper clubs are different. You drop by. But here, this is a theater, and a theater requires a little more theatricality. You have to get them in a mood to listen to you. You might say that what we do here is more like a Broadway show. They come here, and this is an event for them, an evening out. They want to see a whole show, feel fulfilled. That's what we try to give them."

But no country music? He smiled, as if to say, "You noticed," then he pointed out that he had made a country album a couple of years ago. "But," he said, "I'm just a pop singer who made a country album. I don't do country songs in the show because I didn't want to intrude on what's established here. I'm not trying to usurp anyone in the country field. The people who come to see me here are the same who came to see me in Vegas or watched my show on television. I give them Andy Williams, not somebody else.

"Besides, it would be foolish to try to compete. These are great shows here on the strip. I've seen a number of them. I went to the Presley Show not long ago—very nice, completely professional. Everyone on this whole strip is. They just get up and do it. And that's how I was brought up in show business. Just do it."

In his second set, sandwiched somewhere between the religious and the patriotic, Andy does a novel tribute to 76 Country Boulevard, sung to the tune of the old Bobby Troup song, "Route 66." He urges the audience to "Get your kicks on Highway 76." In the course of a number of verses, he names every show in town—Boxcar Willie, Mel Tillis, Jim Stafford, Johnny Cash and June Carter, Shoji Tabuchi—and he ends with "Moe Bandy and another guy named Andy." Last but not least. Some in town may sniff and call the number a peace offering, but others may well recognize it as the good public relations ploy that it is. If Branson wanted an anthem, then Andy Williams has supplied it.

"I wrote 'Highway 76' myself," he said. "Naturally, I called Bobby Troup and let him know what I was up to. He loved the idea, told me to go ahead. There's been some interest among disc jockeys to play it. Also some interest in the gospel medley we do. I'm going to record it with the choir and give it to the deejays around here and see what happens. It could fizzle, or it could become a great thing."

As for the future, he feels as though he's made a sound investment of his time, talent, and money—sure enough, incidentally, that he's bought a condominium over in the Pointe Royale development. "The other day," he said, "we had a thousand for our afternoon show, and Mel had sixteen hundred. *But*"—pointing a finger—"he had thirty buses, which meant he brought in four hundred walk-ins. All of our people were walk-ins. They chose to come here on their own. Now, those buses are booked six months ahead of time. You sign up for wherever the tour is going. Next year the buses will be coming here. It will only get bigger as we go along.

"I feel very happy about the move."

19

Willie Nelson's Roller Coaster

When you come right down to it, there really isn't much to him. A little on the short side and kind of skinny, he has a gray beard and a lot of gray streaking his long reddish hair. By now that face of his has more lines on it than a U.S. Geological Survey map of the Badlands of South Dakota. Physically, he's just not very prepossessing. When he opens his mouth, what comes out is a high, reedy baritone. He says it isn't nasal, but it sounds nasal to me. Anyway, it's not the kind of voice that would win him awards.

But just put him in front of his band facing a full house of fans, and let him start singing his own songs in his own confident way—"Whiskey River," "On the Road Again" (he has over 2,000 to choose from)—and something really remarkable happens. This little gray-haired guy with the thin voice suddenly becomes WILLIE NELSON, writ large, exploding forth, and often stirring a real emotional response in his audience. They're not reacting to his star power alone—although he will go down as one of country's all-time biggest stars. No, they're reacting to his music and to him personally—who he is, what he projects, and what he stands for.

Although some weeks he shares the Willie Nelson Ozark Theatre with Merle Haggard, he's up there onstage twice a day when he's in town, which is most of the time. Audiences catch fire like that at his shows—oh, about half the time. But the house is always full. His name, the biggest in Branson, will always sell tickets. And that, after all, is why he has come here.

Toward the end of his autobiography, *Willie*, which was published in 1988, he remarked that he felt that he was "gathering strength to do something." Maybe it was his Cherokee blood that gave him some sign of the future. But he didn't get it quite right. Knowing what he does today, he might be tempted to edit that passage a little so that it reads, "gathering strength to get *through* something." For it was an ordeal that awaited him, one that many of us have in some sense shared with him, if only in dreading the possibility. In 1990 Willie Nelson got in trouble with the Internal Revenue Service.

"What happened," as reporter David L. Beck of Knight-Ridder Newspapers explained it, "is that at a time when he owed $2 million in taxes, he was advised to borrow not $2 million to pay those taxes but $12 million to put into a tax shelter . . . When those shelters were disallowed by the IRS, he found himself owing about—well, the total in taxes, interest and penalties, after some heavy negotiation with the feds, is about $17 million."

The tax shelter scheme Willie calls, "strange advice"—particularly strange in that it came from the accounting firm of Price-Waterhouse. Not one to be intimidated by their big reputation, he is suing them for $45 million.

One plan to pay off the federal government has yet to succeed. He made an offering of two albums, "Who'll Buy My Memories" and "The Hungry Years"—he calls them "The IRS Tapes"—selling them through commercials on late-night television. To raise the kind of money he needs they would have to sell a total of four million copies. He's still hopeful.

In 1991, the IRS seized much of his property. A small forty-four-acre ranch he owned in Dripping Springs, Texas, was auctioned off for $203,840. A Dallas bank that held a lien on his seventy-six-acre spread near Austin, which included a golf course and Willie's own recording studio, sold it to his friend, Texas football coach Darrell Royal. Other items and holdings in a number of states also went under the gavel, but those handling the IRS seizures were frankly surprised to find that he wasn't nearly as rich as they thought he was. In a television interview about this time Willie shrugged off his losses as "just things" and said that "there was nothing that can't be replaced."

Yet he is serious, as he must be, about settling the tax debt, and that, taking the long and short of it, is why he has come to Branson. Like the rest, he's digging for gold in the Ozarks.

The Willie Nelson Ozark Theatre is just about the farthest west of any on the strip, only about a hundred yards from the junction of 76 and Shepherd of the Hills Expressway, which marks the town limit. This is a theater with a history longer than some in Branson. Before Willie moved in, Mel Tillis had it for two years, and before Mel it was home to Shoji Tabuchi. Both left it to build bigger theaters of their own. Maybe it will prove just as lucky for its present occupant.

The place is in excellent condition and good-sized, seating over a thousand. Arriving a little early, I wandered around the lobby and found my way into the souvenir shop. There, among the sort of Willie and Merle souvenirs you might expect to find in such a place, is one unique to this one—a paperback, *The Willie Nelson Cooked Goose Cookbook & IRS Financial Advisor*, more in the nature of a (bitter) jokebook than a cookbook, and as for financial advice, well . . .

Was it my imagination, as I made my way through the milling crowd in the lobby, or was there not a distinct Texas style evident here? There were women dressed in long-legged jeans and the kind of blouses and gossamer sweaters that could only have come from Neiman-Marcus; and accompanying them were men made many inches taller by Stetsons and high-heeled boots. I overheard those gliding vowels, the statements turned into questions, and saw one man slap his knee and cackle, "Boy, howdy!" They were Texans, sure enough, maybe not the kind who make annual pilgrimages to Willie Nelson's rowdy Fourth of July picnics, but Willie was their boy, pigtails and all, and if driving up from Big-D or Fort Worth might help him a little bit with his tax problems, well, what the hey, huh?

But it wasn't all Texans who came to hear Willie Nelson that night. I found myself in a nest of Minnesotans, fugitives from the late spring cold in their part of the country, tourists from one or more of the big buses parked outside. The lady beside me didn't seem really certain whom she'd come to see, nor did she care especially. His show was on the tour, and that was good enough for her. The audience was diverse, mixed, probably a little older than your basic Willie bunch. I wondered, frankly, how he would go over with a crowd like this.

If he wondered, too, there was no sign of uncertainty. He just went ahead and did it. There was no pitch by a pitchman, no opening act—just Willie and his band, there when the curtains parted, wailing out for all they were worth on the tune he always opens with, "Whiskey River."

He barely gave the audience time to react as he finished up and swung right into "Stay All Night, Stay a Little Longer." But the gang in front—I came to think of them as the Texas bunch—exploded into applause that nearly covered up the hard-driving riff that opens the number. More than to the music, they may have been responding to the big banner behind the band, on which a José Cuervo bottle and a Texas flag were emblazoned. This was a real down-home occasion! Some of the folks around me, on the other hand, didn't put their hands together at all. They seemed confused. Wasn't it polite to wait until the music stopped to applaud?

But Willie wasn't going to stop. The band barely missed a beat as he slowed down the tempo and went through three of his prettiest ballads, "Funny How Time Slips Away," "Crazy" (which became a signature tune for Patsy Cline), and "Night Life." It's on the pretty stuff that he really shines. Up-tempo he sings with authority and a good, tricky, sliding sense of rhythm. But down slow, he's just full of surprises—subtle twists of his own phrases, low drop-downs followed by soaring high flights. You just never know what he'll come up with next, and you have the feeling, too, that at another show it might come out just a little bit different.

It was only then, after he and the band had done five numbers, that he addressed the audience at all. Did he josh the folks up front about Texas? Nope. Did he tell some jokes about his situation vis-a-vis the Internal Revenue Service? Uuh-uuh. Did he attempt in any way to ingratiate himself with the crowd? No, not really. He just introduced the members of the band. He had his sister Barbara do a couple of solos on piano—a boogie-woogie number (they used to call it Texas-style piano) and that pseudo–nineteenth century quickstep, "Down Yonder." He gave special recognition to his drummer, Paul English, who's been with him forever, not by calling for a drum solo but by singing the song that sums up their story, their years together on the road, "Me and Paul." Willie allowed that it was "kind of autobiographical." Then he did Kris Kristofferson's "Help Me Make It Through the Night," remarking laconically, "I never went to bed with an ugly woman, but I sure woke up with a few." And that was as loose as he got with the assembled multitude. It wasn't like he was mad at anybody, or sulking, or anything. He just wasn't much interested in talking to them. He had come to sing and play.

And that's what he did.

They were all his songs, or others that had come to be identified with him—songs he had made his own—like "Blue Eyes Cryin' in the Rain," "Angel Flying Too Close to the Ground," "On the Road Again" (this one won applause from the Texas section right from the opening bars), "Mammas Don't Let Your Babies Grow Up to Be Cowboys," and so on. Then there were a few—"Blue Skies," "Georgia on My Mind," and "All of Me" from the *Stardust* album in which Willie recorded all his favorite pop standards (an album that surprised Nashville by going right through the roof), his duet with Ray Charles, "Seven Spanish Angels," and the one he did with Julio Iglesias, "To All the Girls I've Loved Before."

To mention just a few.

This was really a long set. It seemed to me that intermission had to be coming up pretty soon. It seemed that way to a lot of people around me, too. They were growing noticeably restless.

But no, here came a gospel set—"Will the Circle Be Unbroken," "Amazing Grace," "Uncloudy Day," and "I'll Fly

Away"—and nobody in country does gospel better than Willie Nelson, not even those who have made it their specialty. But wasn't this a long set!

Finally it came through to me, as it must have to others, that there wouldn't be an intermission. Willie was just bound and determined to plow right through to the end. Now, Andy Williams had done a show without an audience break, but it wasn't quite the same thing, for that wonderful juggling comedian, Philip Welford, had spelled him in the middle. Andy then came back refreshed and in a change of clothes, and did a fine final act. His audience took it just fine.

But right here and now, the people around me, the ones I thought of as the Minnesota set, were getting twitchy. As the gospel group concluded with an up-tempo, foot-stomping, "I'll Fly Away," a large number of them broke for the exits. They may have thought, not without reason, that this was the finale.

But it wasn't, and Willie called them back. "Folks," he said, "if you'll just take your seats, we've got a few more songs to do." He said it with remarkable authority. The runners returned. Altogether he did four others, concluding with an equally up, equally foot-stomping rendition of another great gospel song, "I Saw the Light." I mean, if Christians were ever going to jump up into the aisles and boogie, this was their chance. Nobody boogied.

Half the audience was in the lobby by then, and the other half was up on their feet, giving Willie Nelson the long, standing ovation that he deserved. It was a crazy night. Half the people there couldn't wait to get out and the other half couldn't get enough of Willie. But there were no encores. The curtains closed with him waving at the crowd in front, which was still standing and still applauding. As an addendum, I must say, too, that minutes later Willie Nelson was out there at the side of the stage to sign autographs, and all the time I've been in Branson, I've never seen a longer line. He must have been there at least an hour after leaving the stage.

Well, Willie had broken a couple of rules that night. Perhaps not rules, exactly, but a couple of Branson's accepted performance procedures. First of all, and obviously, there was the matter of doing a show without an intermission. Andy Williams had gambled and won. Willie Nelson, to my mind at least, had lost. When you have to call back a sizable fraction of your audience and assure them you won't be taking up much more of their time, then you've lost.

And there was also that principle stated by Bill Mabe of the Baldknobbers, something to the effect that what people expected when they came here was a whole show, one with singing, comedy, and dancing. I remember that he added specifically that when the stars came in and thought they could do the same show they did on the road, they soon found out otherwise. The Baldknobbers have been at it for three decades here in Branson, so they must be doing something right. Still, I can't imagine Willie Nelson changing his show to suit Bill Mabe, or the folks on the tour buses, or anybody else, for that matter. Willie goes his own way. That's the story of his life.

"Funny How Time Slips Away"

He was born May 30, 1933, in Abbott, Texas, a little town closer to Waco than it is to Fort Worth. His parents soon split up and left him and his sister Bobbie (the same sister who plays piano in his band today) in the care of his grandparents. He grew up in Abbott, and it says a lot about him that he has gone back to live there today.

Willie got hold of a guitar very early, and Bobbie began teaching him chords from the piano. She ran away at sixteen and married a local musician. Willie joined their band at thirteen and soon stilled his grandmother's misgivings about his playing with them in beer joints by bringing home enough money to make a difference. Upon graduation from high school, he enlisted in the Air Force. He was soon out on a medical discharge and got married almost immediately.

There followed years of wandering with his young family, up in the Northwest as far as Vancouver, British Columbia (where he worked a deejay show as "Wee Willie"), and all through Texas, of course. There were jobs that had nothing to do with music—he even sold encyclopedias door-to-door

briefly—but whenever he could, if only on the weekend
nights, he would be out playing to dark rooms full of ungrate
ful drunks the songs he wrote during the rest of the week.

Finally: "When I went to Nashville in 1960 as a young
songwriter with ambition to be a singer, it was because Nash
ville was where the store was. If I had anything to sell, it mus
be taken to the store. Nashville, New York, and L.A. were the
big stores. There was hardly any demand for me or my music
outside of Texas, and I knew if I was going to be recognized
widely I would have to make it in Nashville."

That didn't mean he had to like it, though—and he never
did, really. Although he ultimately has had one of the most
successful and richly remunerative careers in country music
he scrambled and struggled like the rest, got skinned on recording deals, went through two marriages, and felt generally
abused and put upon all the time he was there.

Unlike most performers who come to Branson, Willie Nelson enjoys the road. It provided him with escape from Nashville, the deal makers, the lawyers, and the wrangling at home.
As he wrote in *Willie*, "I guess I could have retired modestly
at the age of thirty off of royalties from songs like 'Crazy.' I
might have had to live on a houseboat, but I would have had
enough money coming in to provide me with potted meat
sandwiches for the rest of my life. But I enjoyed playing music
too much to consider just retiring to the life of a writer. If I
had quit playing professionally I would have been out every
night sitting in with somebody anyhow. Working the road kept
me organized."

"On the Road Again" may have been written just to provide a theme song for a movie, but it's one of his best because
it expresses something he feels sincerely: Willie really can't
wait to get on the road again. Although in Branson he sleeps
at the motel next to his theater, he spends an awful lot of time
on that bus of his, the *Honeysuckle Rose*. He's like the captain
of a ship docked too long in port.

The move to Austin in 1971 and the "outlaw" thing he
cooked up with Waylon Jennings saved him in a sense. It
removed him permanently from Nashville and got him to writing those cowboy songs that culminated in the *Red-Headed*

Stranger album, probably his best and certainly his best-selling. It was more than a theme album—more like a western movie on vinyl. (In fact, it was made into a movie with Willie in the starring role some years afterward.) And it proved so successful precisely because it went directly counter to what was then the going trend in Nashville—country pop. He has always gone his own way, never really defiantly; he's just plain stubborn, that's all. And in the end, without ever intending to, Nashville has followed his lead. The "hat acts," the "New Traditionalists" drew inspiration from Willie and Waylon; it's not surprising since so many of them are from Texas and Oklahoma.

That sense of independence that he projects, the ability he possesses to be himself no matter what the circumstances, made him a natural for the big screen and the small. Even that face of his, lined and lean, was exactly right because it was so much more interesting than the usual Hollywood faces. Directors sought him out for "character" roles—Michael Mann for *Thief* and Sidney Pollack for *The Electric Horseman*—and found the man had charisma that came across with surprising intensity. Pollack was so impressed with Willie that he produced *Honeysuckle Rose*, which Jerry Schatzberg directed; it put Willie in an unlikely pairing with Amy Irving, a combination that worked just fine on-screen. If *Honeysuckle Rose* was his most successful picture, his best was *Barbarosa*, a real, old-fashioned western, directed by the Australian Fred Schepsi, a perfect union of style and story with just the right actor. There were a couple of others—*The Red-Headed Stranger* and *Songwriter*—that didn't do so well, but Willie never seemed to mind. If he had actively pursued a film career, taken up residence in Los Angeles and sought roles, he would be making movies today. But that doesn't sound like him, does it?

It's been an interesting life for him so far, a lot of downs and ups—and that's just the way he likes it. He once stated his "philosophy of life" to a lawyer who, unasked, had drawn up an estate plan for him. "I want the people around me to be happy, but I look at life as a roller coaster. When I'm up, I'm up, and when I'm down, I'm down, and when it's all over, the money runs out just about the same time that I'm through with my life . . . No, let's not plan. It's a lot more fun if we don't.''

Off the Road Again

It seemed right to talk with Willie Nelson on his bus, the *Honeysuckle Rose*, because it really is a kind of home to him. Built by the Florida Coach Company at a cost of just about half a million dollars, it has hand-carved woodwork and, as he put it, "a bedroom bigger than some of the joints I've played in." That's it back there with the big six-by-eight American flag over the bed.

He was seated at a little table, pouring a cup of coffee for himself when I was ushered in. So he poured one for me too. He had been shuffling through a clutter of papers and cassettes on the table, but he left off when the questions started and gave his full attention to them. His eyes are remarkable, dark and bright; they hold you.

I was curious about the show, what it was like for him working in a theater. "It's a lot like working a big club, really," he said, "one that doesn't sell alcohol." He laughed. "So it's naturally a little quieter, but that's all right, too.

"I think this theater's fine. Fifteen hundred is a nice crowd. Not too big, not too little. You can go out and do it with your band, or you can go out and do it just with your guitar. 'Course the band would be mad if I did."

Thinking about the performance I'd seen, I suggested tactfully that not everybody who comes to his show is necessarily a Willie Nelson fan. And he answered just as tactfully, "No, not necessarily, but hopefully they will be when they leave."

But why do the show without an intermission? "That's just the way our show is," he said mildly. "It's easier to go straight through than to take a break and try to get the crowd back where they were when we left. I'd rather just keep everything up and build and build and then come to an end."

(*Time out*. He had something interesting to say on this subject in *Willie*, his autobiography: "Bob Wills taught me how to be a bandleader and how to be a star. He would hit the bandstand at 8 P.M. and stay for four hours without a break. One song would end, he'd count four and hit another one. There was no time wasted between songs . . . The more you keep the music going, the smoother the evening will be.")

And about that big line of autograph seekers after the show—I'd never seen a longer one: "I think it's part of why artists do well in this town or why they don't do well. If you spend the time to do that, it'll naturally satisfy the customers a little better. It requires a little time, a little patience. But . . . whether I was here in Branson or whether I was in Fort Worth, I still sign autographs.

"Besides, it's interesting. I enjoy it. It's educational too. You think about someone who'd stand in line like that—you know, some nights it stretches all around the theater—and you see people in there who are getting on up in years standing in line to get an autograph. I think it's great. And I don't usually get complaints from them. Anyone with a complaint wouldn't stand around that long to tell you about it. The people who stand in line are fans.

"It's good for me, too. I get to really talk to the people who come through there and hear their stories. It's good for my ego because they all tell me how much they like me. It's good knowledge for me to take with me when I go out to a town somewhere that's not set up where I can stay for an hour and sign autographs. It's good to stay in touch with the people and not cushion yourself too much. Sometimes they request a song I haven't done. Doing two shows a day, the shows are a little shorter, so I don't do all the songs I normally do on a two-hour show. I usually get called on it if I leave out one of their favorites. They'll tell me about it."

And what are the favorites? "Oh, 'Stardust' and 'On the Road Again' and 'Always on My Mind,' and 'Blue Eyes Crying in the Rain.' "

Does he get tired of playing them over and over again? "Not really," he said. "Those songs I do from the *Stardust* album, for instance, they're such classics, and they're not a piece of cake. You can't just jump out there and think you're going to sing them. 'Stardust' itself is a pretty tricky song to play and sing, so it's a challenge to do these songs and do them well. So no, I don't get tired of them, not any of them."

He remarked that he thought Branson was a "good town, lot of music in this town," and then he went on to explain the arrangement under which he had come. Even though the theater carries his name, he is not the owner. It is owned by promoter John Harrington. It is Willie's for the season—or perhaps longer. "Actually, Johnny Harrington and I are good friends," he continued, "and I came here because I like him and I liked the idea of being here. I've been here a few times before. We did outdoor venues and always had a good crowd. I never did particularly care about doing more than one show a day. But I knew when I came here that I'd have to do two shows a day. That requires a little getting used to. You have to pace yourself a little when you know you're doin' that. You don't party as hard the night before when you know you've got two shows to do. You go to bed early so you can get up.

"But for myself I'm not much of a theater owner type guy. I'd rather have someone else do that and me just come play there. At some point I guess when I really got ready to quit traveling so much that would be an ideal situation to come here and do what some of the other guys have done like Mel Tillis, and he's set for the rest of his pickin' days. If he doesn't want to travel, he doesn't have to. I still enjoy traveling and I miss that part of it.

"But I'll probably be back and do some next season. I thought I would just play it by ear and think about next year when it gets a little closer. It's hard to say if this boom will last, but it's definitely here now. This is a boom period. I think it's got some booming to do. It's not through yet. Just how long it'll last has a lot to do with the economy. But there's sure no recession around this part of the country."

He seems to live pretty quietly here between the theater, the bus, and the motel next door. His family is in Hawaii. I wondered if he had gotten around town at all. Would he get mobbed, if he did? "Well," he said, "if you go out you better expect to see some folks and say hello and sign some autographs and take some pictures, because they're definitely out there watching and waiting and they've got their cameras. But mobbed? Well, nobody ever gets troublesome or threatening. I've never had anything threatening in my career. I think people have a tendency to chase something that's running, but if it's standing there, they'll treat it like anything else standing there.''

About this time one of the guys in the band came into the trailer and asked if he'd gotten the "Graceland" tape yet. Willie said he hadn't, and then explained: "I just did a song with Paul Simon, a song called 'Graceland.' He produced it. It's going to be on my next album. This one we did in New York in Paul Simon's studio he records in up there and then a couple more tracks in Dublin, Ireland, last month when we were over there doing a tour, and then Don Laws, a producer who does Bonnie Raitt, is producing some tracks for my new album. Probably come out the first of the year when we get it all done. Being here, I need to be in the studio more, so I have to wait until I get a few days off to run up to the studio to do some more. It's almost half-done.''

Any more movies? "Well, if it's a good western, and a good horse, and preferably if it's around Austin." He grinned. "I don't want to be picky or nothing.''

About those IRS problems: I placed the question last, thinking he might be kind of touchy on the subject. It had seemed to me, as it had to a lot of other people, that he might just be working for Uncle Sam this summer in Branson. But he wasn't a bit touchy. Here's what he had to say: "When you're looking at $17 million, and you're looking at a building that holds fifteen hundred people, that's definitely a very big debt and a big problem. What it does do is provide a good living for the band, provides us a place to play, and we have an arrangement where I'm allowed to make up to, you know, x-amount of dollars a month, no matter whether it's in Branson or where it is, and they get a percentage. They get half, and I get half after expenses, and that's not really a bad deal.''

Does it depress him? "No," he said. "I've had some serious problems, and that's not one of them.''

Another quote from *Willie*. It's a good book, not squirmy or dodgy, or self-aggrandizing, the way so many of those celebrity autobiographies are. The man reveals himself in it.

"Anybody who went through childhood during the Great Depression—when broke and desperate described nearly the whole country and certainly the farm folks of Central Texas—grew up knowing financial security is an illusion. No matter how high you stuck up money in the stock market or a bank vault, they can take it all away from you in an instant."

Well, they took it away from him in an instant. But Willie Nelson knows that life is a roller coaster ride. If he's gone down, he'll be up again.*

---

*Shortly before this book went to press, Willie Nelson and the Internal Revenue Service came to an agreement whereby he would settle his $17 million debt for $9 million. He announced, however, that he would continue with his suit against Price-Waterhouse.

20

"You Don't Have to Say Missouri Anymore"

By the height of the season, 1992, it seemed certain that the number of visitors to Branson would hit, and perhaps exceed, the predicted five million mark. But a curious pattern took shape. Chuck Barnes, the Rocky's restauranteur, pointed out that the heaviest visitor traffic no longer fell on the weekends, but rather through the week. He read this shift as a temporary falling-off of the town's basic support within the six hundred-mile radius, the weekenders who had filled the theaters, restaurants, and motels in years past. Perversely, it was the national publicity that Branson had received that kept them away.

"They took a look at '*60 Minutes*' on television and read all those magazine stories," said Barnes, "and they said to themselves, 'If it's going to be as crowded as all that this year, then we'll stay away.' Another change here," he went on, "is that it's become less of a family situation. The average middle-class family can't afford to come with kids and go to a lot of shows. It's the recession. It's finally hit Branson."

On the other hand, the national publicity that "the Las Vegas of country music" has received has attracted so many from outside the area that has provided its basic audience that yes, attendance at most shows has increased, motel reservations are up, stays are longer, and more diners than ever are testing the limits of the all-you-can-eat policy that prevails at restaurants up and down Highway 76.

It was Andy Williams who emphasized the importance of the tour buses as the key to success on the strip. And so, when I happened to run into his manager, Tennyson Flowers, just outside the Moon River Theatre, I asked him if the tour bus traffic was building for them. He was very emphatic. "The buses *are* coming," he said. "As an example, we've got forty-three coming in for two different shows this month."

Flowers also remarked on the curious change in the pattern of visiting that had come this season in Branson. "The typical thing," he said, "is that they come in on Sunday afternoon or evening and leave on Friday morning. July Fourth weekend was absolutely dead. As a matter of fact, Shoji shut down on that weekend which by rights should have been big business. But he was right. He saw it coming. On the other hand, July 6th, the Monday after the Fourth, had the heaviest traffic into town we've ever had. And it was a very big week."

He also confirmed what Chuck Barnes had said about the recession having at last caught up with Branson. But Tennyson Flowers also added that not only visitors but also businesses have felt the crunch: "This town really isn't recession-proof. Businesses have folded here. Shows and restaurants have gone out of business. People have come in here thinking this was the pot of gold at the end of the rainbow. But it's not. You've got to come in with big pockets and a commitment to carry on. You've got to be able to be ready to handle it for the long haul."

Between opening day and August, two theaters had shut down. The Celebration Theatre, which had been a venue for traveling attractions, many of them gospel acts, shut down its box office one Monday in July and ceased to answer phone calls. Dino's Theatre, also on the strip, shut down a few weeks later just as suddenly. Dino Kartsonakis, who had patterned his style and show on the late Liberace's, simply hadn't gone over with Branson audiences. (He opened again later in the theater Willie Nelson had vacated for a post-season run.)

This did not mean, however, that the theaters stood empty for long. By August the Osmonds had hung up their sign at the Celebration Theatre. They announced their plans at a press conference and opened September 1. Marie and Donny Osmond would play certain dates through the remainder of the season—Marie would definitely be present for the Christmas shows. They promised an "Osmond Family Christmas." The word around town was that they had leased the Celebration from Bob Mabe for the remainder of the season only and were testing the market. After all, the Osmonds had problems other groups simply didn't have. They announced that they were moving to town with all their kids—forty-eight of them. And as they saw it, "There aren't enough dentists in Branson to take care of all of them." If they solve the dental problem, they will probably decide to stay awhile.

Although it was still known as Dino's Theatre when pop/country singer Jimmie Rodgers spread his banner above the entrance and opened there in September, he soon changed the name. Rodgers (no, not country music's first star, who died in 1933) brings audiences back a few decades with his big pop chart hits from the late fifties and early sixties. He notched fourteen gold records back then, among them, "Honeycomb," "Kisses Sweeter Than Wine," and "Uh-Oh, I'm Falling in Love Again." There was talk earlier in the season that he would buy Boxcar Willie's theater at the end of the 1992 season, and Box would simply lease another, maybe cut back on his play dates and time-share with other shows, as Roy Clark does at his own theater and Loretta Lynn does at Lowes. But with Rodgers established at what he now calls his Honeycomb Theatre, Boxcar Willie seems pretty firmly committed to a full season at his old stand in 1993.

If all this seems a bit tentative, well, it is. As I talked with editor/publisher Ed Anderson at the new offices of *Branson's Country Review* right on Country Music Boulevard, I got the sense that while 1993 was shaping up as a very big year, it was (as of September) still shaping up. He confirmed that it was "a very fluid situation."

He said, "The Wayne Newton deal is about closed. They've called a press conference to make the announcement later on this month." Whether the deal, which has been discussed in town for months, was delayed by the entertainer's financial problems (he filed for bankruptcy with $20 million in debts in the middle of August) would be anybody's guess. However, Newton's local backing is solid and strong. "Gary Snadon of Shepherd of the Hills is the driving force behind that," continued Anderson. "They're building on 248 acres eventually, with a projected theme park of some kind. The immediate plans call for the theater and parking lot and grounds and so on to be put up on forty acres. It'll probably be the biggest one going up next year."

What about the Johnny Cash Theatre? Will it ever be finished? "Oh, yeah," he said confidently, "the Cash property has three people behind it who are going to save it—Jim Thomas and Bill Dailey locally and John Connally, a developer out of Pittsburgh. But . . . "

"But what?"

"It probably won't be the Johnny Cash Theatre."

"Oh. Too bad."

So it goes up and down the strip. Plans for new theaters are announced, unfinished projects are to be completed. You hear, for instance, that Willie Nelson won't be such a presence in Branson in 1993, that he yearns to be on the road again, but he's made it clear that he will be around from time to time. Where he'll hang his hat when he does hit town, however, is not certain, nor for how long. Merle Haggard, who had shared the theater with Willie, was said to be sold on Branson, and in partnership with George Jones and a local developer, he was starting to dig the foundation for a theater of his (their) own. A financial group known as V.O.L., out of Tennessee (the *Vol*unteer State), had put in a bid on the Foggy River Boys Theatre and had installed Johnny Paycheck ("Take This Job and Shove It"). The Foggy River Boys had been a presence in Branson right on the strip since 1972. Where they would go and what they would do would have to be worked out by the group's young new leader, John Sheppard. It was his responsibility from here on out. He had announced that they would restructure and carry on the name, though it was unclear where or if they would continue to appear in Branson.

Not all the potential newcomers had such strong ties to country music as Johnny Paycheck or George Jones. John Davidson, for instance, had been playing matinees at the Jim

Stafford Theatre, said he loved the town, and was looking for a theater in which he could perform full-time. Tom Jones, Neil Diamond, Howard Keel, Bobby Vinton, and Robert Goulet had all come to town and were said to be searching for theaters or land on which to build. First Andy Williams, then Wayne Newton—it seemed that Las Vegas was moving in on Branson.

After outlining all this, Ed Anderson concluded, "We're really in a flux situation. It's murky. I guess you could say that what we've got is an evolutionary process here—the survival of the fittest. I think we're going to have a tremendous year next year. There's no plateau in sight yet for Branson, yet some are built for the long haul and some for the short distance. Here, I think you've got to be ready for the long haul to survive."

His own *Branson's Country Review* is a case in point. After years of squeaking by, the hometown magazine had experienced "a period of nonstop growth since last November." As Anderson explained, "The real growth has been out of town. We've got a national subscription base, which we never had before."

That meant national recognition for the little town in Missouri that Nashville loved to ignore. Folks in Branson knew it, loved it, and reveled in it. As one local booster put it to me, "You don't have to say, 'Las Vegas, *Nevada*.' Everybody knows where Vegas is. Well, that's how it is with Branson now. You don't have to say Missouri anymore."

Even the Mall Looks Different

As if underlining the national (no, *inter*national) reputation of the town, a new voice came on KRZK sometime in August—and it was distinctly foreign-sounding. It belonged to one Bob Morgan, and the spiel he gave accounting for his presence there on Hometown Radio was enough to disarm even a confirmed anglophobe. "What's this English guy doing in Branson?" he asked rhetorically. "Well, they say home is where the heart is, so I guess my home is right here."

Joining the line of traffic up or down Highway 76 with Bob Morgan's picks from Billboard's Country Hot Hundred in your ears, you had to notice that there had been some changes along the way. There were, first of all, the signs marking the turnoffs to shortcuts—Fire Creek Road, Thousand Hills Road, and so on. If you were to take the well-marked Thousand Hills cutoff from the Branson Mall to Missouri 165, you would pass a whole row of brand-new motels, now providing much-needed room space for visitors.

But instead, take the turn into the Branson Mall parking lot and you'll see there have been some changes inside, too. The big Wal-Mart and the equally big Consumers Market still anchor the strip's most prominent retail location. The only notable change there is that Consumers is now open twenty-four hours a day in order to accommodate the night owl shopping habits of the show people in town.

But it's between the two giant buying emporiums that things have altered considerably. Before, going through the middle mall doors that lead into the shopping corridor, you were hit by a sense of emptiness. Many of the small store locations lining the way stood empty. And where there were few shops there were few shoppers.

Now, however, not only is all store space filled, the lobby area is also overflowing with booths and pushcart operations of the kind that attract browsing buyers. Notable among them, right near the front entrance, is a booth outlet for Bransontix, the centralized ticket-selling operation that offers tickets to virtually every show in town and features motel delivery for local phone orders. (There is also an 800 number for out of town advance orders; check the directory in the back of this book.)

Among the new stores that have opened in the mall area is the Branson branch of the Ernest Tubb Record Shop. While not a patch on the mother of all country record stores on lower Broadway in Nashville, it offers the best selection in town, and it's right there on Country Music Boulevard. There is a music shop next door with lots of guitars, fiddles, and maybe even a few dulcimers hanging in racks along the wall. Across the way, you'll see the Elvis-O-Rama, offering all sorts of memorabilia honoring that favorite son of Tupelo, Mississippi.

And of course there are the usual sweet shops, Fabulous Fakes costume jewelry, a women's leisure wear store. And on and on. With all this, the place is really crowded. Are they buyers? Are they browsers? Well, most of the merchants seem to be doing pretty well.

In the middle of it all, on that little stage surrounded by benches and folding chairs is one Vance Greek, serenading the shoppers from behind a grand piano. Although he is no more nor less talented than the anonymous young picker I heard here the last time I stopped in on a Saturday afternoon, Vance Greek is certainly more aggressive about soliciting support. A large hand-painted sign stands near the piano: "If you enjoy my show here are the seven best ways to express your appreciation. 1. Tips. 2. Applause. 3. Tips. 4. Buy my tapes. 5. Tips. 6. Recording contract. 7. TIPS!"

As it turns out, his is not the only live music available at Branson Mall. At the rear of the corridor separating Wal-Mart from Consumers a small auditorium has been installed. The Memory Lane Theatre, seating just 419, was then featuring a 10:00 A.M. breakfast show with the Blackwood Quartet (a second Blackwood unit claiming descent from the great gospel singers of the thirties and forties). The evening show at seven presented Jim Owen, "Star of HANK WILLIAMS movies." TV movies, it turns out, and a PBS special. Prices are a little under the average for Branson shows.

The Gatlin Brothers at the Summit

Across Route 76 and just down the road a little is the site of the Gatlin Brothers hotel and entertainment complex, the Summit, which should be ready in April 1993. It's certainly one of the most ambitious projects to which entertainers have lent their names. It will be their second with the Dallas-based Restaurants of America corporation. The first opened with the huge Bloomington, Minnesota, mall in August 1992. The Gatlin Brothers Music City Grill combines a 250-seat restaurant with an 800-seat showroom. The Branson complex will be even more ambitious.

The word Steve Gatlin used to describe it was "huge." The hotel he assured me, "will be able to house conventions—and really nice accommodations that will include 240 suites. Add onto that two theaters and two restaurants, and you've got an idea of the size of it."*

The association with Restaurants of America came through Rudy Gatlin's father-in-law. "Yeah," said Rudy, "it's my wife's stepdad. We're excited about the Branson project, of course. But you know how it is with us, we sort of divide duties between us. Steve is handling the detail work on the hotel and entertainment complex. I'm more involved with recording. We'll definitely continue to record, but whether any of it will actually be done in Branson depends on Jimmy Bowen and Liberty Records."

The group first played here in 1984. It all started with a surprise phone call from their agent. "I booked you in Branson," he told them. "Three days."

"*Where* is Branson?"

"Trust me," said the agent. "Go."

Steve Gatlin recalled for me that they woke up and looked out the bus windows and found they were at the Roy Clark Celebrity Theatre. Well, they knew Roy, so that was reassuring. "Then, as we waited to do the first show, they saw traffic build during the day to a really impressive flow. We did the shows. We filled the house. And that's how we started here.

"I'm going to keep my house in Brentwood, just outside Nashville," he said. "But while I work here during the heavy months my family's going to live with me here, so I'll really be living in both places. I love Nashville, but I would be crazy to pass up an opportunity to make music in Branson."

Kenny Rogers Synergizes

Just as hotly discussed was the news that Kenny Rogers was coming to town. Born and raised in Houston, Rogers is

---

*As of this writing, plans for the hotel-theater have been put on hold, at any rate for 1993. The Gatlins will be appearing in Branson, however.

one of the superstars of country music. Although he has never really been on the Nashville scene, his huge crossover hits ("Ruby, Don't Take Your Love to Town," "Lucille," "The Gambler," and "Lady") have made his husky voice familiar to many American listeners who wouldn't know Ferlin Husky from Faron Young.

His appearances on television have bolstered his star image. These include not only variety specials but also dramatic roles. A natural actor, he has shown that his strong stage presence transfers directly to the screen. His performances in *The Gambler* and its attendant sequels, as well as *The Coward of the County*, have brought high praise from television critics all over the country.

All this has won him a wide following and made him one of the richest men in country music. So when an entertainer like this establishes a presence in a little town in the Ozarks, it wins attention not just in Branson and Nashville, but in Los Angeles and New York as well. Yet characteristically, Rogers has done it his way, and his way is always a little bit different.

In effect, he has entered into a partnership with the Herschend organization. He is, to be sure, a junior partner, yet he has allied himself so extensively with the Herschends that the arrangement looks, on the face of it, to be something more than the usual for hire situation.

As Kenny Rogers explained it, "I'm going to be involved in all their projects—with the Grand Palace, of course. I play there now, and I'll be doing that a lot in the future. It's a beautiful theater, it really is. But I'll also be involved with the shopping center they're building next to it, and their White Water parks. All their projects."

This will probably also include special appearances at Silver Dollar City, but Rogers will be most prominent a year or two into the future when the Herschends' White River Junction project is completed. In his persona as "The Gambler," he will make appearances on the thousand-passenger showboat that will ply Table Rock Lake. (There will, of course, actually be no gambling on board.)

Why the Herschends? Why didn't Kenny Rogers simply build a theater and let the crowds come to him as so many others have done? "Well," he said, "my original intention was to do something on my own in Branson. But then I talked with the Herschends, and they're really a quality group. They've got concepts that go beyond Branson. So we got involved."

Naturally, coming in as he has, he is optimistic about the town's future. He declared, "The market is still growing, virtually untapped. If people don't overbuild or overextend financially, they'll build something that will last. I think it's really healthy the way we try to solve problems in Branson, like traffic, and building that loop around the town. The way it is now, that two-and-a-half-hour drive down 76, it's like the way the kids used to cruise on Van Nuys Boulevard in Los Angeles."

Using his television power, Kenny Rogers hosted a TV special that was done right there at the Grand Palace, "Christmas in Branson." It featured solid country acts and generated a lot of that warm "Christmas in the Ozarks" feeling. He said that his only real fear was that the town might lose some of that feeling, "what made Branson Branson," he called it. "A lot of these people coming in, you know, are not really country acts."

On the Political Map

Small though the town may be, it does seem to have a future in television. Local and regional investors are putting together a financing package to establish a cable network that will originate from Branson. Such an operation would inevitably come into competition with The Nashville Network and Country Music Television with Gaylord Communications in Nashville. Then won't the fur fly!

Live from Branson? Well, why not? Mel Tillis proved it could be done when he hosted a good-sized chunk of the 1992 "*Jerry Lewis Telethon*" right there from the stage of his theater just off U.S. 65. Mel and other friends raised more money than expected for "Jerry's kids" during the course of the most successful telethon to date.

President George Bush, however, brought even more national attention to Branson when he came to town with the usual host of media mavens in his wake. Advance men for the campaign had been in town a couple of weeks before the Republican National Convention in New Orleans, so it could hardly be said that his visit came as a surprise, especially not since his welcome was so well organized. It was significant, though, that Bush came to Branson the day after the convention. With just a brief morning stopover in Gulfport, Mississippi, Air Force One headed north to Springfield Regional Airport, and the president motorcaded down to a rally in the huge parking lot of Silver Dollar City. You might say he had chosen to kick off his campaign for re-election right here.

After all, these were his people. They stood foursquare for the "family values" that had been extolled so fervently during the course of the convention. This is, as I had been told often, "the buckle on the Bible Belt."

Nevertheless, when George and Barbara Bush arrived, they were met with a scattering of signs in support of Clinton and Gore. No hisses, catcalls, or boos, however. Folks in this part of the country are too respectful of the office of the presidency to jeer the man who holds it, no matter how they may disapprove of his performance.

The arrival had been preceded by a two-hour concert offered by some of Branson's biggest names. As the crowd gathered (estimated at upwards of 17,000) they were serenaded by the likes of Glen Campbell, Loretta Lynn, Boxcar Willie, and Jim Stafford. The president, introduced by Missouri Governor John Ashcroft, echoed most of the themes touched upon in his nomination speech before the Republican Convention. There were, however, added touches given in respect to his audience. He dropped in little references to country music hits of the past. Recalling Bill Clinton's performance on the tenor saxophone on "*The Arsenio Hall Show*," he predicted that after the election, the Arkansas Governor "will be playing that old Buck Owens classic, 'It's Crying Time.' "

Following the afternoon rally, the Bush motorcade headed down Missouri 76 straight into Branson. Once in town, the sixteen Missouri State Troopers assigned as escort saw to it that the president and first lady were not stuck in that notorious creeping traffic jam. And just where were they headed? Well, what do visitors do on an evening in Branson? Why, they take in one of the shows.

The question of which one they would attend was never really in doubt. Moe Bandy had been an active and vocal supporter of George Bush for years. Mississippi-born, an ex-rodeo clown and a one-time sheet metal worker, Bandy is one of the few personalities in country music who might actually name the President among his friends. And so it was to his modest 900-seat theater that the first couple headed that night for a little entertainment and relaxation. It must have helped them to know that some of the proceeds from that sellout show would go to Barbara Bush's favorite charity—her foundation to promote literacy.

The president and his first lady sat modestly back in the sixth row. But at the show's finale, during Bandy's rendition of his flag-waving hit, "Americana," the distinguished guests came up on stage and joined hands with the singer under a great big American flag. Wasn't that a photo opportunity!

Country Continues Strong

If singer Moe Bandy derived distinction from President Bush's visit, then candidate Bush gained equally from the association with country music. More and more, country is perceived as America's music. Rap, hip-hop, heavy metal, even jazz and classical have their constituencies, of course, yet their appeal does not cut broadly across social lines as does country. It is no longer identified solely with the South and Southwest, as it once was. And members of the rock 'n' roll generation of the late sixties and early seventies, who would then have reached for their revolvers at the whining sound of a steel guitar—now listen and love country and pretend that they were fans all along.

The proof of all this was right there on the Billboard Pop Chart. Week in and week out country artists dominated the list as 1992 wound down. Garth Brooks, now hatless and sometimes sporting a thin beard at concerts, had two albums out (one a Christmas special), both sure to be million-copy sellers. Although Clint Black, Randy Travis, and Alan Jackson were all pushing him hard, he had a new challenger in Billy Ray Cyrus, a Kentucky hunk with a ponytail and a bodybuilder's physique. "Achy Breaky Heart," the single from his album *Some Gave All*, went right through the roof. Not to be outdone by all these comparative youngsters who had followed in his wake, George Strait came out with a rodeo movie in the fall, *Pure Country*. Another Willie Nelson? No, smiling George comes off on-screen more like a clean-shaven Kris Kristofferson.

On the female side, Wynonna Ryder continued strong, backing up her debut solo album with a concert tour that proved conclusively that she could make it onstage all by herself. Her audiences seemed to prefer the motorcycle mama side of her split personality; maybe that's the way she'll go. Mary-Chapin Carpenter had a very good year with her two hit singles, "I Feel Lucky" (very big) and "The Bug" (not so big); both were on her album, *Come On Come On*, which enjoyed a short run on the pop chart and a longer one in country. She is the sort of talent that today only country music could contain. Certainly she sings well; hers is a sweet voice reminiscent of those pure folkie sopranos from the past yet one that can take on an edge when the material demands. Yes, the material—she writes practically all of it herself and writes it beautifully, speaking to and for women today. She can be delicate ("Come On Come On") or demanding ("The Hard Way"), yet in either mode, there is an intensity and a sense of felt experience to her lyrics that communicates directly.

With such a glorious present, country music's future is assured. Yet what about Branson? Its growth during the last few years has certainly given it the aspect of a boomtown—bankruptcies, theaters vacated in midseason, the survival of the fittest. There is every reason to believe that the boom will continue before business levels out at some high megabuck level that has not yet been achieved. But the town and the entertainment it offers are likely to be altered in the process.

Gary Presley, who was present at the creation (the first show on the strip), said he was fearful that the specific Ozark flavor of the shows in Branson might be lost. He has reason to fear. A lot of it already has been lost. Yet as long as the Presleys and the Mabes (and their Baldknobbers show) continue, it won't be lost completely. The real fear around town is that the place they call "the Las Vegas of country music" may just become another Las Vegas—that it may lose its association with country music entirely. Yet considering the strength of country today and the immediate radius from which Branson draws its visitors, that's not likely to happen—notwithstanding the success of Andy Williams, the likely entry of Wayne Newton, Howard Keel and John Davidson, nor the possible appearance of Tom Jones, Robert Goulet, Neil Diamond, or any of the rest who are testing the waters. And that's just on the performance side. I'd be willing to bet that you will *never* see Las Vegas–style casino gambling or nudity in Branson. The town has a clear sense of itself as a family recreation spot. That is how it will continue to present itself to vacationers.

If not Las Vegas, then what about Nashville? Will Branson take its place as the country music capital of America? Certainly not. Nashville is where the industry is located—recording, publishing, booking, you name it. And that is where the industry will stay.

Branson became what it is today by providing visitors with what they could not find in Nashville—*easy* accessibility to lots of live country music. There will probably be some industry outposts established here in order to give support to the entertainers who have situated themselves more or less permanently. There will also be more recording right on the spot. Keith O'Neil and his 24-track Caravell Studios should do well in the future, but he is likely to get some competition in Branson. In fact, he already has: Ralph Jungheim, an independent producer from Los Angeles took a mobile recording van from Nashville at the end of the summer in 1992 and recorded Moe Bandy, Roy Clark, and Johnny Paycheck at their theaters and Faron Young live at Mickey Gilley's. By the time you read this, at least a couple of these albums will have been issued on the Laserlight label.

No, you don't have to say Missouri anymore. Today and for the foreseeable future the name of Branson stands alone, increasingly visible, better and better known as more star entertainers move into the town. Visitors who come here like what that name stands for. They know they can be entertained by the best, eat, and get a good night's sleep, maybe even do a little fishing—without being embarrassed in front of their children by rough talk or revealing costumes, and without returning home with empty pockets.

How many other places like it are there in America today?

A Quick Guide to Branson

Just one last word on the traffic. Although the two-and-one-half-hour figure has been cited again and again as the length of time it takes to drive the 76 Strip, it doesn't *always* take that long. Believe me. That's only at the height of the season, when the town is most crowded, and at those hours when theaters are filling up or letting out. There are, as noted in the last chapter, marked sideroad routes that provide shortcuts. When the highway loop around the town is completed, it should alleviate the problem considerably.

That said, it should also be added that the information below is the best that could be provided at this time. Listings on some of the theaters—who will appear, and when—should be taken, in some instances, as tentative. As Ed Anderson, editor of *Branson's Country Review,* said, "We're really in a flux situation." Theaters never stand empty for long in Branson. If an act folds in midseason, as happened in 1992 with Dino's Theatre and the Celebration Theatre, there will be another to take up the lease in a week or two.

If, in planning a trip to Branson, you want the latest on who's playing where and when, your best bet would be to call Bransontix, the local ticket agency. It's always a good idea to order tickets in advance, and they have an 800 number to make it easy for you. All out of town ticket inquiries can be answered at 1-800-888-TIXS. The local number is 334-TIXS; if you use the service in town, they guarantee motel delivery.

On the other hand, calls direct to theaters will also bring prompt, dependable service. You will see that in most cases only telephone numbers have been provided, even with motels and restaurants. There's a very good reason for this: most businesses on Highway 76 don't have addresses posted. They may be there on deeds and licenses, but you're not likely to see them displayed along the road. If you want to know where they are, just call them up and ask them. They'll tell you they're "just across from the Branson Mall," or "right next to Boxcar Willie's." This is just another aspect of small-town America to which big-city visitors must learn to adjust.

MUSIC SHOWS

West Highway 76

Baldknobbers Hillbilly Jamboree Show
(417) 334-5428
Branson's pioneer show offers good country music and comedy.

Moe Bandy's Americana Theatre
(417) 335-8176 or 1-800-424-2334
A patriotic show starring George Bush's favorite country singer.

Boxcar Willie Theatre
(417) 334-8696
The rowdiest show in town and one of the best.

Campbell's Ozark Country Jubilee
(417) 334-6400
The Blackwood Singers have been featured in a predominantly gospel show.

The Johnny Cash Theatre
No longer in bankruptcy, but the future of this theater is uncertain at this writing.

Roy Clark's Celebrity Theatre
(417) 334-0076
Although Roy Clark plays here often, it is also a touring venue for other country and pop acts.

The Foggy River Boys Music Show
(417) 334-7123
One of Branson's longest-running attractions, a feast of home-cooked Ozark entertainment.

The Gatlin Brothers Theatre
Larry Gatlin and the Gatlin Brothers may perform 120–180 dates a year. Tentative.

Gilley's Family Theatre
(417) 334-3210 or 1-800-334-1936
Mickey Gilley, the man from Houston, serves a menu of his many hits.

The Grand Palace
(417) 334-7263 or 1-800-424-7147
The biggest theater in town features a fast-changing lineup of the biggest stars in country.

Lowes Theatre
(417) 334-0428
A touring venue for a variety of country acts—has been headquarters for Loretta Lynn and Ray Price in Branson.

The Memory Lane Theater
(417) 335-3777
The Blackwood Quartet in a gospel breakfast show; evening show features Jim Owen.

The Wayne Newton Theatre
A new venue features one of Las Vegas's brightest stars in frequent appearances; touring acts in between.

The Osmond Family Theater
(417) 336-6100
The Osmonds continue, with frequent visits from Donny and Marie.

The Johnny Paycheck Show
(417) 334-7123
One of country music's renegades makes his comeback and Branson debut.

Presleys' Mountain Music Jubilee
(417) 334-4874
The first show on the Strip continues strong as ever with fine music and great Ozark comedy.

76 Music Hall
(417) 335-2484
Four separate shows are featured through the week, including the excellent Brumley Show.

Jim Stafford's Show
(417) 335-2639 or 1-800-677-8533
The funniest man in Branson does off-the-wall comedy surrounded by a cast of fine singers and country pickers.

Ray Stevens Theatre
(417) 334-2422
Comedy and song from the man who convinced the world that "Everything is Beautiful."

The Texans
(417) 334-0903
A venue for established country acts, most of whom hail from the Lone Star State.

Andy Williams Moon River Theatre
(417) 334-4500
He may not sing country, but he offers one of the classiest shows in town.

Gretna Road

Braschler Music Show
(417) 334-4363
A long-running show that features gospel in the Ozark style.

Shepherd of the Hills Expressway

The Ozark Mountain Amphitheater
(417) 334-7272
A huge (8,000-capacity) outdoor arena that brings in top names on an irregular basis.

The Shoji Tabuchi Theatre
(417) 334-7469
Branson's furious fiddler offers productions of Las Vegas size and quality.

Highway 165

The Buck Trent Dinner Theater
(417) 335-5428
A champion banjo picker and a soulful singer provides good day and evening entertainment and good cooking to boot.

The Wildwood Flower
(417) 335-2700
Branson's only country nightclub has real country music, a big dance floor, and full bar service.

Highway 65

Mel Tillis Theatre
(417) 335-6635
Mel's new showplace offers high visibility from the road, Texas swing renditions of his countless hits, and a full crew of singers and dancers.

THEME PARKS

West of Branson on Highway 76

Mutton Hollow Craft Village
(417) 334-4947
Just outside town, you can take a trip back to the nineteenth century—music, food, and Ozark crafts.

Shepherd of the Hills Homestead and Outdoor Theatre
(417) 334-4191
By day, a preservation and reconstruction of the setting of the Harold Bell Wright novel that started it all; by night, a dramatization of that same novel under the stars.

Silver Dollar City
(417) 338-2611
Marvel Cave, Ozark crafts, family rides (including a steam tour of the park's far perimeter), food, music— all of it in a turn-of-the-century setting just into Stone County.

OVERNIGHT ACCOMMODATIONS

The partial listing of Branson motels that follows should not necessarily be taken as recommendations. I have slept in just a few of them. As for overnight accommodations, there are only three locations that offer anything approaching luxury standards.

THE PALACE INN, big and spacious and right next to the Grand Palace, is the only luxury hotel on the strip; it is well run and usually booked far in advance.

A good distance outside Branson on Highway 165 and on the shores of Table Rock Lake is the POINTE ROYALE CONDOMINIUM RESORT [(417) 334-5614], complete with golf, tennis, and fishing.

Even farther on Table Rock Lake is BIG CEDAR LODGE [(417) 335-2777], primarily for fishing and relaxing.

But if you're going to Branson to fish, there are many cabins, fishing resorts, and trailer parks surrounding the three area lakes.

The campgrounds with easy access to the music shows are PRESLEYS' CAMPGROUND [(417) 334-3447] and the CITY OF BRANSON CAMPGROUND [(417) 334-2915].

West Highway 76

Amber Light Motor Inn (417) 334-7200
America's Inn 4 Less (417) 344-7380
Baldknobbers Motor Inn (417) 334-7948
Ben's Wishing Well Inn (417) 334-6950
Best Western Knights Inn (417) 334-1894
Blue Bayou Motor Inn (417) 334-5758
Caprice Motor Inn (417) 334-8555
Cinnamon Inn (417) 334-8694
Days Inn of Branson (417) 334-5544
Dogwood Park Hotel 1-800-HAVE FUN
Dutch Kountry Inn 1-800-541-5660
E-Z Center Motel (417) 334-8200
Edgewood Motel (417) 334-1000
Family Inn (417) 334-2113
Fiddlers Inn (417) 334-2212
Grand-Vu Motel (417) 334-7474
Hall of Fame Motor Inn (417) 334-5161
Hi-Ho Motel 1-800-235-1094
Hillbilly Inn (417) 334-3946
Holiday Inn (417) 334-5101
Honeysuckle Inn 1-800-942-3553
J. R.'s Motor Inn (417) 334-1241
Jesse James Motel 1-800-648-3155
K Royal Motel (417) 335-2232
Kirkwood Center (417) 334-4177
Lodge of the Ozarks (417) 334-7535
Marvel Motel (417) 334-4341
Melody Lane Inn (417) 334-8598
Mountain Music Inn (417) 335-6625
Mr. Tucker's Inn (417) 334-5497
Music Country Motor Inn South (417) 334-1194
Ozark Mountain Inn (417) 334-8300
Ozark Western Motel (417) 334-7000
Palace Inn 1-800-PALACE-N
Rest-Wel Motel (417) 334-2323
76 Express Inn (417) 334-7500
76 Mall Inn 1-800-828-9068
Shadowbrook Motel (417) 334-4173

> *Southern Oaks Inn (417) 335-8108*
> *Stacey's Ozark Motel (417) 334-8434*
> *Stonewall West Motor Inn (417) 334-5173*
> *Twelve Oaks Motor Inn (417) 334-7340*

Thousand Hills Road

This is a new road just south of Highway 76 which runs almost parallel to it from the Branson Mall to Highway 165. It allows rear access to a number of theaters along the way, including the Andy Williams Moon River Theatre and the Grand Palace. This gives the new motels listed below convenience to some locations on the Strip, yet leaves them outside the heaviest traffic area.

> *Alpine Rose Motel (417) 336-4600*
> *The Atrium (417) 336-6000*
> *Best Inn (417) 336-2378*
> *Big Valley Motel (417) 334-7676*
> *Comfort Inn (417) 335-4727*
> *Hampton Inn (417) 334-6500*
> *Peachtree Motel (417) 335-5900*
> *Super 8 Motel (417) 334-8880*

Downtown Branson and Business 65

Although removed from the center of the entertainment district, these are close enough to provide easy access.

> *Best Western Branson Inn (417) 334-5121*
> *Best Western Rustic Oak 1-800-828-0404*
> *Old Branson Hotel Inn (B & B) (417) 335-6104*
> *Roark Motor Lodge (417) 334-3196*
> *Southern Air Motel (417) 334-2417*
> *Stonewall Motor Inn (417) 334-3416*
> *Travelers Motel Downtown (417) 334-3868*

RESTAURANTS

Again, the listing of these restaurants does not constitute a recommendation. I did make specific recommendations in

Chapter 15, and I'll stick by them. Let me add one postscript, however. McGUFFEY'S, listed on page 260, opened in mid-season. Located between the Andy Williams Moon River Theatre and the Grand Palace on 76, it can claim the most original and eclectic menu in town. The food is great, and it has one of the best bars in Branson.

Family-Style

Apple Mill Restaurant (417) 334-6090
Baldknobbers Country Restaurant (417) 334-7202
Belgian Waffle House (417) 334-6471
Bonanza Family Restaurant (417) 335-2434
Branson Inn Restaurant (417) 334-5121
Captain D's (417) 335 5841
Colonial Restaurant (417) 334-8484
Country Kitchen Restaurant (417) 334-2766
Donovan's Hillbilly Inn Restaurant (417) 334-6644
Duck Cafe (417) 334-5350
The Home Cannery Restaurant (417) 334-6965
Hungry Hog Cafe (417) 334-7535
Long Creek Cafe (417) XXX-1413
Ozark Family Restaurant (417) 334-1206
Penelope's (417) 334-3335
The Plantation (417) 334-7800
Presleys' Jukebox Restaurant (417) 334-3006
Rustic Oak Restaurant (417) 334-6464
Sadie's Sideboard (417) 334-3619
Tommy's Restaurant (417) 334-4995

Specialty

Adam's Rib
(417) 334-8163
Barbecued ribs top a full American menu.

Candlestick Inn (417) 334-3633
American and some Continental.

Confetti
(417) 334-5101
In the Holiday Inn, pastas and American.

Copper Penny
(417) 334-5097
Prime rib and steak.

Dimitri's Restaurant
(417) 334-0888
In the Roark Motor Lodge, Continental specialties.
  Dinner only.

Koi Garden
(417) 334-0687
Oriental menu, predominantly Chinese.

Manny's Restaurant
(417) 334-2815
Mexican specialties.

McGuffey's
(417) 336-3600
Eclectic—Cajun, Tex-Mex, etc.

Mr. Lou's and T.C.'s
(417) 334-8040
Cajun specialties.

Outback Steak & Oyster Bar
(417) 334-6306
Australian theme and specialties—lots of beef.

Rocky's
(417) 335-4765
A complete Italian menu.

The Best in Biographies from Avon Books

IT'S ALWAYS SOMETHING
by Gilda Radner　　　71072-2/$5.95 US/$6.95 Can

JACK NICHOLSON: THE UNAUTHORIZED BIOGRAPHY *by Barbara and Scott Siegel*
　　　76341-9/$4.50 US/$5.50 Can

STILL TALKING
by Joan Rivers　　　71992-4/$5.99 US/$6.99 Can

CARY GRANT: THE LONELY HEART
by Charles Higham and Roy Moseley
　　　71099-9/$5.99 US/$6.99 Can

I, TINA
by Tina Turner with Kurt Loder
　　　70097-2/$4.95 US/$5.95 Can

ONE MORE TIME
by Carol Burnett　　　70449-8/$4.95 US/$5.95 Can

PATTY HEARST: HER OWN STORY
by Patricia Campbell Hearst with Alvin Moscow
　　　70651-2/$4.50 US/$5.95 Can

SPIKE LEE
by Alex Patterson　　　76994-8/$4.99 US/$5.99 Can

Buy these books at your local bookstore or use this coupon for ordering:

Mail to: Avon Books, Dept BP, Box 767, Rte 2, Dresden, TN 38225　　　C
Please send me the book(s) I have checked above.
❏ My check or money order— no cash or CODs please— for $_____ is enclosed
(please add $1.50 to cover postage and handling for each book ordered— Canadian residents add 7% GST).
❏ Charge my VISA/MC Acct#_____ Exp Date_____
Minimum credit card order is two books or $6.00 (please add postage and handling charge of $1.50 per book — Canadian residents add 7% GST). For faster service, call 1-800-762-0779. Residents of Tennessee, please call 1-800-633-1607. Prices and numbers are subject to change without notice. Please allow six to eight weeks for delivery.

Name_____
Address_____
City_____State/Zip_____
Telephone No._____　　　BIO 1192

TAUT, SUSPENSEFUL THRILLERS BY EDGAR AWARD-WINNING AUTHOR

PATRICIA D. CORNWELL

Featuring Kay Scarpetta, M.E.

BODY OF EVIDENCE

71701-8/$5.99 US/$6.99 Can

"Nerve jangling...verve and brilliance...high drama...
Ms. Cornwell fabricates intricate plots and paces the action
at an ankle-turning clip."
The New York Times Book Review

POSTMORTEM

71021-8/$4.99 US/$5.99 Can

"Taut, riveting—whatever your favorite strong adjective,
you'll use it about this book!"
Sara Paretsky

And Coming Soon

ALL THAT REMAINS

71833-2/$5.99 US/$6.99 Can

The WONDER of WOODIWISS

continues with the publication of
her newest novel in trade paperback—

FOREVER IN YOUR EMBRACE
☐ #89818-7
$12.50 U.S. ($15.00 Canada)

THE FLAME AND THE FLOWER
☐ #00525-5
$5.99 U.S. ($6.99 Canada)

THE WOLF AND THE DOVE
☐ #00778-9
$5.99 U.S. ($6.99 Canada)

SHANNA
☐ #38588-0
$5.99 U.S. ($6.99 Canada)

ASHES IN THE WIND
☐ #76984-0
$5.99 U.S. ($6.99 Canada)

A ROSE IN WINTER
☐ #84400-1
$5.99 U.S. ($6.99 Canada)

COME LOVE A STRANGER
☐ #89936-1
$5.99 U.S. ($6.99 Canada)

SO WORTHY MY LOVE
☐ #76148-3
$5.95 U.S. ($6.95 Canada)